The Minds of the Moderns

The Minds of the Moderns

Rationalism, Empiricism and Philosophy of Mind

Janice Thomas

ACUMEN

For Geraint, Gareth and Margaret

First published in 2009 by Acumen

Acumen Publishing Limited
Stocksfield Hall
Stocksfield
NE43 7TN
www.acumenpublishing.co.uk

ISBN: 978-1-84465-186-3 (hardcover)
ISBN: 978-1-84465-187-0 (paperback)

British Library Cataloguing-in-Publication Data
A catalogue record for this book is available
from the British Library.

Typeset in Minion.
Printed in the UK by the MPG Books Group.

Contents

16. Is the mind a substance for Locke?   139
17. Locke's views on self-knowledge   148
18. Locke on consciousness   155
19. Locke on mental causation   163
20. Locke on representation   169

V **Berkeley**

21. Minds are the only substances   181
22. What do we know about our own minds or selves?   191
23. What is the nature of consciousness for Berkeley?   202
24. Berkeley's problem of mental causation   212
25. What is Berkeley's theory of mental representation and
     intentionality?   222

VI **Hume**

26. Is the mind a substance for Hume?   230
27. Hume and self-knowledge   239
28. Hume's notion of consciousness   250
29. Hume on mental causation   259
30. Hume on representation   267

     Conclusion   276
     Bibliography   285
     Index   289

Acknowledgements

I am happy to record a large debt of gratitude to members, both past and present, of the Heythrop Philosophy Department and Heythrop Philosophy Research Seminar, especially Gerry Hughes and the present Head of Department, Peter Gallagher, for help over many years in understanding innumerable philosophical questions including the five topics discussed here. In particular I would like to thank Gerry Hughes and Michael Lacewing for reading and providing useful comments on early versions of the chapters on Descartes on consciousness, Berkeley on substance and Berkeley on mental causation.

The library staffs of both the British Library and the Sydney University Library made my work much easier by their patient help on numerous occasions.

Many thanks to Steven Gerrard for his positive response to the proposal and patient confidence in the project. Thanks also to Acumen's two anonymous publisher's readers and to copy-editor Kate Williams for pertinent and tactful suggestions that enlarged my understanding and saved me from a number of serious errors.

Muriel Hall and Margot Metcalfe both gave generous encouragement at every stage and crucial advice in the final stages of the book's preparation. I would also like to thank Peggy Tilden and Kit Whitfield.

I will always be grateful to my mother whose interest in philosophy introduced me to the subject and my father whose great pride in his children's accomplishments made us strive to achieve more.

Finally and most importantly – although I hope they need no reminders of how much they are appreciated – I want to express my great gratitude to my husband, Geraint *sine qua non* and to our son Gareth and daughter Margaret. They have made invaluable contributions to this book, as to life generally, by their intelligent interest, staunch support, technical help and unfailing good humour. It is dedicated to them with great affection.

Abbreviations

AG   G. W. Leibniz, *Philosophical Essays*, R. Ariew & D. Garber (eds & trans) (1989).

AT   *Oeuvres de Descartes*, 12 vols, rev. edn, C. Adam & P. Tannery (eds) (1964–76).

CSM   *The Philosophical Writings of Descartes, Vols I & II*, J. Cottingham, R. Stoothoff & D. Murdoch (eds & trans.) (1985).

CSMK   *The Philosophical Writings of Descartes, Vol. III*, J. Cottingham, R. Stoothoff, D. Murdoch & A. Kenny (eds & trans.) (1991).

D   G. Berkeley, *Three Dialogues between Hylas and Philonous*, J. Dancy (ed.) (1998)

DM   G. W. Leibniz, *Discourse on Metaphysics*. In his *Philosophical Texts*, R. S. Woolhouse & R. Francks (eds & trans.) (1998).

E   B. Spinoza, *Ethics*, E. Curley (ed. & trans.) (1996).

EH   D. Hume, *Enquiries Concerning Human Understanding and Concerning the Principles of Morals*, L. A. Selby-Bigge (ed.), 3rd edn, P. H. Nidditch (ed.) (1975).

G   G. W. Leibniz, *Die philosophischen Schriften*, C. I. Gerhardt (ed.) (1978).

LA   *The Leibniz–Arnauld Correspondence*, H. T. Mason (ed. & trans.) (1967).

NE   G. W. Leibniz, *New Essays on Human Understanding*, P. Remnant & J. Bennett (eds & trans.) (1997).

M   G. W. Leibniz, *Monadology*. In his *Philosophical Texts*, R. S. Woolhouse & Richard Francks (eds & trans.) (1998).

P   G. Berkeley, *A Treatise Concerning the Principles of Human Knowledge*, J. Dancy (ed.) (1998).

PNG   G. W. Leibniz, "Principles of Nature and Grace, Based on Reason". In *Philosophical Texts*, R. S. Woolhouse & R. Francks (eds & trans.) (1998).

T   D. Hume, *A Treatise of Human Nature*, L. A. Selby-Bigge (ed.), 2nd edn, P. H. Nidditch (ed.) (1978).

WF   G. W. Leibniz, *Philosophical Texts*, R. S. Woolhouse & R. Francks (eds & trans.) (1998).

Introduction

The roll call of great early modern Western philosophers trips readily off any undergraduate's tongue: Descartes, Spinoza, Leibniz, Locke, Berkeley and Hume – the rationalists and the empiricists. Again and again, professional philosophers and students alike come back to these figures for instruction and inspiration. The main objective of this book is to set out clearly views on the philosophy of mind held by each of these six figures. Each thinker has a distinct stance on the nature of mind that can be found in his central text or texts. So I shall be mainly looking at Descartes's *Meditations* and *Discourse on Method*, Spinoza's *Ethics*, Leibniz's *Monadology* and *Discourse on Metaphysics*, Locke's *Essay Concerning Human Understanding*, Berkeley's *A Treatise Concerning the Principles of Human Knowledge* and *Three Dialogues between Hylas and Philonous* and Hume's *A Treatise of Human Nature* (especially Book I).

Students of the history of philosophy will be well aware that most commentaries give some attention to the views on mind held by their subject. However, this discussion is usually restricted to a thinker's position on the metaphysics of mind. My intention here is to go beyond this and try to discover what each of the six philosophers has to say that is relevant to four topics that have been of strong interest to philosophers of mind in recent years. So, in each of the six parts to come, the discussion follows the same pattern. I look first at what each thinker takes to be the metaphysical character of mind (in some cases also mentioning personal identity). But then in the second and third chapters, respectively, I turn to the scope and nature of self-knowledge followed by the nature of consciousness. Finally, the fourth and fifth chapters of each part are devoted to the problem of mental causation and then the nature of representation or intentionality. In the remainder of this introduction I shall give a brief outline of the general concerns and problems to be examined under each of these five topic headings.

The metaphysical character of mind: are minds substances and if so what kind?

The word "substance" in non-philosophical parlance usually signifies a kind of stuff like chalk or cheese, treacle or tea. In philosophical writing, however, the term "substance" has a tradition in Western thought, which goes back at least to Aristotle, in which the word is reserved as a technical term for whatever a particular thinker regards as most fundamental in reality. There are two central Aristotelian criteria of substancehood. First of all, substances are those things that have *ontological* primacy, which is to say they are things that do not depend for their existence on the existence of anything else. Substances are "the fundamental entities in the universe, the ultimate objects of natural science".[1] They are the things on which other things depend for *their* existence. Secondly, substances for Aristotle have *logical* priority in the sense that items in other categories – qualities, quantities and so forth – are predicable of ("said of") them whereas substances are always subjects. They are never predicated of (or "said of") anything else.

According to Aristotle, substances are also genuine individuals or unities not just collections, even collections of parts. They are what might be called "free-standing" things capable of existing and persisting independently in a way that neither their properties nor their parts could do. They can survive change, retaining their identity intact through many kinds of alteration, just so long as they retain those features essential to being the kinds of things they are. For Aristotle two paradigmatic examples of substances – things for which, in each case, it seems to him that all the characteristics mentioned so far are true – are the individual man and the individual horse.

By the time Berkeley came to mount his notorious attack on the hypothesis of *material* substance the Aristotelian criteria for applying the term "substance" had come apart to some extent. Or, rather, some writers highlighted one aspect, while others concentrated on another. For a number of Locke's immediate predecessors "substance" carries much less of a concern for individuality and unity, at least where material substance is concerned. Instead, the term occurs in debates about how many *sorts* of fundamental kinds of stuff reality consists in. This change of emphasis is due, of course, to Descartes, whose very influential view that there are two (but only two) sorts of created substance – material substance and rational souls or minds – was at the centre of his metaphysics. Each type of substance has its essential

---

1. Michael Ayers, *Locke: Epistemology and Ontology*, vol. II (London: Routledge, 1991), 18.

attribute. Material substance, or *res extensa*, has extension in length, breadth and height. The rational soul, or *res cogitans*, is essentially the unextended subject of thought.

Once Cartesian substance dualism has been propounded, the attempt to decide what in reality deserves the honorific title "substance" becomes largely the question whether it is dualism, materialistic monism or idealistic monism that best represents the fundamental character of reality. This is to emphasize, almost to the exclusion of the others, the first of Aristotle's criteria of substancehood, according to which substance is what is *independent in existence*. For Descartes, matter and minds each depend for their existence on nothing other than God, who could, if he wished, create either in the total absence of the other. For Spinoza the interdependence that exists between each thing and the next and that unites each thing with its neighbours and its surroundings is so thoroughgoing that nothing short of the whole of reality qualifies as an independent substance although that one substance is both extended (material) and ideal (mental). On the other hand, for Leibniz, *individuality* is paramount in deciding which things are substances: only his immaterial monads have the simplicity, indivisibility and persistence to count as genuine individuals and thus, for him, substances.

When we come to Locke a different facet of the character of the independence that bestows substancehood comes to the forefront; or at least many of Locke's readers, including Berkeley, found this aspect or emphasis in what Locke says of substance. While Locke explicitly endorsed a dualist metaphysical position recognizing both material and immaterial substance (as well as the one divine substance) he also made the following, and other similar, remarks about "substance in general", describing it as "something ... though we know not what it is" (*Essay* II.xxiii.3, 297),[2] and "the supposed, but unknown support of those qualities we find existing" (II.xxiii.2, 296).

Many readers (including Leibniz) took these "something, we know not what" remarks as evidence that substance, whether material or immaterial, was or should have been for Locke, an in-principle-unknowable thing, a kind of "prime matter", necessary because properties cannot exist unsupported, but itself featureless, an impenetrable mystery at the heart of reality.

To Berkeley it seemed that Locke's view was: (i) that the only things whose existence we are certain of, and about which we have knowledge, are the ideas that come to us in sense experience; but (ii) that we are nonetheless

---

2. John Locke, *An Essay Concerning Human Understanding*, P. H. Nidditch (ed.) (Oxford: Oxford University Press, 1975). References in the form, for example, II.xxiii.3, 297, refer to Book II, Chapter 23, §3, page 297.

constrained also to accept that there is an additional unknown realm or world of mind-independent things that act as the unknown causes of those sensible ideas. We can have no contact with that additional realm of material substance (since it is beyond the reach of sense) and can thus know nothing about it: not even how it accomplishes its supposed task of subtending or causing our ideas of sense. Berkeley thinks philosophers are left to fruitless puzzlement about what could possibly be the nature of the relationship of "inherence" that sensible qualities presumably have to the unknown substance that supports them and the equally mysterious relation of "supporting" or "having" that substances bear to the qualities that inhere in them.

Now it may well be that Locke did not in fact believe material substance in particular to be the in-principle-unknowable, explanatorily impotent thing Berkeley and others took him to subscribe to. I shall look at this question in more detail in Part IV as a preliminary to looking at the relationship Locke recognizes between minds or selves and immaterial substance. For now, it only remains to round off this survey of attitudes to substance throughout this period by noting that Hume joined Berkeley in rejecting the idea of material substance and then went him one better by rejecting immaterial substance as well.

In the chapters that follow I shall be asking, about each philosopher in turn, why he gives the answer he does to the question whether individual created *minds* are or are not substances and looking at the case that each thinker makes for his position. I want to trace the impact of the early modern period's growing scepticism about substance on its evolving theories about the nature of mind.

Self-knowledge and the transparency of the mental

The term "self-knowledge" covers at least two areas. On the one hand, it is often used to mean knowledge of the existence and fundamental or meta-physical nature of an individual mind or self by that self; on the other, it can be used to cover knowledge of what is going on in a particular mind, that is, what that mind is doing, its mental states, activities and contents, its ideas, sensations, thoughts, capacities, beliefs, wishes, fears, hopes, desires – in fact, its whole history of current and past experiences.

In recent philosophy of mind there has been considerable debate about the latter sort of self-knowledge: what is sometimes called "first-person authority" about conscious mental contents. This is the supposedly unchallengeable and non-evidence-based knowledge each of us has of what he or she believes, intends, wants and so forth. It seems that our self-knowledge of at least the conscious contents of our own minds has three significant features – salience, immediacy and authority:

- If I believe dinosaurs once roamed the earth or if I intend to have a pork chop for dinner I do not need to be told that I believe and intend these things. My belief and intention are salient for me.
- I know that these are my present belief and intention without considering any evidence from my behaviour, without having to figure them out from the context or do anything to discover them. My belief and intention are immediate.
- And, as already said, I am authoritative with respect to that belief and that intention. I not only know without evidence that this is what I believe and that is what I intend, but I know in a way that cannot be challenged. No one can tell me that I do not have the conscious mental contents (beliefs, intentions, hopes, fears or whatever) that I sincerely claim to have.

These three features can seem to pose a puzzle: how can any sort of knowledge be correctly so characterized? How can there be knowledge that is in this way salient and immediate for its subject, that does not require evidence and that need not be supported by any justification?

We can ask, of each of our philosophers in turn, whether he thinks we possess either kind of self-knowledge: either self-knowledge of our own nature and existence or the sort of self-knowledge of our own mental contents described above. We can also ask how each philosopher thinks that the sort of self-knowledge he ascribes to human minds is obtained and what justifies our claim to have it. Is it a product of introspection? Or is it gained from some other source, for example, some kind of inference?

Descartes would say that we have both sorts of self-knowledge. For him, certainty of his own existence as a thinker who is essentially an immaterial substance or rational soul comes before all other certainties. He also takes himself to have, if not complete and infallible knowledge of, at least access to, everything going on in his mind. For Descartes, there are no such things as unconscious thoughts.

As we have just seen, Hume stands in sharp contrast to Descartes in that he rejects the very idea of substance. For him, there could not be self-knowledge in the sense of knowledge of the existence of a substantial self. Hume is persuaded of this on empirical grounds: he says that he can find no such thing as a self in introspection. But he does not consider himself as lacking full awareness of what is going on in his mind: "since all actions and sensations of the mind are known to us by consciousness, they must necessarily appear in every particular what they are, and be what they appear" (T I.iv.ii, 190).[3]

So, however great the distance between Descartes's and Hume's verdicts on the existence of a substantial self they are agreed in subscribing to the view that has been dubbed "the transparency of the mind" or "the transparency of the mental". This is the view that there are no hidden corners in the mind, no ideas or thoughts, sensations or feelings, or any other mental functions happening there that are unavailable to the mind in which they occur. In fact, all the philosophers examined here, except Leibniz, subscribe to some part (or version) of the doctrine of the transparency of the mental. All five would reject scepticism about our capacity to know at least a good portion of what goes on in our own minds. However, we should look closely at each thinker's views on mental transparency. Some (both Leibniz and Locke come to mind in different ways) look with sympathy on the common-sense view that there are times when deep sleep or anaesthetic robs us of conscious thought.

For Spinoza, individual human minds or selves, like everything else in nature, are through and through knowable since each mind consists in ideas of its body and ideas are nothing if not knowable. Knowability, however, does not guarantee knowledge. Spinoza is persuaded that considerable effort is required to gain the self-knowledge that a contented and indeed moral life requires. Leibniz, too, believes that we have access to our minds and thus self-knowledge. We have a kind of (self-)consciousness (which Leibniz calls "apperception") that informs us of both the nature of the individual self or spirit and the perceptions and thoughts that it is having.

Like the three rationalists, Locke thinks that we have self-knowledge both in the sense of knowledge of the *existence* of the self and in the sense of knowledge of the *nature and contents* of the mind. This knowledge, which we shall look at in detail in Chapter 17, is not knowledge of a substance, whether material or immaterial. Self-knowledge for Locke comes from "that consciousness, which is inseparable from thinking" and it is knowledge of a "person" or "thinking intelligent Being, that has reason and reflection, and can consider it self as it self, the same thinking thing in different times and places" (*Essay* II.xxvii.9, 335).

Commentators disagree about the amount and type of self-knowledge of which Berkeley thinks we are capable. He certainly says that he has a notion of the self, soul, mind or spirit (these are interchangeable terms for Berkeley)

---

3. David Hume, *A Treatise of Human Nature*, L. A. Selby-Bigge (ed.), 2nd edn, P. H. Nidditch (ed.) (Oxford: Oxford University Press, 1978) [T]. References in the form, for example, I.iv. ii, 190, refer to Book I, Part iv, §ii, page 190.

and that that notion is gained in reflection or "by a reflex act" (D III, 232).[4] In Chapter 22, I shall examine some of the differing interpretations and arguments and try to reach a decision about whether or not Berkeley is really committed to knowledge, not just of the existence, but also of the individual nature and mental contents, of the self.

Finally, to return to Hume, it should be noted that despite his rejection of the notion of the self he never says – nor could he coherently do so – that there is no such thing as a mind. And, as I began this section by saying, nor does he deny that we are able to know what is going on in our minds, what perceptions we are experiencing, whether we are sensing or remembering, thinking about real things or entertaining ideas of a fictional or fanciful kind. There is much to explore in Hume's philosophy of mind notwithstanding his dismissal of the idea of a self and his notorious scepticism about personal identity over time. Self-knowledge is ruled out for him only in that he rejects the term "self" and the notion of an immaterial substance as the principle of identity of that individual bundle of impressions and ideas each of us calls "myself".

Consciousness

The puzzle about consciousness that has so perplexed and fascinated philosophers of mind over the past two or three decades is the puzzle of how to account for the difference between those physical things that are uncontroversially lacking in any kind of consciousness, such as rocks, and those that are beyond dispute conscious, such as human beings. What is consciousness and what philosophical analysis can we give of it? Is it a single sort of thing or are there different types of consciousness? Does it consist in some form of internal monitoring, higher-order thought or special kind of inner sense or self-consciousness? Does it depend on the body for any or all of its features?

For Descartes, Leibniz and Berkeley – each in his own highly distinctive way – it is the existence of a rational soul or mind (and, for Descartes, the rational soul's relationship to its physical body) that accounts for the consciousness enjoyed by individual human beings.

For Spinoza, Locke and Hume – again, each for very different reasons and in different ways – consciousness cannot or should not be accounted for by designating it as the activity of a particular substance. Spinoza recognizes individual

---

4. G. Berkeley, *Three Dialogues between Hylas and Philonous*, J. Dancy (ed.) (Oxford: Oxford University Press, 1998) [D]. References in the form, for example, III, 232, refer to dialogue III, page 232 of the original edition, given by Dancy as marginal numbers.

human minds or consciousnesses but for him they are not substances. On the other hand, we must look at the question whether Spinoza's one substance has, as its mental aspect, what could be regarded as a single "world-mind" or a "collective consciousness" or, alternatively, a "divine mind".

For neither Locke nor Hume is consciousness to be identified with, or explained as the activity of, an individual substance. Locke thinks it is in principle possible that a single consciousness could be associated successively with more than one mental (or physical) substance. And Hume, as has been pointed out several times already, does not recognize the existence of any substances at all, whether mental or physical.

The problem of mental causation

We automatically look to an individual's feelings, desires, wishes, fears and hopes, reasons, thoughts and beliefs for an *explanation* of that individual's actions and behaviour. But do mental items of the sorts just listed literally *cause* actions? Does my thirst cause me to pour a glass of water and drink? Does my fear of the approaching Alsatian literally cause me to cross the road out of its path? Is it the murderer's decision to kill (is it that very state of his mind) that causes him to pull the trigger? It seems to be common sense that feelings cause the behaviour designed to alleviate them; that wishes literally prompt actions thought likely to fulfil them; that decisions produce actions in line with those decisions.

However, this common-sense view about the mind's role in our actions has encountered a strong challenge that present-day philosophers of mind have tried to address in a number of different ways. This challenge is the so-called "problem of mental causation", one version of which goes as follows:

(i)   When I pour myself a drink of water "because I am thirsty" (as I would say), there is a whole state of my body, brain and nervous system that is responsible for initiating and carrying out the muscle movements that move my left hand to pick up the glass and my right to pick up the pitcher and pour.

(ii) But this whole, entirely physical, set-up, if it were preceded by the same causal history of neural and other physical events, would produce the water-pouring activity even without the mental state (i.e. even if I did not feel thirsty).

(iii) And, also, without this brain and body state and physical causal history, the pouring would not take place no matter how thirsty I was.

(iv) So it seems that the physical causes and conditions on their own are sufficient (and some such physical causes and conditions are necessary) to produce my action while my mental state, my thirst, has no causal role in the event that is my pouring the water. The would-be mental cause – my thirst – is actually impotent.

This argument is also sometimes called "the physical exclusion problem" because it maintains that the causal sufficiency of physical properties excludes the causal efficacy or potency of mental properties.

Our six philosophers all believe that human minds and their thoughts, feelings, choices and decisions have a genuinely causal role in human actions. But for each of them there are specific obstacles in the way of justifying this belief. Descartes, notoriously, has great difficulty accounting for any sort of mind–body interaction, including, therefore, causation of physical actions by (wholly mental) beliefs or desires. For both Spinoza and Leibniz there are difficulties explaining how an individual human agent could intervene causally in the rigorously determined or pre-ordained course of history: how a wish or belief or decision by an individual could literally be (part of) the cause of an event that already has a complete explanation in terms of prior circumstances or divine creative will.

Locke clearly believes that individuals merit moral praise or blame for their actions and this can only be fair if the choices and decisions of the individuals in question have some genuine causal role in the motivation of the actions judged. But how is such causal power to be accounted for? Berkeley is convinced that minds are the only causes there are but he has been widely thought to be unable to explain how created minds can even initiate movement in their own bodies let alone make changes in their external environment. Hume, too, seems both convinced of our ability to make moral choices and act on our beliefs and decisions and, yet, to lack a substantial response to the question how exactly mental items are able to affect physical realities. We need to explore whether any of our six philosophers has a substantial answer to the problem of mental causation, one that could defend itself successfully against its critics.

Representation and intentionality

A state of affairs that has seemed to many modern day philosophers of mind and psychology to cry out for philosophical explanation is the way thoughts or ideas, items that ordinary speech would describe as "in the head", can stand for or represent things in the world. It is not as if I *decide* that one of my ideas will stand for something, in the way I can decide to let the pepper shaker stand for the referee's assistant when trying to explain the offside rule at the dinner table. The pepper shaker can be made to stand for or represent something for present purposes and it will thus acquire what philosophers' jargon calls "intentionality" or "aboutness", albeit temporarily. I can create something whose whole purpose is to represent or stand for something simply by drawing a symbol on a map and announcing that that symbol is to stand for, say, a hospital. But these two examples are both examples of what has been called "*derived* intentionality". The pepper shaker and the symbol on the map have their intentionality, their aboutness, bestowed on them by a mind. It is not an intrinsic feature of either to represent what it represents. It seems, however, that ideas or thoughts in a subject's head do not need to be *made* the representatives of what they are thoughts or ideas about. Without being made representatives by any action of their possessors, they just do represent the things they stand for or represent. They have "intrinsic" or "original" intentionality. But how?

What is intrinsic intentionality or "representativeness"? Descartes, like Locke, sees ideas as kinds of "natural" representatives of the things and features in the world that they stand for in thought. Spinoza sees ideas as intrinsic aspects of the portions of the one substance that they represent in our minds. For Leibniz, every monad or basic substance, whether or not endowed with conscious perception, has innumerable representations of everything else in the universe whose representational character is given by God in the pre-established harmony.

Berkeley sees sensory ideas as themselves parts of the external world rather than representatives of things outside the mind, although ideas that are copied from sensory ideas can, in a way, represent what they are copied from. Hume thinks ideas are copies of impressions that they represent although they do not represent anything *extra*-mental.

This is the final puzzle from recent philosophy of mind that I wish to examine in the context of the views of each of the six major early modern philosophers in turn. Here, as with the previous topics, I hope it will not be thought that I am approaching the subject like a prospector revisiting an old seam and hoping to find golden nuggets missed by previous miners. No one should expect to find, simply lying about in Leibniz's *Monadology* or Berkeley's *Treatise Concerning the Principles of Human Knowledge*, novel, fully worked-out answers to modern philosophical questions expressed in a modern idiom or directed explicitly at modern concerns. It is always wise to be careful not to read modern answers to modern problems back into classic works whose authors were addressing quite different problems in quite different terms.

On the other hand, the topics and questions I have chosen all have time-less elements at their core; it would be surprising if they found no echo in the writings of six classic philosophers all of whom were deeply concerned with the nature of minds, knowledge, thought, causation and ideas. It certainly seems worth taking the trouble to try to discover what light each thinker might have to shed on any of the puzzles, even if what we unearth is more likely to be a number of interesting hints and exploratory ideas rather than any full-blown (let alone incontrovertible) solutions.

CHAPTER 1

Does Descartes think minds are substances?

Why start an essay devoted to Descartes's theory of mind with the question whether Descartes thinks human minds are substances or not? Doesn't everyone know that Descartes is a mind–body dualist who thinks that minds are things that are utterly metaphysically different from material bodies? Surely there is no question of deciding – getting on for four hundred years after the publication of the *Meditations*[1] – that Descartes was not a dualist after all?

However, recently a number of commentators have seriously questioned the attribution to Descartes of the sort of black and white, unqualified mind–body substance dualism that Gilbert Ryle captured in his famous expression "the ghost in the machine".[2] For, among other things, such a dualism seems to make the explanation of mind–body interaction impossible and is therefore frequently put up as a hopeless and naive view to be demolished by beginners cutting their teeth in the study of philosophy of mind. Yet Descartes appears not to have worried overly about the problem of interaction. Could it really be right to see "the father of modern philosophy" as stumbling unwittingly into irremediable error in his account of the nature of mind and the self?

---

1. All quotations from Descartes's writings are taken from *The Philosophical Writings of Descartes, Vols I & II*, J. Cottingham, R. Stoothoff & D. Murdoch (eds & trans.) (Cambridge: Cambridge University Press, 1985) [CSM.I and CSM.II, respectively] and *The Philosophical Writings of Descartes, Vol. III*, J. Cottingham, R. Stoothoff, D. Murdoch & A. Kenny (eds & trans.) (Cambridge: Cambridge University Press, 1991) [CSMK]. I also include reference to the twelve-volume standard edition of Descartes's works, *Oeuvres de Descartes*, rev. edn, C. Adam & P. Tannery (eds) (Paris: Vrin/CNRS, 1964–76) [AT].
2. Gilbert Ryle, *The Concept of Mind* (Harmondsworth: Penguin, 1963), 17 and *passim*. The traditional mind–body dualist interpretation of Descartes is challenged in very different ways by Desmond M. Clarke, *Descartes's Theory of Mind* (Oxford: Clarendon Press, 2003); Stephen Gaukroger, *Descartes' System of Natural Philosophy* (Cambridge: Cambridge University Press, 2002); Gordon Baker and Katherine Morris, *Descartes' Dualism* (London: Routledge, 1996); and Joseph Almog, *What Am I?* (Oxford: Oxford University Press, 2002). See also John Cottingham, *Descartes' Philosophy of Mind* (London: Phoenix, 1997), ch. 3.

The answer to this conundrum, as might be expected, is complicated. Yes, Descartes is of course *some sort* of substance dualist: in the *Meditations* and elsewhere Descartes presents arguments to support the view that what he calls "the mind" (or, as he dubs it sometimes, "the rational soul"[3] is an intellectual substance distinct from the body. It is something with a nature fundamentally different in a number of important respects from that of matter. In particular, it thinks and it is not extended.

But on the other hand, arguably, there is much more included in what we would now regard as the province of the mental or of human psychology than what Descartes includes in the preserve of his "rational soul" or "mind". And Descartes has much of interest to say about this "much more". Even in the *Meditations*, for example, Descartes says that animals, although lacking intelligence or reason, possess through sensation much of what human beings, too, obtain in sense perception (AT.VII.32; CSM.II.22). Human imagination and sensation (hunger, thirst, pain) result from an "intermingling" (AT.VII.81; CSM.II.56) of soul or mind and body. And when Descartes talks about the motivation of behaviour he says that much of human movement and behaviour is prompted, just as he thinks all of non-human animal behaviour is, by activity in various bodily systems and different kinds of external and internal physical stimuli mediated through the brain.

Again, when we look outside the *Meditations* at Descartes's earlier and later writings (both published and unpublished, including his correspondence) it can be seen that, far from being naive or blind to the subtleties and also *the body-involving character* of human mental life and experience, Descartes was among the earliest philosophers to move in the direction of a scientifically satisfying physical explanation of numerous aspects of these psychological phenomena.

One recent commentator says that "Descartes the metaphysician" may have been a substance dualist but that "Descartes the natural philosopher" (i.e. scientist or naturalist) merely "flirted briefly with substance dualism" largely out of a sense of duty to his former teachers and religious authorities.[4] This may be a bit over-emphatically put: Descartes the man, who was both a metaphysician and a natural scientist, preserved a more sincere and persistent allegiance to the view that *what he called* the mind is a substance than this interpretation perhaps implies. But it might be better to say that when Descartes equates mind with intelligence, intellect and reason as he does in the *Meditations* (AT.VII.27; CSM.II.18) and denies that such things share any of their nature with that of matter as he does when talking about

---

3. See for example AT.XI.48, 131, 200 and AT.VIIIB.347; CSM.II.97, 101, 107, 296.
4. Clarke, *Descartes's Theory of Mind*, 13.

13

the rational soul ("*l'ame raisonnable*") in the *Discourse on Method* (*Discourse*) (AT.VI.46, 59; CSM.I.134, 141) he means by "mind" something very much narrower than is meant when that term is employed by present-day philosophers of mind. In particular, he believes that many of what we would now call "human mental abilities and subjective experiences" (i.e. important parts of what present-day readers would call "the mind") are to be explained in large part by reference to human physiological systems including the brain and (what is now called) "the central nervous system". Examples of such elements of the mind are: a good deal of sense perception including the receiving of ideas and representations in the brain; imagination; feelings and responses to them; pain and pleasure; and the emotions.

What Descartes refers to as the rational soul, mind or intellectual substance is, in two senses, something "left over". It is the slim core of indubitable existence with which the meditator is left in the Second Meditation after doubting away everything about which he is able to suspend belief. It is also the one mysterious agency that, if known, would explain the elements of human mental life that cannot be accommodated in the system of animal physiology to which Descartes was lead by his researches, dissections and experiments over a number of decades of study.

The real distinction argument

Descartes does not define "substance" in the text of the *Meditations*; nor does he offer a proof that either body or mind is a substance. However, elsewhere in his writings he gives definitions of the term that, although they are to some extent at odds with one another, give a good sense of what he regarded as important in deciding whether or not something is a substance. One of these is to be found in the *Principles of Philosophy* (I.51, I.52: AT.VIIIA.24–5; CSM. I.210), where he defines "substance" as something "which exists in such a way as to depend on no other thing for its existence". He hastens to point out that this definition applies in strictness only to God: "But as for corporeal substance and mind (or created thinking substance), these can be understood to fall under this common concept: things that need only the concurrence of God in order to exist". So it appears that Descartes thinks that mind is a substance because it depends on nothing other than God to come into and remain in existence, as indeed does material substance as a whole.

The second definition occurs in an appendix to the Second Replies. There, Descartes defines a substance as anything in which resides "any property, quality or attribute of which we have a real idea" (AT.VII.161; CSM.II.114).

So, spotting, and having a real idea of, a quality or attribute entitles us to say that the thing which has that attribute is a substance. Since I am aware that I am thinking, I am entitled to conclude that that thinking is the property of a thinking substance. I am a substance that thinks.

Thus Aristotle's two criteria of substancehood mentioned in the Introduction – ontological independence and logical primacy – are both relevant in Descartes's decision to call anything a substance. But what makes Descartes go further and say that mind and body are not just two substances as Aristotle's individual man and individual horse are two (material) substances, but that they are utterly metaphysically different *kinds* of substance? Descartes is convinced, as he says in the synopsis of the *Meditations*, that they are "not only different but in some way opposite" (AT.VII.13; CSM.II.10). He thinks that inert extended matter, regardless of what kind or how arranged, cannot think and also that thought is completely unextended. As a result, he maintains that neither could be reduced to the other. Thought is not just a capacity belonging to a particular arrangement of matter. Extension is not a notion or property that could ever be discovered among the properties of a mind.

But how does Descartes *argue for* this utter difference between minds and bodies and the impossibility of reducing one sort of substance to the other?[5] Famously, his main argument in the *Meditations* is what is known as "the real distinction argument" (AT.VII.78; CSM.II.54). It is an argument intended to prove that his own mind and his body are not identical: that they are numerically distinct. He believes that he has established earlier in the *Meditations* that because God exists and is no deceiver, "everything which I clearly and distinctly perceive is of necessity true" (AT.VII.70; CSM.II.48). He also believes that "everything which I clearly and distinctly understand is capable of being created by God so as to correspond exactly with my understanding of it" (AT.VII.78; CSM.II.54). Thus:

---

5. Descartes has a number of arguments for his dualism. Here I discuss at length only the real distinction argument. The interpretation of this argument has inspired a great deal of controversy: to take just one example see the symposium articles: Joseph Almog, "Précis of What Am I?"; Michael Della Rocca, "Descartes–Inseparability–Almog"; and Stephen Yablo, "Almog on Descartes's Mind and Body", all in *Philosophy and Phenomenological Research* **70**(3) (2005), 696–700, 701–8 and 709–16, respectively. There are excellent chapters on Descartes's arguments for dualism (and related material in the Second and Sixth Meditations) in Catherine Wilson, *Descartes's* Meditations: *An Introduction* (Cambridge: Cambridge University Press, 2003); Gary Hatfield, *Descartes and the* Meditations (London: Routledge, 2003); and Margaret D. Wilson, *Descartes* (London: Routledge & Kegan Paul, 1978).

> on the one hand I have a clear and distinct idea of myself, in so far as I am simply a thinking, non-extended thing; and on the other hand I have a distinct idea of body, in so far as this is simply an extended, non-thinking thing. And accordingly, it is certain that I am really distinct from my body, and can exist without it.
>
> (AT.VII.78; CSM.II.54)

The last phrase, "and can exist without it", is crucial. Descartes is arguing that, because he has a clear and distinct idea or understanding of his own mind, God could create that mind without Descartes's body and, indeed, in the absence of *any* other created thing, material or immaterial. That is, Descartes is arguing from his clear and distinct understanding of his mind to the conclusion that his mind (and by extension any created mind) is truly numerically distinct (i.e. separable) from all other substances, including the body with which it seems to have a special relationship.

Descartes's contemporary critics were not convinced by this argument. Arnauld, for example, wondered whether Descartes's understanding of his mind was sufficient to let him know that his thought does not depend on anything material (AT.VII.201–4; CSM.II.141–4). After all, it seems possible to have a clear understanding of something and yet to think it lacks features that, unbeknown to you, it *must* possess since they are essential to the existence of such a thing. Descartes's response to this is to acknowledge the latter point but to claim that his understanding of his mind certainly *is* sufficient to enable him to conclude that it is independent of matter since he can categorically deny to his mind "all the attributes which belong to a body" (AT.VII.227; CSM.II.159).

This reply is unpersuasive. Simply to deny that his mind has any of the attributes of extended substance looks very like begging the question. But Descartes would say that his clear and distinct idea of his mind or rational soul gives him thoroughgoing knowledge of its essence: the essence of his rational soul is thought. To him this means, in turn, that all his mental properties are what he would call "modes of thought" rather than "modes of matter". He tells Thomas Hobbes that the various forms of thinking (understanding, willing, imagining, having sensory perceptions, etc.) are utterly different from the properties "which cannot be thought of apart from local extension" (size, shape, motion, etc.) and that "acts of thought have nothing in common with corporeal acts" (AT.VII.176; CSM.II.124, reply to Hobbes's second objection). This is reminiscent of the truism that it is nonsense to ask, about a thought or idea, "How long is it?" or "How much does it weigh?" Everyone would agree that spatial notions such as length and weight seem wholly inapplicable (in any literal sense) to mental things.

But even if we agree with Descartes that the essential natures of mental and material things are, in his phrase, "some way opposite", we may be reluctant to accept that this establishes substance dualism since, like Hobbes, we may still want a demonstration that mental things do not depend for their existence on physical things. In other words we may still want a proof that mind is what Descartes himself, using his independence criterion, would call a substance.

And if Descartes were to say, using his second criterion, that awareness of thinking entitles him to say that the thinking must be the property of a substance, why must the substance in which thoughts inhere be a different substance from the one in which corporeal properties inhere? What is to stop one substance – say an individual human person – being a multi-purpose device that can both take up space and think?

Descartes himself has made an important concession on this point in the Second Meditation:

> And yet may it not perhaps be the case that these very things [i.e. the body or some ingredient of the body] which I am supposing to be nothing, because they are unknown to me, are in reality identical with the "I" of which I am aware? I do not know, and for the moment I shall not argue the point, since I can make judgements only about things which are known to me. (AT.VII.27; CSM.II.18)

But the real distinction argument does not succeed in making up the deficiency in knowledge that Descartes here confesses. Surely the problem Descartes needs to address is that, as Arnauld says, the power of thought "appears to be attached to bodily organs" (AT.VII.204; CSM.II.143). It is not enough to respond, as Descartes does to Arnauld, that this appearance is no *proof* that the bodily organs cause the thought. In the *Meditations*, Descartes has taken on himself the burden of demonstrating that the body has no essential role in thought. The burden of proof lies with him and it is not clear that he ever succeeds in discharging it.

The nature of matter and the rational soul

Since his main metaphysical argument for dualism does not appear sufficiently compelling to win over his critics, it might be wondered what else – aside from the self-knowledge delivered by reflection, which will be discussed below – sustains Descartes's conviction that there is some non-material part of himself that is the true subject, so to speak, of the first-person pronoun.

17

One obvious answer is that he believes on religious grounds in immortality. But, as he says in both the synopsis to the *Meditations* (AT.VII.14; CSM.II.10) and the Sixth Meditation (AT.VII.85–6; CSM.II.59), any material thing can easily be destroyed by dividing or separating one part of it from another. So he has a strong motive for believing and attempting to show that there is in himself, and by extension every human being, a rational soul, a substance that is not material or dependent for its existence on anything material and thus that its indestructibility and immortality are genuine possibilities (see also *Discourse*: AT.VI.59; CSM.I.141).

A deeper and more complex reason for his persisting belief in the immaterial rational soul lies in his convictions about matter or, rather, his views about what matter is *not*. When writing about inanimate nature Descartes's considered view is mechanism: crudely put, this is the view that all physical phenomena can be explained entirely in terms of matter in motion. Descartes saw no reason why the same view should not be extended to yield true understanding in the study and explanation of living things. This was to adopt a revolutionary – even dangerous – approach given that the orthodox view among Descartes's contemporaries was a traditional Aristotelian account of the natural world according to which all living things are animated by, and are caused to function in all their various ways by, a number of individual souls. Even plants are seen as needing a "vegetative soul" to account for life and nourishment. Animals, in addition to their "vegetative soul", also have a "sensitive (or sentient) soul" to enable physical activities such as breathing and walking; sensing and feeling (seeing light, feeling pain, anger, etc.); remembering and expecting; desire and aversion. On this account, all human animals have, in addition to the two sorts of soul already mentioned, a rational soul as well to make possible thinking, judgement, moral deliberation and choice.

Descartes wants science to move away as far as possible from such accounts of living things since he regards them as explanatorily empty, irrelevant and in some ways seriously misleading. Because he holds that matter is not ensouled in this way but is completely inert, he believes what is needed to understand the activities and physiological systems of living things is nothing but the same sound knowledge of the laws of mechanics that his early work convinced him is sufficient for the detailed and complete understanding of non-living nature. So he says in the *Treatise on Man* that mechanism would explain all the following functions in human beings:

> the digestion of food, the beating of the heart and arteries, the nourishment and growth of the limbs, respiration, waking and

sleeping, the reception by the external sense organs of light, sounds, smells, tastes, heat and other such qualities, the imprinting of the ideas of these qualities in the organ of the "common" sense and the imagination, the retention or stamping of these ideas in the memory, the internal movements of the appetites and passions, and finally the external movements of all the limbs ... these functions follow from the mere arrangement of the machine's [the human body's] organs every bit as naturally as the movements of a clock or other automaton follow from the arrangement of its counter-weights and wheels. In order to explain these functions, then, it is not necessary to conceive of this machine as having any vegetative or sensitive soul or other principle of movement and life, apart from its blood and its spirits, which are agitated by the heat of the fire burning continuously in its heart – a fire which has the same nature as all the fires that occur in inanimate bodies.

(AT.XI.202; CSM.I.108)

These are conclusions that Descartes has reached, not by any sort of *a priori* argument, but on the basis of empirical research and dissections conducted, as he tells one of his correspondents, over a period of eleven years (Letter to Mersenne, 20 February 1639: AT.II.525; CSM.III.134).

Rigorous and protracted though Descartes's researches, experiments and dissections have been, however, there are two remarkable and uniquely human features that stubbornly resist mechanical explanation in terms of human physiology. First of all, mechanism seems unable to explain the kind of flexible human intelligence that can be turned to solving any sort of problem in any area of life. Secondly, when it comes to accounting for our ability to employ language to make our thoughts known to others there seems to be no physiological or material explanation to be found.

In Part V of the *Discourse* Descartes says that, although it is conceivable that a machine could be constructed that could utter words – even words that seem appropriate to several different situations – it is not conceivable that such a machine should "give an appropriately meaningful answer to whatever is said in its presence, as the dullest of men can do". He also observes that: "even though such machines might do some things as well as we do them, or perhaps even better, they would inevitably fail in others, which would reveal that they were acting not through understanding but only from the disposition of their organs". This is because reason is "a universal instrument" whereas a machine, however cunning, has to be designed so that each of its actions is performed by one dedicated device, with the result that for all practical purposes it would be "impossible for a machine to have enough different organs to make it act in all the contingencies of life in the way in which our reason makes us act" (AT.VI.56–7; CSM.I.139–40).

The conclusion that Descartes shortly reaches in the *Discourse* is that the rational soul "cannot be derived in any way from the potentiality of matter, but must be specially created". So Descartes is convinced by his scientific work that there is something *super*natural or beyond the reach of scientific explanation and natural law in each human being and this he calls the "rational soul" or "mind". Imagination, sense perception, and reception of ideas or representations as a result of the activity of the bodily senses are all explicable to some extent within the mechanistic physiology Descartes has devised. But thinking, he believes, requires more than the resources of a machine that is nothing but a material object. So Descartes would say that machines could never be programmed to think and understand. And this is not because, unfortunately, he lived before the invention of really sophisticated electronic material objects such as the latest generation of computers. He believes that thinking and the sort of consciousness he is aware of in himself are beyond the resources of any material, mechanical device, no matter how sophisticated. Thinking and human consciousness can only be achieved by a spiritual substance.

But whereas the description of physical systems such as the circulatory, visual and respiratory systems gives genuine information and understanding about these complex systems, structures and organs, the description of the rational soul as "the 'I' whose essence is thinking" does little more than label the point at which understanding of human animals in terms of their bodily systems runs out. Descartes's mind is a thing that thinks. *How* that thinking is accomplished, he believes, defies explanation. Again, this is not because Descartes, unfortunately, lived before the accomplishment of the sort of sophisticated neurophysiological research that has occurred in the past half century. He would maintain that thought and the sort of consciousness of which he is aware in himself are not the kinds of things that can occur without supernatural agency or that can be explained by any sort of physiological research, however sophisticated. At some stage in the attempted explanation there will come a claim that, say, the thought that "health is undoubtedly the chief good … in this life" (*Discourse* pt 6: AT.VI.62; CSM.I.143) is correlated with this or that brain state or pattern of neuronal firing and the mystery will persist why *just that* physical–mental correlation should obtain. For Descartes this is something that lies beyond the reach of science.

CHAPTER 2

Descartes on self-knowledge

In the letter to the Sorbonne that prefaces the *Meditations* Descartes writes that whereas "many people have considered that it is not easy to discover [the soul's] nature" he thinks the nature and existence of the soul are matters capable of demonstration, that is, they are knowable with the utmost certainty (AT.VII.3; CSM.II.4). He concludes the synopsis by declaring his intention to prove that "knowledge of our own minds and of God ... are the most certain and evident of all possible objects of knowledge for the human intellect" (AT.VII.16; CSM.II.11).

These passages, together with the fact that he subtitles the Second Meditation "The Nature of the Human Mind, and How it is Better Known than the Body", strongly suggest that Descartes thinks self-knowledge of some kind is within the grasp of anyone who makes the effort to reflect and find it. But what sorts of self-knowledge does Descartes think possible? Does he take himself to have knowledge of his existence and essential nature? Does he think that it is possible to obtain knowledge of the contents and capacities of one's own individual mind?

Interwoven with these questions is another question: what does Descartes regard as the referent of the word "self" and also the words "mind", "soul" and "human person or man"? In other words, *what is the self* whose self-knowledge is in question? On the one hand, we have Descartes's explicit statement (in reply to Pierre Gassendi) that he considers the mind "not as a part of the soul but as the thinking soul in its entirety" (AT.VII.356; CSM.II.246). On the other hand, there seems to be a shifting referent for the first-person pronoun throughout the *Meditations*: in Lilli Alanen's apt phrase "Descartes's use of the term 'I' is somewhat floating".[1] So sometimes the "I" Descartes talks about is the "I" of autobiography, which at least purports to refer to the

---

1. Lilli Alanen, *Descartes's Concept of Mind* (Cambridge, MA: Harvard University Press, 2003).

historical personage René Descartes. But sometimes the "I" is nothing but the pure, incorporeal subject of thought. Sometimes, too, it is the embodied soul: "my whole self, in so far as I am a combination of body and mind" (AT. VII.81; CSM.II.56), that is, the full living human person consisting of mind and body united by what he calls elsewhere a "substantial union" (e.g. Fourth Replies: AT.VII.228, 219; CSM.II.160, 154–5; Letter to Regius, January 1642: AT.III.493; CSM.II.206).

In Chapter 1 we saw reason to think that Descartes, if writing today, might be persuaded to apply the term "mind" more broadly to include the human animal's sensations and passions – which account for so many features of our subjectivity including phenomenology (see Chapter 3, § "Phenomenal consciousness") – while keeping the term "rational soul" for the pure self-consciousness (or whatever it is) that he thinks is provided by the immaterial substance he distinguishes from everything material. In Chapter 3 I shall look at what Descartes thinks is contributed by the rational soul to the consciousness and self-consciousness of the human person consisting of rational soul and human body substantially united. But, first, I want to look at what Descartes has to say about self-knowledge in the sense of knowledge of the existence, nature and contents of the rational soul.

The first sort of self-knowledge: knowledge of the existence and essential nature of the rational soul

Descartes assuredly believes he is possessed of certain knowledge that his rational soul *exists* on the basis of what some commentators call "the *cogito* reasoning". After applying his method of doubt throughout the First Meditation, Descartes says at the outset of the Second Meditation that he has come to the view that he could, for all he knows, be suffering a systematic illusion that he possesses a body and bodily senses. Happily, however, if that were the case, the existence of something-suffering-an-illusion could not itself be an illusion or be doubted. So if he is deceived then he undoubtedly exists to be deceived. If he thinks anything at all then he exists to do that thinking. Thus emerges Descartes's certainty of his own existence: "this proposition, *I am, I exist*, is necessarily true whenever it is put forward by me or conceived in my mind ... [This is] the very item of knowledge that I maintain is the most certain and evident of all" (AT.VII.25; CSM.II.17).

In the rest of the Second Meditation the method that Descartes uses to gain self-knowledge of his *essential nature* replicates his First Meditation procedure. There, he peeled away beliefs provided by sense perception and even those provided by logic and mathematics until he was left with the single belief that cannot be doubted because it confirms itself even in every attempt to doubt it. Now, in the Second Meditation, Descartes cleverly begins by asking the question the reader is probably asking: "What is this 'I' whose existence has just been established?" In the investigation that follows, Descartes again employs the method of doubt and canvasses a number of possible identities for the "I".

He had formerly thought himself a man but this suggestion leads into an endless regress of useless technical subtleties generated by traditional philosophers' attempts to define "man". Better simply to use common sense and ask what anyone might think pertains to being a man. Surely it would ordinarily be taken to involve having a face, hands and body, being nourished, moving about and having sense perceptions. But the body and the senses are at present being treated as illusions so these beliefs about what the "I" is are peeled away and discarded, at least for the time being.[2]

Likewise, suggestions from the imagination – for example, that I am a vapour of some kind or the bodily limbs which that vapour is imagined to permeate – all invoke something bodily so they too must be peeled away. Only pure thought is left. "What then am I? A thing that thinks. What is that? A thing that doubts, understands, affirms, denies, is willing, is unwilling, and also imagines and has sensory perceptions" (AT.VII.28; CSM.II.19).

Descartes has now reached a first certainty about the nature of his mind that most readers therefore think he regards as a truth and thus a piece of self-knowledge. He knows from the *cogito* that he exists and he knows through this procedure of peeling away what could be illusory that he is at least (and possibly at most) a thing that thinks. Not that he takes himself to know, at this stage at any rate, that he is a persistent or enduring individual. Nor does he know what a thing capable of thought is or what it requires for its existence.

It is appropriate to point out that the sort of enquiry just described, which issues in "an easier and more evident perception of my own mind than of anything else" (AT.VII.34; CSM.II.23), despite the presence in this quotation of the word "perception", is *a rational or intellectual process* that leads to knowledge in the sense of "understanding" of the thinking thing rather than any sort of sensory or sense-like glimpse or inner view of the self. There is a tradition, associated with Ryle among many others, of interpreting Descartes as claiming that we gain all our knowledge of our own minds by introspection, construed as inner sense. This interpretation seems to me very far off

---

2. Michael Ayers, "The Second Meditation and Objections to Cartesian Dualism", in *Early Modern Philosophy: Mind, Matter, and Metaphysics*, C. Mercer & E. O'Neill (eds), 24–45 (New York: Oxford University Press, 2005).

the mark where Descartes's knowledge of his own existence and nature (as essentially a thing that thinks) are concerned. The latter part of the Second Meditation is precisely devoted to trying to establish the *unfitness* of any sort of sensory mechanism for furnishing knowledge and understanding of the true natures of things. Descartes uses the example of a piece of wax that he sees and handles but comes to *know*, not by this employment of his senses, but only by reasoning and judgement. What he concludes to be true of the wax is clearly meant to apply to the mind as well: "bodies" Descartes writes, "are not strictly perceived by the senses or the faculty of imagination but by the intellect alone, and … this perception derives not from their being touched or seen but from their being understood" (AT.VII.34; CSM.II.23).

The "I", the thinking thing, is likewise known, not by any sort of inner *sense*, but by the intellect that discovers that the "I" exists (necessarily) whenever it is thinking and is essentially a thinking thing. It does this by doubting away and rejecting every other suggestion as to what, including everything material, the mind might be taken by ordinary common apprehensions to be. The *cogito* reasoning that assures me of my existence is clearly not a form of inner sensation or interior glimpsing. My perception of my mind and discovery of its essential nature (by doubting away everything that might be delusory in my idea of myself) are no more exercises of inner sense than true perception of the wax is an exercise of the outer, bodily senses.[3]

How seriously does Descartes intend us to take his claim to know his own mind better than he knows anything else? Does he really claim that what is known through self-knowledge by the understanding is more certain or better known than anything known through the senses? I think that, at the very least, he believes he has established that he knows his own existence and essential nature as a thinking thing better than he knows any sense-perceived object since, for example, every time he thinks he sees an object he cannot be sure that there is an object or that he does in fact see it but at the same time

---

3. An anonymous helpful reader has suggested that it is unclear what "inner sensation" is or would be. When Descartes claims that the *cogito* is "self-evident by a simple intuition of the mind" (and not "by means of any syllogism") (AT.VII.140; CSM.II.200) might he not mean that the conclusion that I exist is one given in inner sense? But intuition is not a sensory or quasi-sensory mechanism for Descartes. He writes: "By 'intuition' I do not mean the fluctuating testimony of the senses" (AT.X.368; CSM.I.14). A Cartesian "simple intuition of the mind" is a swift exercise of the intellect, as when one realizes in a single mental grasp or operation that a proposition in geometry follows from its premises; it is not anything like a mental glance or glimpse. And sensation, syllogisms and deductions are not the only means by which the intellect can arrive at understanding; there is also (at least) the method of doubt.

he does know that he is *thinking* he sees that object and thus that a thinker exists to do that thinking.

So far I have just been talking about the self-knowledge of his existence and nature as a rational soul that Descartes discusses in the Second Meditation. When, in the Sixth Meditation, he turns again to a question about his essence, namely the question whether it involves having and using an imagination, he once again employs a method that bears little resemblance to introspection conceived as use of an inner sensory mechanism as a source of evidence. He comes to know that his essence does not involve imagination, not by looking (however metaphorically) at his inner self and seeing that imagination is not one of its parts, but by considering whether he could possibly have existed, or now continue to exist, without that faculty. His reason tells him that this would be perfectly possible; there is no logical contradiction in supposing that he might lack (or always have existed without) imagination (AT.VII.73; CSM.II.51).

The second sort of self-knowledge: knowledge of the contents and capacities of the individual rational soul

The previous section looked at the question whether Descartes believes that we can have self-knowledge of the existence and essential nature of our minds and concluded that he does indeed believe this and also that human beings come by this knowledge about themselves not by introspection, but by successive applications of the method of doubt. We now turn to the question whether Descartes thinks that self-knowledge of the *contents* of our minds is possible and, if so, how such particular self-knowledge (as it might be called) is acquired and how far it extends.

The answer to the first part of this question is that Descartes does think that each human mind has some sort of access to its own contents. He is sure that, in some sense or other, we are all able to know what ideas, sense perceptions, beliefs, desires, wishes, hopes, fears and so on we have, and also what mental activities such as reasoning, deciding, judging, remembering, willing and so forth are taking place at any given time in our minds. And most of Descartes's present-day readers would say, quite correctly, that he thinks we each employ what is sometimes called "the Cartesian introspective model" (or "inner observation model") for acquiring this self-knowledge of our individual mental contents, activities and powers. Most of these readers would also say that such a view is open to several trenchant criticisms that it cannot survive.

So we need to ask, "What is the Cartesian introspective model?",[4] "What are the criticisms levelled against this model?" and "Is Descartes guilty of falling into the errors of which his critics accuse him?" In particular we need to ask whether Descartes can be acquitted of the charge that he is strikingly inconsistent in several of his claims about the nature of our self-knowledge of the contents of our minds.

What is the so-called Cartesian introspective or "inner observation" model of self-knowledge? According to this view, the mind is a kind of inner realm where thinking takes place and that also acts as a private container holding all of a subject's ideas, including sense perceptions and sensations, beliefs, desires, reasonings, acts of will, decisions, imaginings and so on. Further, on this view we each have a kind of inner sense that is strongly analogous to the outer bodily senses in its operation, providing private observational access to this storehouse of mental states or ideas that exist as independent entities, always available to be encountered in such introspection.

This brief outline accurately captures the main features of Descartes's position provided we make two vital qualifications. First, he does not regard the sort of inner observation by which we know our own thoughts as literally the exercise of any sort of sensory mechanism; nor is it clear that he ever presses the analogy between mental inspection of ideas and bodily sensation very far. Secondly, it is not obvious how autonomous or independent Descartes takes individual mental contents or ideas to be. He sometimes writes as if he thinks the mind is pre-stocked with all its ideas (not just the so-called "innate" ones), which are there to be found – or not – depending on the subject's circumstances and history. On the other hand he also sometimes seems to say in a Berkeleian (or Lockean) manner that the existence of ideas depends on their being had or thought by their subject.

What critics find objectionable about this so-called "Cartesian introspective model" of self-knowledge of mental contents is the implication they find in it that the deliverances of introspection are automatic and also infallible so that: first, I cannot help being aware or conscious of any and every mental state or activity that is in any way in my mind; and secondly, I cannot be mistaken about any of my mental contents. The first of these is the view that Descartes believes that the mind is completely transparent to itself. The second is the view that he thinks every individual is infallible about each of his or her mental states. Both mental transparency and such infallibility seem

---

4. Crispin Wright, Barry C. Smith and Cynthia Macdonald (eds), *Knowing Our Own Minds* (Oxford: Clarendon Press, 2006), 2–4, 23.

to their critics to be shown false by everyday experience and thus to be indefensible claims about self-knowledge of mental contents.

But does Descartes's view of introspection actually commit him to either of these positions? Does his notion of inner inspection amount to the belief that there are no ideas or mental states that exist without their owner's knowledge or even noticing? And does he think that every mental state or event is known through and through in every aspect by its subject so that subjects can never be mistaken about any aspect of their own mental contents?

Descartes does not himself use the term "introspection", unsurprisingly, since it seems that the word was not actually coined or in use in any language until after his death.[5] He certainly sometimes uses expressions that suggest that he sees mental activity as a kind of non-sensory inspection of ideas. For example, when he comes to contrast the mind's use of imagination with the mind's pure understanding he says that "when the mind understands, it turns towards itself and inspects one of the ideas which are within it" whereas the imagination "turns towards the body and looks at something in the body which conforms to an idea understood by the mind or perceived by the senses" (AT.II.73; CSM.II.51). He is here making the point that pure thought and understanding are not directed on the body or corporeal things.

In this passage, however, Descartes does not write as if the mind's capacity to turn inwards towards its ideas and "inspect" them means either that introspection is automatic, irresistible and total, or that such inspection confers complete and infallible knowledge of its objects. On other occasions, however, in sharp contrast, Descartes does say explicitly that there is nothing in his mind of which he is not in some manner conscious and that that consciousness or knowledge is certain and infallible so that his judgements about his own mental states or ideas cannot be erroneous.[6] In the First Replies he says that "precisely in so far as I am a thinking thing ... there can be nothing within me of which I am not in some way aware" (AT.VII.107; CSM.II.77; see also Fourth Replies: AT.VII.246; CSM.II.171). In the Second and Third Meditations Descartes writes, among many such comments, that "I think", "I will", "I affirm", "I deny", "I imagine" and "I seem to feel heat (seem to see

---

5. William Lyons, *The Disappearance of Introspection* (Cambridge, MA: MIT Press, 1986) cites *A New English Dictionary on Historical Principles*, J. A. H. Murray (ed.) (Oxford: Clarendon Press, 1888), in turn citing Sir Matthew Hale: "The actings of the Mind or Imagination it self, by way of reflection or introspection of themselves" (*The Primitive Origination of Mankind, Considered and Examined According to the Light of Nature* [London, 1677], I ii 55).
6. For an excellent discussion of this topic and a detailed presentation of the textual evidence for both parts of this assertion see Wilson, *Descartes*, 150ff.

light, etc.)" are all indubitable: I am infallible when I make any of these judgements. I cannot think that I am feeling heat or imagining or thinking and turn out to be mistaken.

Can anything be done to defend Descartes against the charge of simple inconsistency here? We might begin by noting the phrase "*in some way* aware" in the quotation above. Descartes certainly holds that there can be and are numerous ideas in a person's mind of which he is at most minimally aware at any given time. There are, for example, all the many ideas stored in memory of which a subject is not currently thinking no matter how much he might be disposed to assent to them once he recalls them. Descartes certainly does not believe or say that he is actively aware at every moment of every idea of which he has ever been fully aware at some point in the past and could now remember.

The same is true of the many ideas that Descartes believes are innate in the human mind. He says both that prejudice can prevent an individual from seeing the truth of an innate idea and that it is even possible for an inattentive or distracted mind to fail throughout its human life ever to come to awareness of an innate idea such as the innate idea of God. And this is despite the fact that innate ideas, as the phrase implies, are inborn and potentially knowable even in the womb.

Again, far from claiming that he knows everything there is to know about all his current fully conscious ideas, thoughts, emotions and experiences he sometimes explicitly denies this. In the Fifth Meditation he says that certain ideas, such as the idea of a triangle, can be discovered to contain features that he had not thought of at all when previously, for example, imagining a triangle (AT.VII.64; CSM.II.45).

Further examples of Descartes's recognition and understanding of the existence of ideas of which their subject is only minimally or partly aware (and their importance in human psychology) can be found repeatedly throughout his writings. This is especially true in his correspondence, where Descartes shows that he is subtly aware of many ways in which a person's mind and behaviour can be influenced not only by the body's state of health but by long-forgotten incidents, thoughts and experiences and by perceptions and sensations not noticed in detail at the time. He also shows in his understanding of his philosophical opponents' psychological motivation that he is very much alert to the effect that unacknowledged preferences, biases, pride, envy, fear and so on (of which their subject would sincerely deny awareness) can have on their subject's behaviour. Descartes is as ready as most present-day psychologists to recognize that a person can have mental states of which he is to some degree unaware and that a person's ideas can have features that remain to some degree hidden from him.

So how is Descartes to be rescued from the charge of glaring inconsistency? The discussion so far has simply made clear that Descartes does in fact say *both* that the human mind is conscious of all the ideas it has *and* that there are some ideas in every mind that are invisible to their possessor until attended to. I have been attempting to show how Descartes might have thought that these two positions were not inconsistent by interpreting Descartes as saying that there is a kind of bare or minimal awareness or consciousness of one's ideas that consists simply in being able to access those ideas in the right circumstances. According to this view the many innate and memory ideas of which we are only minimally aware at a given time are not "invisible". They simply occupy the margins of our minds and are there to be seen when we turn our concentrated attention to them in reflection. They are conscious in the sense that they are potentially fully conscious. As Descartes says at the beginning of the Fifth Meditation, I seem with respect to such ideas to be "noticing for the first time things which were long present within me although I had never turned my mental gaze on them before" (AT.VII.64; CSM.II.44).

It has to be admitted that this can, at first sight, seem a feeble defence against the inconsistency charge. Surely an idea I have never turned my mental gaze on before is not a "minimally conscious" idea: it is one that has been *un*conscious until now. Would it not have been much better for Descartes to do as Leibniz was later to do and abandon the view that absolutely all ideas are conscious? It seems so clear that Descartes – every bit as much as Leibniz – recognized that there can be and are many ideas in any given mind of which that minded subject is wholly unaware and that pass utterly unnoticed for some or all of that individual's mental history.

But there is a way of rescuing Descartes from this renewed accusation of glaring inconsistency. If Descartes recognized more than one type of consciousness or sense for the term "conscious" then it is entirely possible that, for him, some ideas (e.g. memories and innate ideas) might be conscious in one sense while remaining unconscious in another sense.

The inner observation model of introspection encourages the view that the only sort of conscious awareness is that analogous to inspecting a visual field. The analogy pictures the rational soul as scanning or directing a mental gaze on a mental visual field or array of ideas that are somehow there to be "seen" just as objects in the visual field may be there and visible even if not yet attended to. But this account seems to come unstuck when we realize that consciousness is being treated as equivalent to "falling under the gaze of the mind". How can ideas that have not yet fallen under the mind's gaze be conscious at all, even minimally or barely so? How can ideas be there in the mind (i.e. conscious) awaiting the mental gaze on which being conscious depends?

But there are many indications in Descartes's writings that he was alive to the existence of a number of other sorts of consciousness or awareness other than introspective noticing: ones where the rational soul need not be engaged. For him, to take one example, physical states that arise in the subject when the bodily sense organs are physically affected give rise to brain states that (in us) in turn affect the rational soul. Non-human animals that lack a rational soul can nonetheless experience such physical states: they can have an affected sense organ and the brain state resultant from it, and are said by Descartes to have, in this way, sensations such as seeing light and hearing sound. If these physical sensations – for any sort of animal, human or not – are regarded as conscious in their own distinct way (call it "perceptually conscious") then that could go some way to explain how Descartes could think there was nothing in the mind that was not conscious and yet think that the mental gaze of the rational soul was needed to make some ideas in the mind conscious in the fullest, perhaps most significant, possible sense.

In the past, commentators have taken Descartes to identify thinking (the essential activity of the rational soul) with the whole of, and every sort of, mental activity and conscious awareness. This would make Descartes committed to the implausible view that there can be no thoughts, ideas, sense perceptions or any other mental states of any kind that are outside the realm of the rational soul. In the next chapter I shall argue in detail that this view seriously distorts our understanding of Descartes's extensive and sophisticated grasp of human psychology. It misses Descartes's implicit recognition that human selves or persons, consisting as they do of a substantial union of rational soul and living human animal, experience different sorts of consciousness. It thus misinterprets Descartes as inconsistent in his claims about the scope and limits of our self-knowledge of the contents of our minds.

CHAPTER 3

Human consciousness and the rational soul

A misleading interpretation[1]

Descartes has often been portrayed as restricting consciousness of all kinds to those animals that possess rational souls, that is, to human beings. Supporting this conclusion is the claim that Descartes regards consciousness as equivalent to thought and also that he always gives the verb *cogitare* a much wider sense than that of the English verb "to think". According to this view, Descartes includes in "thinking" not only the having of sense perceptions and feelings like pains but even the sensations of walking and of uttering something aloud.[2] So this interpretation sees Descartes as equating consciousness with thoughts, that is, mental states of all sorts, which, therefore, because these all require a rational soul, human beings alone can experience.

There is so much in this that is wrong, seriously misleading or both that it is difficult to know where to begin in trying to correct it. For a start, it assumes Descartes has a clear, unequivocal sense or meaning for the term "consciousness" (and that we can be certain what that meaning is). In fact, the term "consciousness" is very rarely to be found anywhere in Descartes's writings and, crucially, in talking about the distinction between human beings and other creatures Descartes never uses the term "consciousness".[3] So anyone wishing to defend the view that Descartes restricts consciousness to beings possessed of rational souls (and to the operation of those souls) owes us a great deal of supporting argument that is seldom to be found in writings where this conclusion is asserted. Again, the view outlined in the first paragraph assumes that Descartes explicitly denies that non-human

---

1. This chapter uses material about consciousness and the rational soul adapted from my paper "Does Descartes Deny Consciousness to Animals?" *Ratio* 19 (2006), 336–63.
2. A. Kenny, *Descartes A Study of His Philosophy* (New York: Random House, 1968), 44–5.
3. J. Cottingham (ed.), *Descartes* (Oxford: Oxford University Press, 1998), 23.

31

animals, because they lack rational souls, possess whatever feature the term "consciousness" designates. But he never makes any such denial.

As to the supposed broadening of "*cogitare*" to include all conscious mental activity including sense perception, this again is more frequently simply asserted than argued for. And where it is defended the offered defence depends almost entirely on what is by no means a universally agreed reading of two passages from the Second Meditation. First: "But what then am I? A thing that thinks. What is that? A thing that doubts, understands, affirms, denies, is willing, is unwilling, and also imagines and has sensory perceptions" (AT.VII.28; CSM. II.19). This passage occurs at the start of Descartes's first attempts to discover the nature of the thinking thing whose existence has been established by the *cogito*. To some readers it seems to be a declaration that it is the rational soul alone that does all these things, including the imagining and the having of sense perceptions, which are added to the list after "and also". But Descartes is about to consider whether or not it is in fact one and the same "I" that does all these things. His answer is importantly qualified and therefore not as helpful to the interpretation I am criticizing as its friends might have hoped. He says that it *is* the same "I" who doubts, and so on, and who also:

> has sensory perceptions, or is aware of bodily things as it were through the senses. For example, I am now seeing light, hearing a noise, feeling heat. But I am asleep, so all this is false. Yet I certainly *seem* to see, to hear, and to be warmed. This cannot be false; what is called "having a sensory perception" is strictly just this, and in this restricted sense of the term it is simply thinking.
> (AT.VII.29; CSM.II.51)

So no sooner has Descartes said that the same subject who doubts, understands, and so on also has sensory perceptions than he qualifies what he has said by drawing a distinction between, on the one hand, seeing light, hearing a noise and feeling heat and, on the other, *seeming* to see, to hear and to be warmed. Surprisingly, it is the latter that Descartes says are cases of "having a sense perception" *in the strict sense*, that is, being "aware of bodily things *as it were* through the senses".

Descartes is saying that phrases such as "seeing light", "hearing a noise" and "feeling heat" are ambiguous. They refer in strictness to the mind's seemings, to the awareness the rational soul has of how things *appear*. I may think I see light, hear a noise, feel heat when my bodily senses are in fact actually in contact with light, sound, something warm. But, I may also have these same seemings when no such real sensory contact is happening.

However, this is not just a point about the possibility that my seemings may mislead me about the physical world because of a lack of true sensory contact through my senses: the cited passage is making the crucial point that awareness of bodily things through the senses on the one hand, and the rational soul's seemings on the other, can come apart so that each can occur in the absence of the other. Shortly, we shall see that Descartes says that I may also have true sensory contact or awareness through the senses when my rational soul is *not* engaged, either because I am asleep, or in a fit, or because I am distracted, perhaps by some strong feeling or emotion, perhaps by more interesting or pressing concerns or deliberations where my reason is wholly occupied. Or I may simply have no time to think before I perform some needed action. Again, I may be immersed in routine to which I am not giving any attention with my reason. In all such cases I have a sort of animal sensory awareness because my sense organs, nerves and brain are suitably engaged even though this is "thoughtless" because it takes place in the absence of input from the rational soul.[4]

The reading I have just given owes a debt to, among others, the work of Gordon Baker and Katherine Morris,[5] who have argued persuasively *against* the view that Descartes intends to include sensations and feelings such as pain, love, fear, hunger and joy, sense perceptions, and exercises of the imagination in "thinking". They point out that Descartes regards phrases such as "seeing light" and "feeling heat" as ambiguous and contend that he is better interpreted as keeping the term "thought" for the faculty that is aware that (and what) the agent *seems* to be sensing, perceiving, feeling and imagining and for the more narrowly reason-involving activities of reflection and moral deliberation. This means that there is more to human mental life, subjective awareness, feeling and experience than just conscious *thought*. In what follows I shall argue that there is indeed more to human consciousness and subjective experience on Descartes's view than the reason and self-consciousness provided by the rational soul.

Human consciousness

In the Introduction I remarked that consciousness has had a curious treatment by philosophers of mind in the past hundred years. Initial almost total neglect – or even denial – has been followed recently by careful attention

---

4. In the rest of this chapter the term "thoughtless" will be used in exactly this way to mean without input from, or engagement by, the rational soul.
5. For example see Baker & Morris, *Descartes' Dualism*, 25.

leading to the recognition of an array of numerous types of consciousness (or senses of "conscious") all jostling for inclusion in our understanding of human subjectivity. At least the following are distinguished by many authors: organism consciousness, perceptual consciousness, access consciousness, phenomenal consciousness and introspective consciousness. On some theories, consciousness is seen as a sort of second-level or higher-order thought or awareness that a subject obtains by means of some variety of inner monitoring or interior scanning that may or may not be equated with introspection or inner sense. Theorists continue to debate the nature and operations of the different sorts of consciousness just listed and whether one or another can exist in the absence of one or another of the others. There is also dispute about whether there is, in fact, only one sort of consciousness that manifests itself differently in different subjects (and different species of subject) or whether there are several comparatively autonomous and unconnected sorts of consciousness that cannot be reduced one to the other.

It can be maintained that Descartes recognized, in his theory of the mind of the "substantial union" (of rational soul and living human body), all the different senses or types of consciousness just listed, not that he used present-day – or any – technical labels for all the different sorts of conscious experience or awareness he was able to distinguish. But Descartes's many different examples of types of "thoughtless" human actions (in many different writings)[6] point to a subtle understanding on his part of the numerous different varieties of conscious awareness of which both human minds alone, and also human minds in common with those of other creatures, are capable. The mistaken interpretation sketched in the first paragraph above usually includes the explicit claim that Descartes's view of consciousness is an all-or-nothing view: that Descartes thinks that "either a creature has the full range of conscious powers, and is capable of language and abstract thought as well as sensation and feelings of hunger, or it is an automaton, with no experience of any kind".[7] It seems to me, on the contrary, that there is much evidence, in Descartes's writings on animal motivation and behaviour, to support the contention that he does not subscribe to this austere either/or view but rather

---

6. There are passages in a number of letters: to Newcastle, November 1646 (AT.IV.569–76; CSMK.302–4); to More, February 1649 (AT.V.276–9; CSMK.365–7); to Reneri for Pollot, May 1638 (AT.II.39–41; CSMK.99–100); Fourth Replies (AT.VII.229–30; CSM.II.160–61); to Plempius for Fromondus October 1637 (AT.I.413; CSMK.61–2); *Treatise on Man* (AT. XI.143ff.; CSM.I.99–108).
7. Bernard Williams, *Descartes: The Project of Pure Inquiry* (Harmondsworth: Pelican, 1978), 284.

recognizes many sorts of conscious awareness for the mind–body union that do not involve thought, that we share with (some) animals and that thus do not rely on the presence or workings of a rational soul. Some of our conscious awareness is thanks to the rational soul but some is simply down to our animal nature.

This is not to downplay in any way the contribution of the rational soul to human mental life. Abstract thought and flexible reasoning such as are demanded by language use and by complex problem-solving as well as science, moral deliberation and choice – all these on Descartes's view are made possible for human beings (and for them alone in the animal kingdom) by possession of a rational soul. But much of human conscious experience for Descartes also is, as it is for all the other animals, a matter of the operation of the sensitivities and autonomous mechanisms of the bodily organism, just as are the vital functions of nutrition, breathing, circulation of the blood and so on. He wants to persuade his readers that no "vegetative souls" or "sensitive souls" such as natural historians of his time often appealed to in explaining animal (and plant) behaviour are needed to account for these vital functions.

And it can be argued that the physical sensitivities and mechanisms with which Descartes wants to replace these sorts of animal souls need not be regarded as a behaviourist would regard them. Descartes regularly ascribes passions to animals – fears, hopes, joys, pleasures and pains, recognitions and expectations – with no suggestion that these purely physical states and episodes are not also *experienced* by their animal subjects. It is not even the case that Descartes maintains that human animals alone can express their passions. Rather, he says that human animals alone can express in language *something other than* their passions. For all Descartes explicitly says to the contrary, he could be a committed non-reductive materialist about feelings and sensations, regarding them, for human animals as well as non-human ones, as supervening on or emerging from the inner workings of the animal-machine *and being experienced by their animal subject* even in the absence of a rational soul.

Consciousness without the rational soul

Organism consciousness

One relatively uncontroversial sort of consciousness that present-day writers often introduce early in their discussions of the nature of consciousness is what is called variously "organism consciousness" or "minimal consciousness".

This is the sense of "consciousness" in which a subject is conscious if it is capable of being awake although also capable of being asleep or of being rendered unconscious by a blow, illness, drugs and so forth. Clearly Descartes holds that human beings are conscious in this sense and equally clearly he does not think consciousness in this sense is restricted to human beings. Such conscious awareness is a product of the complexity and physical capacities of the animal organism.

In the course of explaining what motivates the actions of non-human animals (and human beings at times when their rational soul is not operative) Descartes considers the case of the sleepwalker (and also the sleepswimmer). A sleepwalker, like an animal that lacks a rational soul, can often perform actions that are purposive and appear guided by intentions of the subject. These actions may occasion astonishment since they are done while the agent is asleep yet may display more competence in execution than their agent is capable of when awake. However, the point of the example is to show Descartes's readers that apparent genuine purposiveness is no proof of the presence and influence of a rational soul. For Descartes would say that a sleepwalker, being asleep, is not guided by his rational soul and yet, nonetheless, he does what he does on purpose and sometimes in order to achieve a discernible end.

This "thoughtless" walking or swimming differs from two other Cartesian illustrations: the example of the man who parries a blow before he has time to think what to do (Letter to Newcastle, November 1646: AT.IV.569; CSMK.302); and the example of the man who blinks at a playful mock blow from a friend even though he wills not to (*Passions of the Soul* I.13: AT.XI.338–9; CSM.I.333–4). Both recipients of blows, unlike the sleepwalker, are awake but they have no time to deliberate or plan and simply act on a reflex. Here are two further cases of "thoughtless" action (where the rational soul is not involved). But Descartes does not say or imply that the reflexive blow-parrying and blinking are done without the subjects' being aware of what they are doing. Both are aware of what is happening and each is aware that, on his part, there is no thought involved. What differentiates the two is that one does and the other does not act "on purpose", "intentionally" or "as he wills to act". The second man acts against his own will. So, action of which the subject is conscious that is reflexively triggered gives us another sort of conscious awareness enjoyed by human beings without the involvement of the rational soul. Such an action can be experienced by the subject as being either willed (intentional) or not.

By using both examples Descartes is strengthening the case he is making in these passages that behaviour apt for its circumstances is no proof of the presence or guidance of reason. But he is also simultaneously making clear that acting intentionally or on purpose (on a purpose of which the actor is aware) and acting under the guidance of reason are not equivalent, and that awareness or consciousness by the subject that he is acting on purpose and for a particular end of which he is aware are not necessarily restricted to human minds and are, in human beings, not necessarily provided by the rational soul.

Perceptual consciousness
The example of the sleepwalker is very reminiscent of David Armstrong's oft-discussed example of the long-distance lorry driver,[8] which Armstrong uses to illustrate what he calls "perceptual consciousness". The driver, following when tired a route with which he is familiar to the point of tedium, goes into a state of automatism where nonetheless he manifestly still retains the sensory awareness necessary to obey traffic lights, avoid ditches and parked cars and steer through the convolutions of the route without accident. He is not asleep (unconscious in that sense) but in another sense he *is* unconscious. He might afterwards deny that he had been aware of what he was doing while driving and say that he can now recall no features of the journey. He might also say that this is because, while he was en route, "his mind was elsewhere".[9]

Similarly, in all Descartes's examples discussed so far the behaviour attributed to the subject attests to the possession by that subject of sensory awareness of his changing situation. The sleepwalker or sleep-swimmer must see and hear in order to navigate and deal with the features of the route he takes. The blow-parrier must sense the direction from which the impending blow is coming and use his senses to direct whatever he uses to ward off the blow when it comes.

Descartes has further examples of behaviours that he would say do not involve thought but that certainly involve sensory awareness of the subject's surroundings and situation. In routine activities – walking to the shops, singing at choir practice, eating dinner – my mind may not be "on" how to walk, sing or ply my cutlery. I have long since learned how to do these things so thought will only be required if I run into some snag: broken pavement, trouble keeping correct pitch, a tricky piece of gristle. Reason is not needed

---

8. D. M. Armstrong, "What *is* Consciousness?", in his *The Nature of Mind and Other Essays*, 55–67 (Ithaca, NY: Cornell University Press, 1981), 59, and *A Materialist Theory of the Mind* (London: Routledge & Kegan Paul, 1968), 93.
9. As Descartes says too: Letter to Plempius for Fromondus, 3 October 1637 (AT.I.413; CSMK.61–2).

when I am doing any of these activities in a straightforward, routine way. So I am not ordinarily conscious *that* I am aware of the things of which I must, nonetheless, be perceptually conscious in such circumstances. Descartes is not prepared to say that matter, however cunningly arranged, could *reason*. This, however, leaves a great deal of capacity for sensory awareness, feeling, emotion and guidance of behaviour by the light of remembered perceptions still within the scope of the bodily machine functioning without the participation of the rational soul.

Access consciousness

Cases like those just discussed of perception that is to some degree automatic or inadvertent call to mind the sorts of states that Ned Block dubs "access conscious" states. Block's notion of access consciousness is, as he says, a *functional* notion. It is the notion of a subject's being in possession of a representation that is "poised" *inter alia* "for direct … control of action".[10] The man who puts out his arm on purpose to protect his head when he falls, although he has no time to work out what he ought to do, is simply guided by his perception of the approaching fall. He has access to the information that he is about to fall. This perception is a representation poised to guide action and it does so: Descartes is crediting the man with Blockian access consciousness of the imminent accident.

But someone might say that, on the contrary, Descartes would not accept that the man has access consciousness of the danger. Admittedly, what happens is not simple reflex or stimulus response. But the man's action is much more like the switching on of the heating by the thermostat when the room temperature drops. It is a response to circumstances triggered entirely mechanically in the absence of any impetus deriving from awareness or interpretation of those circumstances.

But as noted in Chapter 1 (p. 19), Descartes does credit human (and other) animals with ideas or representations that arrive in the brain entirely independently of the rational soul. What is controversial in the example is the claim that these representations have significance or meaning for their subject, whose action is guided by an appreciation of that significance. The man who braces himself to break his impending fall, like the sheep that runs from a wolf but not from the shepherd (Fourth Replies: AT.VII.229–30; CSM.II.161),

---

10. Ned Block, "On a Confusion about a Function of Consciousness", in *The Nature of Consciousness*, N. Block, O. Flanagan & G. Guzeldere (eds), 375–415 (Cambridge, MA: MIT Press, 1997), 382. See also his "Consciousness", in *A Companion to the Philosophy of Mind*, S. Guttenplan (ed.), 210–19 (Oxford: Blackwell, 1994).

sees his circumstances as dangerous. The justification for this claim is that the action prompted by the representation is appropriate to a perceived danger but would be wholly inappropriate to something not taken to be dangerous. Moreover, if the subject did not interpret his circumstances as dangerous the action would not happen; it is much more than simply the inescapable result of a mechanical push–pull.

Phenomenal consciousness

Some writers about consciousness clearly feel that the only kind of consciousness of any interest is what is called phenomenal consciousness. This is the consciousness or awareness of the *feel* of experiences, their *distinctive sensory or emotive character*. In Thomas Nagel's famous phrase there is "something it is like" to taste a lemon, see an expanse of blue sky or smell gorgonzola.[11] To be truly aware of these things is to experience their distinctive qualitative character, not just to be affected by them in a mechanical way.

It might be suggested that, contrary to the interpretation I have been offering, Descartes does not really think there can be "thoughtless" consciousness of the kinds talked about so far because without the activity of the rational soul these experiences would not have any phenomenology and thus they would not actually be *experienced* by their subject at all: they would be unconscious. In support of this objection it might be said that Descartes's description of reasonless animals as "automatons made by God or nature" (Letter to Reneri for Pollot, April or May 1648: AT.II.39–41; CSMK.99–100; see also Letter to Mersenne, 30 July 1640: AT.III.122; CSMK.149) shows that he thinks a creature without a rational soul is like a robot or mechanical toy: insensible and incapable of genuine perceptual, or any other kind of, consciousness.

But we should not ignore the historical context of Descartes's remark; the term "automaton" signified for Descartes and his contemporary readers only that the things to which it was applied were self-moving. He was saying that animals do not need any sort of soul to animate them. They are like clocks in having a purely mechanical source for their movements and behaviour. Of course they are also *unlike* clockwork in being alive. But Descartes thinks that life, whether for human or for non-human animals does not require possession of a soul of any kind. Indeed, as he protests, "I do not deny life to animals", and he goes on to say, "and I do not even deny sensation, in so far as it depends on a bodily organ" (Letter to More, 5 February 1649: AT.V.278; CSMK.366).

---

11. Thomas Nagel, "What Is It Like to Be a Bat?", reprinted in his *Mortal Questions*, 165–80 (Cambridge: Cambridge University Press, 1979), and originally published in 1974.

For Descartes, then, being an automaton – a self-moving, exclusively physical being – does not preclude being the subject of conscious sensation. But still it might be held that this sort of sensation is at best a poor second-class thing, hardly worth calling sensation at all. Such sensation is a conduit of information much of it important, even life-preserving, for the animal possessed of it. But would Descartes not say that a rational soul is needed before there can be a distinctive phenomenal feel: a "something it is like" to experience any sense perception or passion?

The answer is that Descartes nowhere suggests that the feelings or phenomenal character of human sensations require thought in order to exist. When he comes to say anything about the phenomenology of our experience (e.g. in the *Passions of the Soul* and the *Principles of Philosophy*) he always explains the difference between one sort of sensation or feeling and another, not in terms of the involvement or otherwise of the rational soul, but in terms of bodily factors and differences: "The wide variety in sensations is a result, firstly, of differences in the nerves themselves, and secondly of differences in the sorts of motion which occur in particular nerves" (*Principles* IV.190: AT.VIIIA.315ff; CSM.I.280–81). Moreover, in the same passage Descartes specifically divides each of our sensations and emotional states into "animal" and "intellectual" versions. So he contrasts "intellectual joy" with "animal joy", maintaining that it is entirely in virtue of being human *animals* that we have the latter to experience. Descartes says explicitly that we can experience both, on the one hand, animal joy, sadness, hunger and thirst and, on the other, intellectual joy and sadness and the volition to eat and drink. This is because we are each composed of both a living (physical) animal and a rational (immaterial) soul.

It seems likely, then, that Descartes judges the thoughtless animal seeing, hearing, thirst, hunger, joy and pain we sometimes experience to be different in some way from what we experience when our rational souls are engaged. But it is also *unlikely* that he would have recognized a category of animal (including human animal) passions, impulses and sensations and yet regarded them as involving *no* sort of feeling or phenomenology for their possessors.

Introspective consciousness
Armstrong argues that what he calls "perceptual consciousness" differs from something he calls "introspective consciousness",[12] which consists of self-scanning activity by the subject: a variety of "inner sense" or higher-order

---

12. Armstrong, "What *is* Consciousness?", 59–67.

perception of what is occurring in the subject's mind. With such self-conscious awareness of the contents and present activities of one's own mind we reach a kind of consciousness that Descartes regards as a central capacity and proper purpose of the rational soul. In Chapter 2, § "The second sort of self-know-ledge", we saw that Descartes thinks the rational soul gives me introspective immediate awareness of all my ideas, including what sensations and sense experiences I am having. When I look out over the bay and see the dark blue of the sea it is my rational soul by which I am aware that I am seeing this blue. The rational soul gives me a sort of higher-order awareness of what it is that I am aware of through my senses. In doing so it gives me a reflective and height-ened awareness of the nature of the world and surroundings that I sense.

Of course, this is only the beginning of what the rational soul does for me. It also enables me to exercise flexible intelligence in dealing with the full range of problems and practical challenges that life may present. It is the part of me with which I engage in abstract reasoning, or work on problems in logic or mathematics, or do scientific research. It is also fully in play when I deliberate and make moral choices and develop long-term plans and strat-egies. Again, the rational soul comes into its own when I engage in philo-sophical reflection.

And, of course, as noted several times above, the use of language to express something other than the passions or feelings of the subject is something that human beings alone in the animal kingdom possess because they are endowed with rational souls, which make the use of language possible.

The conclusion of this chapter is that the rational soul for Descartes is the hub of human consciousness. It is the central intellectual component of that subject which is formed by the substantial union of rational soul and living human body. But it is not lodged in its body like an (immaterial) pilot in a (physical) ship; it is not an autonomous subject somehow isolated within that substantial union. Having experiences and enjoying or enduring certain forms of awareness such as perceptual consciousness, access consciousness and even phenomenal consciousness are shared activities that can and do at times happen without any contribution from the rational soul. Rather, the rational soul is the self-aware part of the person that renders much of the mental life of that substantial union *self*-conscious. It provides the mental gaze that can, as occasion demands, attend to any sensory or other idea and make it fully, introspectively conscious.

CHAPTER 4

Mental causation

Notoriously, Descartes's dualism is afflicted with a deeply serious and potentially fatal difficulty: the difficulty of explaining mind–body interaction. To many it has seemed that, just in so far as Descartes is able to support the claim that body and mind are metaphysically utterly different from each other, to that same extent he is unable to explain how two such different substances could affect one another. If mind or rational soul and physical body are really as different from each other as he claims, how can changes in physical sense organs (for example) cause changes in the subject's ideas? And how can the mind make the body do things? Yet Descartes is in full agreement with those who say that when I look at the sea it is the sea that causes my perception of blue, and when I decide to cross the road it is my decision and the thoughts leading to it that cause my body to perform that action.

On the surface it appears that the modern-day "problem of mental causation" outlined in the Introduction (and sometimes called "the physical exclusion problem") is just a modern version of this Cartesian difficulty.[1] Granted, this more recently fashionable problem is usually raised as a challenge to property dualists rather than substance dualists. But it, just like the problem raised by Descartes's critics, asks how our mental lives can possibly exercise any causal influence over physical events, particularly our own actions. Recall that the new problem very briefly goes as follows: for any actual physical event selected as an example, the physical properties of the causes of that event are sufficient to account for its occurrence, no matter what the antecedent wishes, hopes, intentions or decisions of any mind are. The physical properties of things appear to be sufficient to account for each physical happening in the

---

1. This chapter is greatly indebted to Sarah Patterson's persuasive interpretation of this topic; see her "Epiphenomenalism and Occasionalism: Problems of Mental Causation, Old and New", *History of Philosophy Quarterly* **22** (2005), 239–57.

world. So how can a distinct mental property of any mental event have any physical effects at all?

This chapter will look at Descartes's problem about mind–body interaction, asking, among other things, whether it is the same as what was just called the modern-day problem of mental causation. Whether the answer to this question is yes or no, we need to know what answer Descartes can offer to anyone who is sceptical about the mind's capacity to affect physical behaviour.

Descartes's problem of mental causation

Critics sometimes ridicule Descartes for failing to realize how the problem of mind–body interaction – as they see it – undermines his whole metaphysical position. How could a philosopher of his stature be apparently so untroubled by such a threatening and intransigent problem? The properties of the two kinds of substance he recognizes seem to put those substances in such disparate categories that it is hard to understand how they could possibly interact. And yet Descartes continues to speak of the relationship between mind and body in unashamedly causal terms.

But Descartes has a crisp answer for anyone like Arnauld who raises this problem of the heterogeneity or disparateness of mind and body:

> That the mind, which is incorporeal, can set the body in motion is something which is shown to us not by any reasoning or comparison with other matters, but by the surest and plainest everyday experience. It is one of those self-evident things which we only make obscure when we try to explain them in terms of other things. (Arnauld, 29 July 1648: AT.V.222; CSMK.358)

It would be foolish to question whether our mental states can initiate and guide our actions when the matter is confirmed daily and repeatedly by our "everyday experience". That the mind influences the body, that decisions and other mental states produce physical actions, is, for Descartes a brute fact that cannot be explained or accounted for "in terms of other things": in terms of anything more basic, more primitive or more intuitively certain.

But this hardly seems an adequate response to Arnauld's worry. The question that exercises him is not whether mind and body do interact but rather whether substance dualism can account for this interaction successfully. If Cartesian dualism makes mind–body interaction inexplicable – or, indeed, if it makes such interaction impossible – this seems good grounds for rejecting the metaphysical theory that has such consequences. Stubborn insistence that mind–body interaction certainly takes place or that it cannot be explained in terms of anything more basic will not answer the case.

But Descartes is not unaware of the full challenge that critics are directing at his dualism. He tells Gassendi that there is an argument with an unstated premise or "supposition that is false and cannot in any way be proved" (AT.IXA.213; CSM.II.275), which leads some thinkers to conclude that, on his substance dualism, minds and bodies cannot interact. The premise that *is* stated is the truth that "minds and bodies are substances with very different natures". The premise that is left unstated is the proposition that "things of entirely different natures cannot act on one another". And Descartes is adamant that there is no reason to accept that things that are dissimilar in nature cannot affect each other. So he has no hesitation in rejecting this whole argument.

Descartes's position here may seem initially persuasive. It is easy to think of examples of pairs of things that apparently have little or nothing in common and yet are well able to influence each other: rough sandpaper makes wood smooth; a small spark can ignite a blaze that destroys a forest. It would seem silly to say that these things are "too disparate" to be causally related: that they must share properties if they are to interact.

The trouble is that, for Descartes, the living human body and the rational soul or mind differ from each other far more radically than do the pairs of things in these examples. Cartesian mind and body are wholly different in nature, to the extent that the defining and essential properties of each can be categorically denied of the other. Another of Descartes's correspondents, Princess Elisabeth of Bohemia, with whom he had a lengthy exchange on the nature of the relation between mind and body and on the emotions, questioned Descartes closely about this issue. Elisabeth wanted to know how "the human soul, which is only a thinking substance, [can] determine the movement of the animal spirits in order to perform a voluntary action" (16 May 1643: AT.III.661).[2] It seems that Descartes's own strictures about the nature of physical movement on the one hand, and the properties of the rational soul on the other, rule out any possibility of the mind's moving the body. Bodies move when they are pushed and contact is necessary for pushing. What pushes must have extension but Descartes "excludes extension completely" from his concept of the soul or mind: "immaterial" and "extended" are mutually incompatible properties. To Elisabeth it looks as if Descartes's own principles commit him to the view that only a body can move a body.

---

2. See also R. Descartes, *Meditations and Other Metaphysical Writings*, rev. edn, D. M. Clarke (ed. & trans.) (Harmondsworth: Penguin, 2001), 148.

Descartes does not deal with Elisabeth's objection at all well. He tries several different ways of escaping her conclusion. First he talks of the need to keep the concepts by which we understand body separate from those by which we understand the soul and separate again from those by which we understand the union of mind and body, the everyday human self. We ought not to try to understand how the mind moves the body in terms of the concepts that help us understand how bodies move bodies. He offers instead the notion of gravity and its power to move bodies towards the centre of the earth as an *analogue* for the mind's power over the body: gravity is not a physical substance that physically contacts what it moves and nor is the mind.

Are these responses to Elisabeth's questions as unhelpful as she and subsequent critics have found them? If Descartes's dualism is correct then notions and concepts honed for understanding how bodies move bodies are, as he says, likely to mislead us when we are trying to understand how minds move bodies. And the mind's governance of the body does seem more like gravity's overarching but contact-free dominion over the physical than like the mechanics of a series of literal pushes and pulls.

Anyway, it is clear that Descartes intends these two responses to Elisabeth's problem not so much to demolish the objection raised as to assuage her anxiety about the possibility of a solution. He does not expect an outmoded view of the nature of gravity (which, as Elisabeth notes, he himself no longer accepts) to do much to explain how the mind initiates physical motion. For this he knows he needs to produce a much fuller account of the nature of the substantial union between rational soul and body than he has given in the *Meditations*. Of course, the question is: what will that fuller account be and will it really provide the desired resolution of Elisabeth's problem?

Descartes's answer

The answer is that Descartes's attempts to account in greater detail for the substantial union and interaction between mind and body may eventually satisfy Elisabeth, who shares his religious convictions and his dualism, but they are never going to satisfy a materialist critic. For they *start* from the unshakable certainty that there are two radically different sorts of substance. As we saw in Chapter 1, for Descartes the rational soul enters the picture in accounts of human nature only at the point where accounts in physical (specifically physiological) terms run out. Although Descartes is convinced that physiological explanations of human capacities and experience can extend much further than most of his contemporaries are prepared to accept, such explanations cannot explain *all* of human sensation, feeling, motivation and psychology. The rational soul is needed to account for superior human mental activities, particularly reasoning, language-use and moral judgement. As we saw in Chapter 3 it is also needed, for human beings alone among earthly creatures, to enable the sort of higher-order thought by which our inner states are scanned, monitored and made introspectively conscious.

Because these distinctive human mental capacities have, in his view, no discoverable physiological origins or explanations, a supernatural source and non-physical nature are necessary for the rational soul. So he is left with no other possible thesis about how the mind or soul moves the body than to compare it, as he cautiously (but also daringly) does when writing to More, to the power of God to move bodies: a power that God has despite the fact that he is completely incorporeal (Letter to More, 15 April 1649: AT.V.347; CSMK.375). Descartes can thus vigorously resist the contention that only a body can move a body. There is a viable alternative: human minds are spiritual substances that – like God – can move bodies simply by deciding or willing to do so. But he never promises or attempts to give an explanation of how that supernatural source works or how spiritual substances do what they alone can do.

As Sarah Patterson points out, Descartes's comparison of the power of human and divine minds to move bodies "neatly turns the tables on Descartes's [contemporary] opponents".[3] None would want to dispute that God is incorporeal or that he can move bodies by force of will alone. So Descartes's only problem here is that he risks angering religious authority by comparing the human soul's powers with those of God. He is, therefore, very careful to say that he does *not* hold that "any mode of action belongs univocally to both God and his creatures" (Letter to More, 15 April 1649: AT.V.347; CSMK.375). God's power to move bodies by thought alone and Descartes's analogous power are not the same. God's power is beyond Descartes's understanding. But daily experience gives him a kind of understanding of his own power: something God has given him so that he can have an idea or inkling of what divine or angelic power to move bodies might be.

In effect, then, Descartes's answer to Elisabeth's query is that, for human beings, there can be no positive answer to the question *how* the mind moves the body any more than there could be an answer (for us) to the question how God creates and moves physical bodies. All there can be is greater understanding of the nature of the experience (the mind–body interaction) enjoyed

---

3. Patterson, "Epiphenomenalism and Occasionalism", 243.

and suffered by human beings: those beings who combine body and soul in a substantial union. It is to supply that promised further, greater understanding of the nature of human experience, feelings and psychology that Descartes writes his *Passions of the Soul*, working out many of his ideas in further correspondence with Elisabeth.

But is Descartes himself satisfied with his "there-is-no-answer" answer to the question how mind moves the body? It is sometimes said that if he really thought that there could be no explanation of how human mind–body interaction works he would not have suggested the pineal gland as the point in the brain at which the causal leap between mind and body takes place. So a recent commentator complains that "perhaps Descartes thought that, because the gland was so small, the problem of interaction was made so small as to cease to be a problem" but "if a body can be moved only by a body, then no matter how small the body is, it must be moved by a body; nothing else".[4]

As we have seen, however, Descartes does not accept that a body can be moved only by a body. And he certainly does not think that the mind–body problem is negligible because the pineal gland is small, or for any other reason. He believes that the body takes sensory stimuli that impinge on it and focuses them at a point in the brain where they are available to, and in a form to be registered by, the mind. That same spot can then be used by the mind as a locus for its immediate action when motivating the body via the body's extensive systems of nerves and blood vessels that meet there. But in nominating the pineal gland as a possible location for this interchange Descartes is not still searching for an answer to the question *how* the mind and body affect one another. He thinks we can safely relegate the problem of mind–body interaction from the top rank of philosophical problems because he has given it all the answer possible: human minds move their bodies – as God moves matter – by force of will.

The new problem of mental causation and Cartesian dualism

In the preceding sections we saw how critics of Cartesian substance dualism try to use a mental causation problem to undermine that dualism: if it cannot account for the mind–body interaction that we are all intuitively certain really occurs then such substance dualism cannot be the correct account of the metaphysics of mind. Descartes's response is to assert that his dualism *can*

---

4. A. P. Martinich, Fritz Allhoff, & Anand Jayprakash Vaidya, *Early Modern Philosophy: Essential Readings with Commentary* (Oxford: Blackwell, 2007), 140.

account for the mind's ability to move the body. The mind moves the body in the way that all spiritual substances including God initiate physical movement. We may not have any detailed knowledge of how this is done (we lack a sort of "spiritual mechanics") but we cannot deny that it happens in the divine case and know from experience that it happens in our own. The weight of defending dualism thus falls back where it belongs in Descartes's view – on the arguments for the distinctness of mind and body presented in the Sixth Meditation – and ultimately on Descartes's proofs of the existence of God. Of course, if he cannot establish that at least one indisputably non-corporeal substance exists then his explanation of mind–body interaction in terms of spiritual power crumbles to nothing.

Does the modern problem of mental causation differ from the problem of mind–body interaction that Descartes is accused of being unable to resolve? It was Donald Davidson's anomalous monism[5] that triggered the recent discussions of the question how much, if any, power the mind has to cause actions. Davidson, as the name of his theory implies, is a monist: for him the only substances are material substances. He is, however, a property dualist. He does not believe that mental properties are reducible without remainder to physical properties. Rather, he thinks that single events can have both mental properties and physical ones.

The word "anomalous" ("non-law-like" or "non-law-governed") appears in the name of his theory to signify that, for him, mental states and events are not related to physical states and events in a law-like way. There are no strict laws determining that this or that mental state will result in this or that behaviour by its possessor. Nor are there any laws dictating that, when an agent is thinking or feeling a particular type of thought or sensation, his brain and central nervous system will be in a particular state.

There *are*, for Davidson, strict causal laws governing all physical causal interactions. This means that if I stretch out my hand to take a glass of water there must be a physical cause (some configuration of neuronal firings triggering muscle movements) that obeys physical laws and that is responsible for that hand movement. The physical cause just mentioned is responsible for the hand movement in the sense that it is necessary and sufficient for that movement. The movement would not have happened without it and, given that it occurred, the movement had to happen. So, for Davidson, the physical realm is causally closed. Every physical event has a complete wholly physical

---

5. Donald Davidson, "Actions, Reasons and Causes", in his *Essays on Actions and Events*, 3–20 (Oxford: Clarendon Press, 1980). See also Jaegwon Kim, *Mind in a Physical World* (Cambridge MA: MIT Press, 1998).

cause that is sufficient to guarantee that it happens. This view is, of course, not restricted to Davidson. Most materialists accept it unreservedly.

So what would Davidson say about my desire for a glass of water; that is, what role does he assign to what seems to me to be the *mental* cause of my action? Davidson would say that the brain event that is my desire can be described in two different ways: it is a physical brain event and it is also experienced by me as a mental event, an occurrent desire for a drink. Under the first description it falls under physical laws that relate it to its physical effect: namely, the movement of my hand. Under its description as a desire it explains *why* I moved my hand; it gives the reason for my action. For Davidson, the single event that is describable in both ways provides both the (physical) cause and the (mental) explanation of my hand movement. It is right to say that my mind causes my bodily action because the cause of that bodily action is a physical-event-that-is-at-the-same-time-a-mental-event.

Critics hold that Davidson's theory, despite his evident intentions to the contrary, actually makes the mental causally impotent. This criticism goes as follows. Davidson holds that events are causes or effects only in so far as they instantiate physical laws. But this, his critics say, amounts to claiming that mental events are causally efficacious only in virtue of their physical features and not their mental ones. The mental does not cause anything *qua* mental (in so far as it is mental). Davidson's anomalous monism leads directly to epiphenomenalism: the view that physical processes in the brain produce and sustain mental states but these mental states are powerless to affect the physical processes on which they depend, or any other physical thing or event. Davidson's account of mind–body interaction seems to his critics to render mental properties mere danglers, impotent to produce any bodily effects.

Davidson's reply is to repeat his conviction that causal relations hold only between events, however they are described. So it is not in virtue of having these or those mental properties *or these or those physical properties* that an event produces its effect. Events do not cause other events *qua* mental or *qua* physical; they just cause what they cause. This reply gives Davidson's critics no more satisfaction than Descartes's critics felt at his reassertion that we know from daily experience that the mind can and does move the body. Both sets of critics are dissatisfied because neither theorist explains *how* the distinctively mental features of the cause are responsible for the physical effect achieved.

It is my sudden desire for water, I want to say, that moves my hand, not some brain event that I know nothing about. At least Descartes agrees that it is my mental state as such that produces the physical action even if he is unable to explain how exactly my mind moves my body. Davidson *is* able to explain how exactly my body is moved, but at the expense, it seems, of removing my desire for water from the equation. Davidson would say that my desire is still there since it just is the single causally efficacious event that can be correctly described in either physical or mental terms. The critic replies that this still leaves the mental as such with no work to do. Had my brain event been exactly what it was when I reached out for the glass, but without my experiencing any desire for water, my hand would still have moved in exactly the same way. Had I wanted water but lacked the right brain event I would not have extended my hand.

It is difficult if not impossible for twenty-first-century readers, most of whom lack all Cartesian faith in the existence of spirits, to question Davidson's commitment to the causal closure of the physical world. But if it is right that every physical event has a complete physical cause sufficient to produce it, it becomes impossible to see how the mental properties of mental events could have any power to influence any physical happening.

This new problem of mental causation is sometimes called "the physical exclusion problem". This is because it argues that the physical properties of a mental event are sufficient to account for all that event's effects so that physical properties exclude the causal claims of mental properties. Is this exclusion problem – articulated in recent times as a challenge for property dualism – just a modern version of the problem that contemporary critics including Elisabeth addressed to Descartes?

Clearly the two arguments have a common conclusion: that the mental is impotent to cause physical movements. Elisabeth's argument is that a body can only be moved by something extended and capable of contact, features that Cartesian minds do not have. The exclusion argument says that in fact all bodily movements have physical causes sufficient to ensure their occurrence so that the mental is causally redundant. So the two mental causation arguments are importantly distinct: they rely on different premises and take different routes to the same conclusion.

Faced with the physical exclusion argument Descartes would have to say that the material realm is not causally closed. Divine and other spirits can influence matter and intervene in physical history. But it is not clear what philosophical, as opposed to theological, arguments he could muster to support this claim. Nor is it easy to see how he would square this with his insistence in the *Principles of Philosophy* that God "always preserves the same quantity of motion in matter" (AT.VIIIA.62; CSM.I.240).

Repetition of the claim that I know from my daily experience that spirits can and do move bodies cannot help. As Spinoza points out, no matter how strongly I *feel* that I am making my body move by willing it to do so this is no proof that it is my will that does the moving.

CHAPTER 5

Mental representation

Ideas, images and resemblance

There are numerous ways for one thing to represent another thing. Paintings and portraits can represent their subject matter. Maps represent geographical areas and features. Graphs can represent economic, political, criminal, medical, virtually *any* kinds of trends or features. A red light means stop or danger. Diagrams and blueprints represent methods of assembly and details of construction. More obvious than any of the things mentioned so far, words – bits of language – stand for things and states of affairs.

But if all these things are rightly regarded as representational they are also alike in having what is sometimes called "*derived* intentionality or aboutness". An object is not a map unless it has been made with the intention of representing a particular region. A graph exhibits what it does because someone draws it, meaning it to illustrate just that trend or statistic. Words denote the situations and objects they do because speakers have a convention that those words have their prescribed senses. The listed items represent their objects because of the intentions, decisions or conventions of beings with minds. It is only the mental states of thinkers that are generally taken to have underived or "original" intentionality.

The original intentionality or representational character of the mental, it is generally also agreed, is the source of the aboutness that thinkers are able to bestow on their words and the other significant objects they create and use. The question is: how does underived or original intentionality work? What accounts for the fact that we are able to think about things employing mental states that, apparently without our endowing them with this capacity, *just are* about the objects of our thought?

Surprisingly often, students suggest that Descartes's answer to this question is that ideas in our heads represent their objects by resembling them. There is a difficult-to-eradicate perception that all the classic philosophers of the early modern period who embraced what Locke called "the way of ideas" – that is, those who began to present their explanations of the workings of the mind in terms of what they called ideas – thought of ideas principally as images or little pictures. And this perception leads to the view that the ideas or images said to be in our minds for these thinkers naturally represent things in the world by resembling them just as pictures or portraits can represent their subject matter by conveying a likeness of the subject.

This mistaken view is encouraged by the frequent use of the term "image" made by some of those philosophers: as Spinoza writes, it is "customary" to call the ideas of things outside the mind "images" even though "they do not reproduce the figures of things" (E2p17s).[1] Even Descartes, at the outset of his discussion early in the Third Meditation of ideas and what they represent says "some of my thoughts are as it were the images of things, and it is only in these cases that the term 'idea' is strictly appropriate" (AT.VII.37; CSM.II.25).

This is partly a hold-over from Descartes's earliest work in natural history and philosophy. Descartes's first writings about the ideas acquired in sense perception show that he was very tempted by the view that sensory ideas resemble their objects (and thus represent them) because the bodily senses literally take the physical impress of what is perceived. They then transfer that impression to the brain (and somehow on to the mind) so that sensory ideas are representations that keep the same shape and features as the object perceived just as a wax impress retains the features, and is the image, of the seal that made it (see *Rules for the Direction of the Mind*: AT.X.411–14; CSM.I.40, 41).

But the remainder of the Third Meditation's discussion of ideas and what they represent makes very clear that Descartes has not retained the view that ideas represent their objects in the way that pictures or portraits do. Yes, in the past he has unreflectively believed "that there were things outside me which were the sources of my ideas and which resembled them in all respects" (AT.VII.35; CSM.II.25). But now he has realized how limited is the scope for mental items to resemble the physical objects for which they stand and he begins to steer the meditator towards a different view. He qualifies his remark that ideas are "as it were the images of things" by listing five examples, two of which are ideas of immaterial things: an angel and God. But these are things of which, according to Descartes, no sensory images are possible so, of course, they could not be represented by any picture.

---

1. All references to Spinoza's *Ethics* are to the translation by Edwin Curley (ed.) (Harmondsworth: Penguin, 1996) [E] in the form E2p17s, which means the scholium (note) to *Ethics*, Book 2, Proposition 17.

Moreover, Descartes swiftly introduces a distinction among his ideas that divides them into three kinds according to their source. Ideas of the first kind – such as those of God, the nature of truth, the nature of thought and the nature of things – are all pronounced to be *innate ideas*. These ideas are placed in their possessor by God and thus owe their "aboutness" or intentionality to God. Despite appearances, these ideas thus have intentionality that is derived, rather than original. Descartes believes that his idea of God is about God because that is what God intended it to be about. God placed that idea in his mind to be, from birth, the mark signifying that Descartes was God's creature. He placed other innate ideas in the mind to represent non-sensory items that the under-standing would need from the earliest time in order to function appropriately.

Descartes's other two sorts of ideas distinguished in this part of the text are what he calls "*adventitious ideas*" and "*invented ideas*", that is, ideas invented by the subject himself. Adventitious ideas come from sense experience and thus might seem suitable candidates to represent their subject matter by picto-rial resemblance. However, as Descartes shortly points out, it would take a separate proof to establish that these ideas are not simply a subset of invented ideas produced by a faculty of his own of whose existence and operation he is unaware. And anyway, as he goes on to say, "even if these ideas did come from things other than myself, it would not follow that they must *resemble* those things" (AT.VII.39; CSM.II.27; emphasis added).

At the point in the meditation where he is just beginning his search for the source of error, Descartes writes: "And the chief and most common mistake which is to be found here consists in my judging that the ideas which are in me resemble, or conform to, things located outside me" (AT.VII.37; CSM.II.26). Merely having an idea that seems to be "of" an external object cannot be any sort of error or mistake. But to judge that there is in fact an external object to match that idea, solely on the basis of the content of that idea, is a mistake. An idea of a fictional item such as a chimera affords, to the thinker who has it, exactly the same justification for thinking a real external indi-vidual matching that idea exists as does the idea of a horse. That is, neither idea gives sufficient justification for concluding that there exists an external object matching that idea. Famously, Descartes does claim that the idea of God must represent something really existent that matches its idea perfectly. But he specifically argues (in a way that relies on his doctrine of degrees of reality and whose details need not detain us here) that the defence of this claim is applicable only to God: the idea of God is a completely unique case.

Innate ideas have intentionality derived from God. But where does the "aboutness" of the ideas in each of Descartes's other two categories come from? Adventitious (sensory) ideas, remember, represent sensible objects external to the body. Invented ideas represent mythical creatures and other things that do not exist. It might seem that my idea of a chimera, say, represents what it does by my fiat since such a being is a myth, something that does not exist anywhere outside my mind. However, a little thought will show why the intentionality or aboutness of a thinker's ideas, of whatever category, could not be something that *their possessor* bestows on them. Imagine yourself thinking up a mythical beast, inventing, for example, the idea of a winged hippo. You can create an idea to represent such a thing in your mind but it will succeed in representing just such a creature only because it is a composite idea whose two parts already represent, on the one hand, a hippo and, on the other, having wings. The representational character of invented ideas is not bestowed by their inventor. It is parasitic on or derived from the representational character of the ideas of which it is composed.

Moreover, it is not possible to have what Descartes would call an "adventitious idea" with a distinct character that identifies it as the particular idea it is but which is not yet *about* anything and *then* decide to assign it to be "the idea of a horse". For what idea would you be using to think of exactly the sort of animal you want to represent with your chosen idea? You would have to have an idea of a horse *already* in order to think of horses for any purpose, even as the possible representational content of a new idea. In addition, it is not at all clear that the hypothesized "idea with a distinct character that identifies it as the particular idea it is but which is not yet *about* anything" is a genuine possibility. Surely the only distinct character that an idea could possess which would fit it to be used as the idea of a horse would be the distinct character or content "idea of a horse".

Ideas and their causes

So, for Descartes, innate ideas have their intentionality bestowed by God and invented ideas represent what they do by combining elements from preexisting ideas that already represent their objects. What of the third kind of ideas? What does Descartes think accounts for the aboutness or representational character of his adventitious (sensory) ideas? As we saw in the previous section, even though he has not yet begun to try to prove there is a God who does not allow him to be systematically mistaken about extended things, Descartes is prepared to deny that it is because they *resemble* external things that his sensory ideas represent what they do.

The example he regards as decisive is the idea of the sun: Descartes says that he has two ideas of the sun: one "which is acquired as it were from the senses and which is a prime example of an idea which I reckon to come from an external source, makes the sun appear very small"; the other "based on astronomical reasoning ... shows the sun to be several times larger than the earth" (AT.VII.39; CSM.II.27). Reason tells Descartes that the second idea more truly captures the nature of the sun and thus that the first idea has "no resemblance to it at all". Still, the sense-acquired idea does, nonetheless, represent the sun. How is this to be explained?

The explanation has two parts. The first comes here in the part of the Third Meditation that I have been discussing. The second requires a more complicated account and can only be given in the Sixth Meditation after the existence of extended things has been established. In the Third Meditation Descartes says that until now he has always believed that "there exist things distinct from myself *which transmit to me ideas or images of themselves* through the sense organs or in some other way" (AT.VII.40; CSM.II.27; emphasis added). His hitherto unquestioned view is that external objects themselves "transmit" or cause ideas, which in turn are "of" or about their objects because those objects cause them. This may be a theory that Descartes has so far accepted only on "a blind impulse" but he declares his determination to establish that there are indeed external objects and sees no reason to doubt that these objects, if they exist, are the causes of the ideas in his mind that represent them in thought.

Misrepresentation

It is a popular view in recent philosophy of mind that our ideas of objects outside the mind such as Descartes's towers and stars, cloaks, hats, fires and dressing gowns are caused by sensory encounter with those objects and stand for those things in our thinking because they are *regularly* so caused. It is because those ideas turn up in the course of our experience in such a way as to be reliable indicators or signs of the presence of those objects in our vicinity that they come to represent those objects in our thought. Another way of putting this is to say that our ideas covary with the presence of what they are ideas of and that is why they can represent the objects with which they covary.

The notions of "reliable indication" and "covariance" are easy to grasp. Take, for example, the images that appear in your rear-view mirror when driving. Because those images alter exactly in parallel with the comings and goings of the cars driving behind you, you can use the rear-view mirror to give you vital and accurate ideas about the movement of the traffic on the road behind. The mirror images covary with the traffic movements and indicate them to you reliably as you drive. The mirror images represent (they are about) the movements of the cars behind you.

But the reliable-indicator theory of mental representation has been criticized for being unable to account for *mis*representation.[2] For, unfortunately, there is a very significant difference between the way in which the representations in the mirror stand for the movements of the traffic behind you and the way in which ideas represent the objects that, on this view, are their causes. If there is an image of a red car in the mirror that entails that there is a red car behind. Mirror images cannot reflect what is not there. But you can have an idea of a red car at any time: there is no necessity for there to be a red car anywhere nearby causing that particular token idea in you. And, contrariwise, a red car may fail to raise in your mind the idea of a red car and trigger instead some quite different idea, if encountered under certain sorts of conditions (say on a dark and heavily foggy night).

It seems that it is neither necessary nor sufficient to have a red car present for the idea of a red car to arise in the mind of a thinker. But if that is true what becomes of the notion that it is *because* (and only because) that idea is a reliable indicator of the presence of X that that idea represents X? It would seem that no idea can misrepresent. On this theory an idea cannot, say, *mis*represent a red car as a brown van. Any idea does in fact represent what it covaries with and, in so doing, indicates – whatever that may be.

Is Descartes's view of the representational character of his so-called "adventitious" ideas afflicted with the same problems just now attributed to the reliable-indicator theory? In fact, is Descartes's theory a reliable-indicator view? Well, in several places in the *Meditations* Descartes does discuss the question how to account for the way many adventitious ideas seem to misrepresent reality. In the Third Meditation, as we have seen, he maintains that, for example, my sensory idea of the sun represents the sun in my thought, even though it represents the sun as being much smaller than its real size: that is, it misrepresents the sun in that way. Nonetheless that idea represents the sun for me because it was in fact caused initially by sensory encounter with the sun. When I see the sun and feel its warmth it impresses itself on my mind: I thus passively acquire an idea of the sun.

The point is, however, that Descartes says nothing here about regularity or anything that could be called "covariance". A single encounter is enough to put a representative of the sun in my mind. And he leaves entirely blank at

---

2. Fred Dretske, "Misrepresentation", in *Belief*, Radu Bogdan (ed.), 17–36 (Oxford: Clarendon Press, 1986).

this point *how* it is that impressions on the senses get translated into something mental: how they are transferred to the mind so as to represent external things in thought. So Descartes's theory of mental representation would seem not to be a reliable-indicator theory although he is aware of the challenge of having to explain misrepresentation nonetheless.

The Third Meditation contains a number of further examples of cases where different types of adventitious ideas could potentially mislead a perceiver about the nature of reality. There is a class of ideas that Descartes dubs "materially false", which it would be ill-advised ever to take at face value. Or rather, such ideas can never be other than what he calls "confused and obscure". These are the ideas of "light and colours, sounds, smells, tastes, heat and cold and the other tactile qualities", that is, the things that will come to be known to philosophers as the ideas of "secondary qualities". Such ideas can never by themselves tell us, for example, "whether cold is merely the absence of heat or vice versa, or whether both of them are real qualities, or neither is". Materially false ideas, Descartes says, are false in that "they represent non-things as things" (AT.VII.43–4; CSM.II.30).

But if adventitious ideas, as described above, represent their sensible causes, how can materially false ideas ever occur? For surely a non-thing cannot cause anything, even a confused and obscure idea. If cold is really nothing at all and thus, seemingly, can have no affect on my physical senses, how can I come to have an idea of it in sense experience? Descartes must wait until the Sixth Meditation to return to the ideas of secondary qualities and the question how, and what exactly, they represent. He does so in the course of exploring how yet another sort of idea can sometimes misrepresent reality.

The man suffering from dropsy and the solution to Descartes's problem of misrepresentation

Although a couple of paragraphs of the Sixth Meditation are devoted to attempting to prove that mind and body are distinct substances, the meditation's main concern is to establish that material things really exist and then to explain how we can acquire knowledge of them and what that knowledge is for. That material objects exist is proved, Descartes thinks, once he has shown that God exists and is not a deceiver and thus that he would not allow Descartes to believe that his ideas of sensible things come from corporeal things when all along they come from some other source such as God himself or an angel. However, corporeal things "may not all exist in a way that exactly corresponds with my sensory grasp of them, for in many cases the grasp of the senses is very obscure and confused" (AT.VII.80; CSM.II.55).

Descartes is concerned to acquit God of any responsibility for misleading us about the nature of the material world. The trouble is that God is the creator: material nature and all the created minds are exactly as God chose to make them. So if we follow what we appear to be "taught by nature" we are actually following God's instructions and thus it would seem to be God who is to blame if we get into difficulties when doing so. And we certainly do frequently err and get into difficulties at times when we seem only to be acting as nature teaches us to act. Take, for example, the case of the patient with excess water building up in his soft tissues who is caused by his condition to have a sensation or idea of thirst that misrepresents as "need of water" what is in fact a bodily state of *dangerous excess of water*. This is a condition that used to be known as dropsy. It is often a symptom of congestive heart failure so the dropsy patient who drinks because he is thirsty could die as a result of his mistake.

But Descartes has an explanation of why God should not be blamed when ideas of thirst from this source misrepresent the patient's bodily state in such a potentially disastrous way. And here at last Descartes finally rounds off his account of the source of the representational character of our sensory ideas. Remember that, in the Third Meditation, Descartes left unexplained how it is that sensations that originate in the encounter between bodily senses and their objects get transferred to the mind and translated into ideas. Now he returns to this question and says that what happens in sense perception is that the nerves transfer the pattern of movement or agitation from the affected sense organ to the centre of the brain. In the brain, that movement is then transferred again, this time to the mind. But "any movement occurring in the part of the brain that immediately affects the mind produces just one corresponding sensation … a given motion in the brain must always produce the same sensation in the mind" (AT.VII.87–8; CSM.II.60–61).

Nature has created our bodies and united our minds to them in the best way possible but it has not been possible to unite more than one "movement" or pattern of agitation in the central nervous system to each feeling or idea and vice versa. A sensation of "dryness in the throat", for instance, which is transferred by the nerves to the brain and on to the mind as a particular movement, can rouse only one particular idea in the mind, namely the idea of thirst.

The sensory system can work only if it is restricted in this way to a single sensation per particular bodily stimulus. Therefore "the best system that could be devised is that it should produce the one sensation which, of all possible sensations, is most especially and most frequently conducive to the preservation of the healthy man" (*ibid.*). Unfortunately for the dropsy patient, dryness in the throat has been correlated with the idea or sensation of thirst so that he feels impelled to drink just as do the vast majority for whom drinking water frequently is a requisite of staying healthy. In his, very un-ideal, un-standard circumstances the patient's sensations misrepresent his bodily state radically and could mislead him into self-destructive activity instead of activity likely to preserve his health and well-being.

Descartes gives a second example to reinforce the point: if I injure my foot, thus agitating the nerves in that part of the body:

> this motion, by way of the spinal cord, reaches the inner parts of the brain, and there gives the mind its signal for having a certain sensation, namely the sensation of pain as occurring in the foot. This stimulates the mind to do its best to get rid of the cause of the pain, which it takes to be harmful to the foot. (*Ibid.*)

Sensory ideas, Descartes thinks, are specifically designed to conduce to actions that preserve and foster health. And the designer is of course God:

> God could have made the nature of man such that this particular motion in the brain indicated something else to the mind; it might, for example, have made the mind aware of the actual motion occurring in the brain, or in the foot, or in any of the intermediate regions; or it might have indicated something else entirely. But there is nothing else which would have been so conducive to the continued well-being of the body. (*Ibid.*)

The sensory ideas we receive through our exterior sense organs and from the somatic field within our bodies represent what they do because God has designed our sensory system just as he has. Thirst represents need of water. Pain in a particular part of the body means injury or disease at that location, which calls for action by the sufferer. Our adventitious or sensory ideas, like our innate ideas and invented ideas, owe their intentionality, their aboutness, ultimately to God. None of them has original intentionality in the sense of "pure, unassigned, non-derived aboutness". God has laid down what each particular sort of sensation or sensory idea will mean or represent.

Similarly, in the case of the secondary qualities, when I see the white or green of a flowering bush or taste what I call "the sweetness of the honey", I am experiencing the sensations that have been ordained to result from the respective particular motions in my various sense organs. I will be misled only if I judge that there are, or could be, in the insensate perceived objects, "the self-same whiteness or greenness … or sweetness which I perceive" (AT. VII.82; CSM.II.57). For these are all experiences. They are things that only a mind–body union, or at least a creature with sense organs, can have.

> Similarly, although I feel heat when I go near a fire and feel pain when I go too near, there is no convincing argument for supposing that there is something in the fire which resembles the heat, any more than for supposing that there is something which resembles the pain.   (AT.VII.83; CSM.II.57)

Ideas do not represent by resembling their objects but by being appointed by God to signal what in the environment should be sought or shunned to ensure the individual's well-being. I must still make a judgement about what to pursue or avoid. I am not *determined* in my actions by my sense perceptions. But since God is not a deceiver there can be "no falsity in my opinions which cannot be corrected by some other faculty supplied by God" (*ibid.*). Reason should tell the man with dropsy, for example, that he must resist the impulse to drink more than his doctor advises until his condition is restored to normal, after which his thirst will return to being a safe guide.

So despite initial appearances, Descartes's account of where the about-ness of our ideas comes from is not an account, certainly not a resemblance account, of original intentionality. Nor is it a reliable-indicator theory. Rather, it is an account of how a creator might have established sensory ideas to do vital tasks for us that nowadays are more likely to be accounted for by reference to evolution. Sensory ideas, keyed as they are to the beneficial or harmful properties of things in the material world, help us in our struggle to survive and indeed thrive when faced with all the many and strenuous biological imperatives of human life in a very complex, often dangerous world.

CHAPTER 6

Is the mind a substance for Spinoza?

It is something of an irony that Spinoza's thoroughgoing dedication to some of the basic principles of Cartesian thought results in his concluding that the human mind is *not* a substance. Spinoza believes that if you follow Descartes's principles to what he regards as their logical conclusion you wind up a monist, not a substance dualist. In fact, for Spinoza there is only one individual substance and that one substance is, and can be, nothing less than the whole of reality. Reality or nature is a single substance, a single individual that exists necessarily and is characterized throughout by both the attribute of extension and the attribute of thought. As we shall see, Spinoza is neither an idealist nor a materialist since he thinks that every bit of reality has both a mental facet and a physical or material one so that every portion of reality is through and through *both* ideal (of the nature of ideas) and material (extended). As he writes, "The mind and the body are one and the same thing, which is conceived now under the attribute of thought and now under the attribute of extension" (E3p2s).

So, although the main lines of Spinoza's theory of mind are expounded in Part 2 of the *Ethics*, large constraints on that theory have already been spelled out in Part 1. Spinoza defines "substance" as "what is in itself and is conceived through itself; that is, that whose concept does not require the concept of another thing, from which it must be formed" (E1d3). Recall that Descartes's notion of substance contains both the notion of being the subject of a distinct attribute or essence and the notion of (comparative) independence in existence. Spinoza's notion of a substance focuses particularly on the second of these Cartesian ideas: the idea of something independent, something that relies on nothing but itself in order to come into and remain in existence. Spinoza takes this idea utterly seriously.

So, to qualify as a substance for Spinoza a thing must be such that it can exist and be wholly comprehended (understood, known) *without reference to any other thing*. A substance cannot share any feature with anything else;

otherwise complete understanding of it would require reference to features of that second thing and it would thus fail to be a substance after all. A substance cannot share existence with any other thing because substances are by definition self-contained, not defined or limited by something external. Yet a putative second thing *would* limit any substance with which it co-existed. A complete account of the first substance would have to specify that it occupied only part of reality, running out, so to speak, at the point where the other thing began.

Of course, Descartes too would say that, strictly speaking, there is only one thing that deserves the title substance, namely God. But Descartes believes that reality contains things additional to God and that those things can be called substances in an extended sense because they depend on God alone for their existence. Unlike Spinoza, he believes that numerous individual mental substances and material substances (or parts of the single great material substance of which all physical bodies are parts) can co-exist. For Spinoza this view simply refuses to follow the definition of substance to its logical conclusion, which is that only one thing properly called an individual substance can exist.

Spinoza devotes the whole of Part 1 of the *Ethics* to exploring the implications of his definitions of "substance", "attribute", "mode" and "cause-of-itself", so that by the start of Part 2, "Of the Nature and Origin of the Mind", the term "substance" has been shown to be wholly inappropriate for individual human minds. Unlike anything entitled to be called a substance (on Spinoza's use of the term) human minds do not cause themselves, do share features with each other and with other sorts of things and are highly dependent for their, entirely contingent, existence on things other than themselves.

Not a substance but a bundle?

If human minds are not substances (either material or mental) what *does* Spinoza take them to be? And how is one human mind to be individuated and distinguished from the next? For Spinoza is as aware as anyone of the fact that human minds and bodies are both (comparatively) discrete and, so to speak, "free-standing" particulars that we can distinguish from each other and that last and can be re-identified. Moreover, Spinoza is as keen as any of the philosophers of the early modern period to establish that some part at least of the human mind might rightly regard itself as in some sense immortal or eternal. So we need to ask what Spinoza's positive account is and what he means by "mind".

In Part 2 of the *Ethics* he tells us that "The first thing which constitutes the actual being of a human Mind is nothing but the idea of a singular thing which actually exists" (E2p11) and he goes on to affirm that "The object of the idea constituting the human mind is the body" (E2p13). Putting the two together we have Spinoza's view that *the human mind is the* idea *of the human body*.

But what does the statement "the mind is the idea of the body" mean? A first attempt to grapple with this notion might yield the suggestion that Spinoza thinks my mind is a composite, a bundle made up of my ideas of my left foot, my right foot, my heart, my liver, my skin, my blood vessels and so forth round all my limbs and parts, all my organs and other physical constituents. This suggestion certainly captures Spinoza's belief that "the idea of my body" is a highly *multiple* idea, itself containing many ideas. But it misses the fact that what Spinoza means by "the idea of the body" is the idea of something (the human body) that is in turn best understood as a unity – a complex organic system with subsystems and sub-subsystems nested within it – not just a pile or jumble of parts. This view of the body as an organic systematic unity would naturally lead to the view that the *idea* of the body, too, is not just a hodgepodge or bundle of ideas of parts but a rich complex system of complicatedly interconnected ideas (see E2p15d).

Even with this sympathetic elaboration, however, Spinoza's definition of the human mind as "the idea of the body" is bound to be confronted almost immediately by the following natural objection. Surely a mind is an active agent. It seems right to think of it as the producer of ideas, or at least the passive receiver of ideas from sense perception and other sources that then operates on those ideas, employing them in imagination, accessing them in memory, making judgements about the world and choices based on them. Could an idea – even a complex rich idea composed of many ideas, such as Spinoza deems the human mind to be – be itself the producer and receiver of ideas? Any theory of mind that can in any sense be called a "bundle theory" is bound to attract a version of this criticism. That Berkeley consciously avoided a bundle theory of the mind because of its vulnerability to such an objection is discussed below in Chapter 21, and in due course we shall also look at Hume's response to such a challenge to his theory of the mind.

Chapter 8 will consider the question whether Spinoza can or could provide an account of the human mind as an active agent or conscious subject rather than just a collection of ideas. For the moment it is vital to make explicit that, whereas Hume's theory may with some truth be described as the view that, at any given time, my mind is constituted by some sort of bundle of *my* ideas, on Spinoza's theory of the human mind my mind consists of ideas of my body that are not just mine but also *God's*. It is very difficult to interpret this claim but we should note that one of its supposed consequences is that my mind is in fact a part of the infinite mind of God.

Neither a substance nor a hodgepodge of ideas but a discrete and re-identifiable individual

Earlier I mentioned the question whether Spinoza's theory of mind could accommodate the ordinary common-sense view that human minds are discrete individuals and also stable, persistent, re-identifiable particulars that can be re-encountered after a lapse of time. What are Spinoza's criteria of individuation for minds and what are his criteria of personal identity?

To answer these two closely related questions we need to look at what Spinoza says about what he calls "attributes" and "modes". At the beginning of Part 1 of the *Ethics*, Spinoza defines "attribute" as "that which intellect perceives of substance, as constituting its essence" and "mode" as "the affections of substance, or, that which is in something else, through which it is also conceived" (E1d4&5). As so often with the technical, brief and – it must be admitted – cryptic definitions, propositions, postulates and lemmas of Spinoza's *Ethics*, these definitions need a good deal of amplification before we can glimpse what Spinoza means and is trying to achieve. Unfortunately, whether the amplification comes from Spinoza himself or from his commentators it is usually as much a source of controversy as of illumination.

So, among some of Spinoza's readers,[1] it seems evident that attributes are "basic and irreducible properties" that characterize every portion of reality. Every part of reality has the properties characteristic of extension (taking up space and having some quantity of what Spinoza calls "motion-and-rest") and also every part of reality has or, rather, *is* an idea whose existence and nature are accounted for exclusively in terms of previously existing ideas. This makes thought and extension, and hence the one substance or God composed of them, two great explanatory orders such that every object and event has a complete description and account in terms of each. Others read Spinoza as saying that thought and extension are subjective appearances, cloaks with which we clothe the one substance when we encounter it in thought or sense experience whereas its real objective unperceived nature remains hidden, mysterious and unknown.

---

1. For example, see J. Bennett, *A Study of Spinoza's Ethics* (Cambridge: Cambridge University Press, 1984). But contrast E. Curley *Spinoza's Metaphysics: An Essay in Interpretation* (Cambridge, MA: Harvard University Press, 1969).

Because it is not of the first relevance for our topic, I will not spend time pursuing this question but simply accept here the first, arguably more plausible, of the two views of Spinoza's attributes. It is much more important for our purposes to understand the difference between an attribute and a mode. To the modern ear the two terms may sound like mere verbal variants both meaning something like "property" or "quality". But whereas Spinoza's attributes are all-pervasive characteristics, modes, in Spinoza's terminology, are individual particular things:

- Modes under the attribute of extension are individual material things.
- Modes under the attribute of thought are individual ideas and, among them, minds.

Spinoza believes that there exist an infinity of other attributes aside from thought and extension that human minds have no knowledge of or access to. These other attributes are all, like thought and extension, attributes of God or the one substance. Unfortunately they are undetectable to us, lying as they do beyond the reach of our cognition.

The crucial point to notice is that any particular thing or mode we encounter in our experience can be explained or understood *as a body* only by reference to other physical things and laws while it can be explained or understood *as a thought or mind* only by reference to other ideas or minds. There are two great causal or explanatory chains or realms available to human understandings: the chain of physical causes and the chain of ideas or mental causes. These two chains are incommensurable and no item from one ever intrudes on the other. Notwithstanding this incommensurability, however, the two great causal or explanatory chains characterize only the single reality, the one substance that Spinoza calls alternately "God" or "Nature".

So an individual human mind is a mode of reality under the attribute of thought. Its individuality and also its capacity to endure through time[2] as a single individual are a result of the unity and individuality of the body whose complex idea it is. Its body is individuated from all others and from things of other kinds by the fact that the human body is a highly complex self-contained and comparatively independent organism whose parts convey energy (or "motion-and-rest", as Spinoza calls it) reciprocally in a fixed ratio.

---

2. Or so it would seem: "The object of the idea constituting the human mind is the body, or a certain mode of extension which actually exists, and nothing else" (E2p13). This appears to say that the death or termination of the body extinguishes the mind but this is not Spinoza's declared final view on the possibility of some kind of immortality.

Numerous bodily systems interact and exchange energy. There is no loss of identity for a human body when there is a loss or gain of matter changing the body's overall size. Rather, it is only when the law-governed regular exchange of energy between constituents alters significantly or breaks down that the stability of the organism and, hence, ultimately, its identity, is lost.

This sophisticated account of mental individuation and identity as being somehow dependent on bodily identity (itself subtly conceived) offers some hope of Spinoza's being able to give a plausible account of personal identity. But that hope will be fully realized only if he can overcome other difficulties in his theory of mind such as the difficulty already mentioned of explaining how the mind can be nothing but an idea or assemblage of ideas and yet, also, the active agent or subject that creates and deploys ideas as well as passively (or even actively) receiving and accumulating them. In other words, he needs some sort of account of consciousness or subjectivity. Spinoza's theory of mind must also be able to give something other than a causal reading of "depend" in the proposition "mental individuation and identity depend on bodily individuation and identity", since Spinoza denies any sort of causal relationship in either direction between mind and body (see Chapters 8 and 9).

Spinoza's identity theory of mind

Commentators disagree about whether or not Spinoza can consistently subscribe to an identity theory of mind. In this subsection I shall look first at an argument that Spinoza's would-be mind–body identity theory is inconsistent with his denial of mind–body interaction and then, secondly, examine the case for saying that his identity theory is inconsistent with what he says about the distinctness of the attributes of thought and extension. Finally, I want to consider briefly whether Spinoza's theory of mind and body has any important affinities with any recent theory of mind.

First argument

The first argument[3] goes as follows. Suppose it is the case that a certain mode of extension, A, causes mode of extension B. Spinoza would say that "A causes B" is a truth. However, if A is numerically identical with mode of thought I, then it would seem also to be true that "I causes B". But this is precisely what

---

3. R. J. Delahunty, *Spinoza* (London: Routledge & Kegan Paul, 1985), 197. It is usefully elaborated and subtly responded to in detail by Michael Della Rocca *Representation and the Mind–Body Problem in Spinoza* (Oxford: Oxford University Press, 1996), ch. 7.

Spinoza denies: that an idea can cause something physical; that there can be mind–matter causal interaction. The conclusion of this objection is thus that Spinoza must either reject the claim that my mind and my body are the same single portion of reality under two different descriptions or he must acknowledge that mind and body can and do interact.

One possible response to this argument is to say that there is a third alternative: Spinoza could say that the argument appears to succeed only because it relies on his agreeing that a causal proposition's truth-value is preserved when identicals are substituted one for the other into that proposition. But he need not agree that "… causes …" is, as logicians would say, a "referentially transparent context". Take away the technical jargon and this means Spinoza could insist that it is true that *A* causes *B* only in so far as *A* is a mode or individual under the attribute of extension. That the same portion of reality that is a mode of extension is, as a matter of fact, also a mode of thought goes no way towards establishing that it caused, or could have caused, any body (material mode) *as a mode of thought*. Only its status as a body has any causal relevance to the production of any other body. To argue otherwise would be like claiming, for example, that the purple colour of some poison killed a rat whereas Spinoza's position is like that of the exterminator who says that the toxicity of the poison was the sole cause of the rat's death, *not* the poison's purple colour. At the very least one could say that "idea *I* causes body *B*" is not true if looked on as an explanation of the coming to be of a body. Thought and extension are (at least) *explanatorily* independent.

Second argument

The second argument mentioned above[4] asks the question how Spinoza can consistently maintain that thought and extension are really distinct attributes and at the same time hold that there is only the one substance pervasively characterized by both. Spinoza makes very clear that he regards thought and extension as completely distinct. We know that he takes it as proof of the distinctness of an attribute if that attribute is conceivable "without the aid of the other" (E1p10s) and he argues that "each attribute is conceived through itself without any other" (E2p6). On the other hand, he says "the thinking substance and the extended substance are one and the same substance, which is now comprehended under this attribute, now under that" (E2p7s).

---

4. An objection along these lines is raised by Alan Donagan, "Spinoza's Dualism", in *The Philosophy of Baruch Spinoza*, Richard Kennington (ed.), 89–102 (Washington, DC: Catholic University of America Press, 1980), esp. 93ff.

The problem is that the orthodoxy of the period has it that attributes do not just add a property to what they are said to be attributes of: they constitute the *nature* or *essence* of what they characterize. And Spinoza agrees. So how can he say that two distinct attributes are instantiated in a single substance? Surely there should be two substances, one for each attribute? Put another way, the question is: how can a single individual thing have two genuinely distinct *essences*?

This objection seems plausible up to a point. Something certainly cannot have two *incompatible* attributes at one and the same time. Again, it is natural to think that a single individual cannot be essentially, "through and through" or "at its very core" characterized by two distinct natures. Surely a single thing can have either one essential nature or another but not both.

In the Third Replies Descartes comes close to saying that thought and extension are not just distinct but incompatible. "Acts of thought", he says, "have nothing in common with corporeal acts" (AT.VII.176; CSM.II.124). Thus, Descartes maintains, it makes sense to hold that thought and extension are the essential attributes of two distinct substances. Has Spinoza any effective response to this Cartesian position?

Spinoza clearly wishes to address the tension he finds in Descartes's philosophy between substance dualism and allegiance to the idea of a substantial union between mind and body in each individual human being. Far from trying to maintain against Descartes that both thought and extension are, after all, natures that presuppose some common feature or character and thus could both at the same time characterize a single thing, Spinoza maintains that they have nothing whatever in common but that this fact creates no barrier to identifying the subject of thought with the subject of extension. We could say that Spinoza thinks thought and extension, different as they are, are not incompatible features since they do not compete over the same territory in any way. What does this mean? Well, a particular shape could not be both circular and square at the same time. These two properties compete over the same descriptive or explanatory territory: a single figure cannot fulfil the conditions for exemplifying both shapes at the same time.

But Spinoza would say that just as an object can easily be red and at the same time round, so too a portion of reality can be a living, lasting human body and at the same time a mind, a subject experiencing a succession of psychological states, features and occurrences. Physical histories and explanations exist for every physical feature of a body. Psychological histories and explanations exist for every mental feature of any mind. For Spinoza the two great explanatory systems explain different sorts of things. No item from one need *or could* figure in the explanation or description of any item in the other. The two explanatory systems do not interpenetrate in any way. And this means that a (the) single substance can have both natures essentially.

Anticipations of non-reductive materialism

Present-day holders of non-reductive materialist theories of mind such as Davidson would agree with Spinoza that my mind is an aspect of myself that is not reducible to any portion or set of properties of my body or brain. According to such a theory mental properties are different in kind from physical properties and not ontologically reducible to them. On either view there are not two sorts of substance, mental and physical. Rather, there is only one sort of substance, which Davidson would call physical or material while Spinoza, as we have seen, would say it was *both* mental and physical. He would agree with Davidson that there are and could be no bridging laws that connect events under their mental descriptions with those events described physically. (For more on the affinity between Spinoza's views and non-reductive materialism see below Chapter 8, § "A materialist in spite of himself?".)

However, Spinoza's theory of mind is certainly not just an early version of Davidson's anomalous monism. They part company at the point where Davidson would explain the existence of the mental as dependent in a non-law-governed way on the physical. For Davidson, mental properties supervene on and depend on the physical properties to which they cannot be reduced but with which they covary. Spinoza believes that mental properties depend only on the one great substance in so far as it is a mind just as physical properties depend exclusively on the one great substance in so far as it is a body. So although Spinoza agrees with Davidson that mental and physical events covary in the sense of having a thoroughgoing parallelism with each other he would deny mutual *dependence* in either direction. He would not allow the sort of supervenience that Davidson believes in. For him a mental property can never be explained by reference to anything physical; no physical property can ever be explained by reference to anything other than the great chain of physical causes.

And yet, in Chapter 9 below we will look at the denial of any kind of interaction between mind and body and see whether Spinoza's theory of mind does in fact have the resources to defend what can seem a highly counterintuitive position with respect to mental causation. For common sense suggests that my desires and feelings, my intentions and choices, are the causes of my actions and are themselves – although one and all psychological things – mostly caused by physical things that affect my mind by affecting me physically. If common sense is wrong about all of this then we are owed an explanation of what is wrong with it, and also why common sense so strongly suggests the opposite.

CHAPTER 7

Spinoza and self-knowledge

Spinoza is convinced that it is only by seeking and obtaining as much under-standing as we can of our passions and emotions, beliefs, intentions and wants, and so on, that we can have any hope of balancing or subduing them in order to achieve happiness and whatever salvation is possible. And we can know that this individual personal self-knowledge is a worthy, and to some extent attainable, object of our efforts by coming to know the shared funda-mental nature of human minds and their place in reality as a whole.

However, Spinoza also thinks that there are severe limits on individual human self-knowledge. Knowledge of my own body is said to be very limited,[1] and what there is is necessarily indirect. Worse still, knowledge of my own mind is said to be, to a great extent and unavoidably, inadequate and confused.[2] And although Spinoza is sharply critical of Descartes for not providing us with a clear and distinct conception of the union of mind and body (E5 Preface), it is difficult to find in Spinoza's own writings a cred-ible attempt to furnish such an account.[3] So it is equally difficult to see how Spinoza could hold that individual persons can have self-knowledge of the mind and body union that we all take ourselves to be.

Yet Spinoza's metaphysical system has often been seen as committed to the principle that individual thought can match reality, that there are ideas adequate to every object, that reality is through and through intelligible and thus that our knowledge of reality cannot fall prey to wholesale and ines-capable epistemological scepticism. One of his main tenets is that reason tells us what the attributes of substance really are and allows us insight into

---

1. For Spinoza, "we have only a completely confused knowledge of our body" (E2p13cs).
2. Spinoza writes that the human mind "does not have an adequate, but only a confused and mutilated knowledge of itself, of its own body, and of external bodies" (E2p29c).
3. Spinoza writes that he has just made clear "what should be understood by the union of mind and body" (E2p13cs), but it is doubtful that many readers would agree.

the principles and conditions governing the two great explanatory or causal systems of thought and extension. In so far as each of us is a chunk of reality that is both a part of extension and an (exactly parallel) item in thought, it seems reasonable to think that Spinoza believes it possible for us to obtain: (i) understanding of ourselves as bodies and minds *in general*; (ii) at least the same knowledge of ourselves *as particular bodies* as we are able to obtain of any material mode; (iii) knowledge of the contents of our own individual minds; and (iv) knowledge of the mind–body union we all take ourselves to be. Spinoza distinguishes three kinds of knowledge (E2p40s2):

- "knowledge of the first kind, opinion or imagination", that is, sensory experience, which yields inadequate and false ideas and may involve induction;
- "reason", that is, knowledge that is adequate and true, also universal and possibly involving deduction; and
- "intuitive knowledge"; this is certainly the most difficult of Spinoza's three kinds to interpret but it is said to provide "adequate knowledge of the essence of [particular] things".

So, what kinds of knowledge does Spinoza allow (i) of the nature of the human mind in general, (ii) of my body, (iii) of my own individual mental history and contents and (iv) of the union of mind and body, which each of us takes himself or herself to be?

The human mind in general

The brief answer to the first part of this question is that Spinoza holds that I can come to know of the fundamental nature of human minds (my own among them) by employing my reason. Just as, using Euclid's *Elements*, I can prove various propositions and obtain knowledge about geometrical figures, so too I can apply my reason to philosophy and in particular the arguments and systematic views found in Spinoza's *Ethics* to reveal the nature of the human mind as God's complex idea of each human body, to discover all the general truths of a detailed philosophical psychology and to make a meticulous description and catalogue of the passions and emotions (as Spinoza has done in the fourth and fifth parts of the *Ethics*, respectively).

This is possible because the view of former thinkers (including Descartes) that man is some sort of "dominion within a dominion", and not subject to the laws that govern the rest of creation, is completely mistaken (E3 Preface).

Far from being exceptional or a law unto itself, the human mind is wholly natural, subject to, and wholly explicable by reference to, the *necessary* laws that govern all of nature.

So it is certainly not by any sort of inner sense, nor by a Cartesian method of doubt, but by metaphysical reflection that I find out the nature of the human mind in general: as we saw in Chapter 6 it is not a substance but rather an individual contingent *mode* under the attribute of thought. Each such mode of thought corresponds exactly to the individual contingent mode under the attribute of extension that is its particular individual human body, its object. This is said to be because mind and body are not only parallel but literally numerically identical. There is just one portion of reality for each human being and each such portion has a mental aspect (its mind) and a physical one (its body). If my knowledge that the human mind is God's full complex idea of the individual human body (and thus that my mind is the idea of my body) counts as a species of self-knowledge then I obtain that self-knowledge with my reason by doing philosophy. That knowledge, in Spinoza's scheme, is evidently knowledge of the second kind: knowledge from reason.

The mind as the idea of the body

It is one thing to say that "the mind is the idea of the body" and that each human being is a portion of reality with two utterly distinct aspects. It is another thing to try to work out what these sayings mean and to understand their implications. For a start, as Margaret Wilson points out,[4] the formula "the mind is the idea of the body" seems to mean that each of us is omniscient about his or her individual body. Spinoza at first seems to draw this conclusion himself: "Whatever happens in the object of the idea constituting the human mind must be perceived by the human mind ... nothing can happen in that body which is not perceived by the mind" (E2p12). However, as Wilson reminds us, there is a vast amount of minute activity in any human body at any given time: "changes of the relation of the simplest parts – the smallest molecules, the atoms, the electrons of each of the millions of cells".[5] Arguably, it passes credence that my mind could hold the sheer volume of ideas involved. And this would be true even if a large proportion of those ideas were the non-conscious ideas that Spinoza, unlike Descartes, is

---

4. M. D. Wilson, "Objects, Ideas, and 'Minds': Comments on Spinoza's Theory of Mind", in Kennington, *The Philosophy of Baruch Spinoza*, 103–20, esp. 107–8.
5. *Ibid.*, 108.

prepared to allow. Even if we alter the idiom and speak of the individual mind "being constituted by" rather than "having" all of these ideas of the body, this account of mind seems inflated and mysterious to the point of incomprehensibility if not incoherence.

Apprehension only deepens when we look ahead to Spinoza's apparently conflicting contention that, far from having complete knowledge "we have only a completely *confused* knowledge of our body" (E2p13cs, emphasis added; and see E2p24). Why would Spinoza contend both that the mind has or consists of ideas of every minute happening in its body and then, only a few paragraphs later, that we have only confused knowledge of our own body? It is equally unappealing to conclude either that he changes his mind abruptly or that he is simply and blindly inconsistent.

A suggestion that allows Spinoza to escape both charges is that he does not regard *having ideas* of any particular object as equivalent to or sufficient for *having complete knowledge or understanding* of that object. As Edwin Curley writes in the index to his translation of the *Ethics*, Spinoza's calling something "knowledge" must not be taken "to imply that what is 'known' is true". So what must I possess, besides a complete set of ideas of my body, before Spinoza will credit me with complete knowledge of (the truth about) that body? A crucial problem with expecting the idea-collection-that-is-my-mind to provide me with complete or adequate knowledge of my body is that, for Spinoza, knowledge of any material body whatsoever requires knowledge of things *other than* that body. Since any body, B, is a mode and not a substance, there are many things outside B on which it depends, which have played a causal role in its coming to be and continuing in existence, which help to define it and would need to be referred to in any adequate understanding of it. No matter how vast the volume of ideas packed into that complex idea of my body that is my mind, that complex idea by itself can amount to no more than "a confused and mutilated knowledge" (E2p29c) of my body. It lacks the required ideas of *other* objects.

This is not to say that I cannot gain *some* understanding of my own body in the same way and to the same extent that I can obtain (limited) knowledge of other material modes. When I employ any of my bodily senses to examine any physical object there is a physical change in my body of a type appropriate to the sense in question. All such changes in my body are reflected in the mental side of my being: new ideas reflecting and corresponding to those physical changes occur in my mind. Spinoza nowhere suggests that I could not be physically affected by my own body. In fact he goes on to say that the mind perceives its own body only through the affections of the body (E2p29c), that is, through ideas of the physical changes wrought on its sense organs in sense experience. So I could come to know something about some part of my body indirectly using sight, touch and so forth. But even if this is right, it would seem that the knowledge of my body that Spinoza would allow me is only ever going to be the sensory or empirical knowledge, his "knowledge of the first kind", which, because it is inadequate, mutilated and confused, lacking in clarity and distinctness, present-day readers would be very reluctant to call "knowledge" at all.

Particular self-knowledge of my mental contents

At the beginning of this discussion of self-knowledge I said that Spinoza believes that it is only by seeking and obtaining as much understanding as we can of our emotions and feelings, beliefs, intentions and wants, and so on, that we can have any hope of balancing or subduing them in order to achieve happiness and whatever salvation is possible. The question now is: what knowledge of our own particular individual mental life does Spinoza think we can obtain and how does he think we acquire it?

Again we find an appearance of self-contradiction when we compare something Spinoza says early in the *Ethics* with what he says towards its conclusion. In the second part of the *Ethics* he is apparently very sceptical of our ability to know without confusion anything much of what occurs in our minds. He writes: "So long as the human mind perceives things from the common order of Nature, it does not have an adequate but only a confused and mutilated knowledge of itself" (E2p29). Spinoza explains his use of the phrase "from the common order of nature" a few lines later: "that is, so long as [the mind] is determined externally, from fortuitous encounters with things, to regard this or that". At those special times when I am exercising my reason and thus wholly occupied with comparing, contrasting and drawing conclusions from necessary truths my ideas are adequate, true, clear and distinct. But things are otherwise most of the time when I am engaged just in ordinary daily life and thought; then my mind is mostly receiving and operating on the myriad ideas of sense perception, that is, those that turn up in my mind to reflect my body's endless encounters via my sense organs with the external world. These ideas of my body that are my sense perceptions are necessarily inadequate since they are partial and patchy.

However, it is not just my perceptions of the world external to me that are inadequate. Since my mind consists largely of these confused and inadequate ideas and my awareness of my own mind consists in whatever ideas I have of these ideas, my ordinary everyday knowledge of my own mind is equally inadequate. Such self-knowledge is knowledge of Spinoza's first kind, that is, it is confused and mutilated knowledge. Like my limited knowledge of my body, my knowledge of my own mind so far seems hardly worthy of the name. It does not seem to be that authoritative knowledge-properly-so-called about one's own beliefs and intentions that modern-day philosophers of mind find so difficult to explain. For example, I may have this sort of knowledge or awareness that, as it seems to me, I am sad about something or resentful of someone. But Spinoza would say that this is or need be only a partial, inadequate understanding of an insufficiently comprehended part of my inner life and my mind. It does not reflect how I am really placed in the world or "how I am" considered timelessly, relative to an eternal perspective.

By Part 5 of the *Ethics*, however, Spinoza is much more upbeat about the possibility of my knowing, and, perhaps more importantly, influencing, what is really going on in my mind, controlling what ideas, emotions and passions I am subject to. He writes: "each of us has – in part, at least, if not absolutely – the power to understand himself and his affects, and consequently, the power to bring it about that he is less acted on by them" (E5p4s). Spinoza has spent the intervening parts of the *Ethics* since Part 2 elaborating a detailed account of human motivation (Part 3) and human "affects" (the general term for feelings and emotions) (Part 4). The supreme motive is *conatus*, that is, the striving or endeavour for self-preservation: for Spinoza "the good" for human beings is defined as what is useful in that it conduces to survival. The emotions are compounded out of the feelings aroused in this endeavour to sustain ourselves. All our appetites and desires are ultimately reducible to the striving for survival that human beings have as the necessary and fundamental core of their nature.

Now, in Part 5, Spinoza aims to show that these emotions and appetites can with effort be controlled so that we become reconciled to what is inevitable and sometimes are able to shape our own fates by dealing with such threats to our happiness and emotional well-being as can be changed or avoided. The key to accomplishing such feats of reconciliation and reshaping of our fates lies in a particular sort of self-awareness, a particular sort of knowledge of our inner states and feelings. The sort of knowledge required is not the impoverished "confused and mutilated" awareness of what I am feeling and thinking, which comes in the course of ordinary experience. Rather, what is needed is the knowledge of my particular feelings and emotions, which is provided by Spinoza's third sort of knowledge, intuition.

And this, in turn, is achieved by means of an application of the second sort of knowledge: one uses reason to gain Spinoza's second kind of knowledge or understanding of *the nature of the emotions in general*: love and hate, joy and sadness and all the different shades of feeling built out of these, such as confidence and fear, gladness, ambition, envy, humility, mockery, pity, hope, self-esteem and so on. Every increase in such general understanding bestows more control over *one's own particular instances of those emotions and feeling*. Or, at any rate, the more general understanding one has, the less one is enslaved by those particular feelings.

The method by which this is to be accomplished is by seeing that the singular affects we are subject to in everyday experience are necessary: that they could not have been otherwise. For example, "we see that sadness over some good which has perished is lessened as soon as the man who has lost it realizes that this good could not, in any way, have been kept" (E5p6s). A number of such "remedies for the affects" – sometimes referred to by Spinoza's commentators as "emotional therapies" – are advocated in Part 5 of the *Ethics*. To take just one example, the understanding leading to resignation and reduction of sadness that has just been mentioned can be aided by the memorizing of maxims such as "hate is to be conquered by love, or nobility, not by repaying it with hate in return" (E5p10s). This maxim should be repeated while meditating on its truth with the aid of images of wrongs responded to in a noble way. By such means the dangerous or excessive emotions that threaten our emotional balance are subdued or even extinguished and with them the desires and appetites that they produce, which, when they are frustrated, are highly detrimental to our well-being and contentment.

Spinoza's notion of self-understanding is thus what might be called a dynamic and prescriptive rather than a static one; reasoned self-understanding, for Spinoza, alters the mind that is understood. No sooner do I understand that I am pining for something that is essentially, and thus necessarily, unobtainable than I cease to feel the pull of that object of desire and become reconciled to its absence. Or so Spinoza believes.

As I mentioned earlier, because Spinoza holds that what I have been calling "our everyday self-awareness" of our feelings, beliefs and intentions does not involve any sort of true or clear knowledge of our mental contents, we would look in vain for hints of Spinoza's being interested in the modern problem of accounting for first-person authority about one's mental contents. He might agree that such feelings and thoughts as I am conscious of in myself at any given unreflective time come without observational or behavioural evidence by which I am informed of their presence in my mind. My awareness of them is immediate, non-inferential. But it falls well short of being complete and therefore from being authoritative. Spinoza is far from subscribing to any sort of "mental transparency" doctrine. He believes that many of our beliefs, intentions, feelings or motives are unconscious or, if not strictly unconscious, then disguised, hidden, truncated, confused and unclear to their possessor. And we are anything but infallible with respect to them. Thus, as we have seen, Spinoza denies that I can have true knowledge of my own mind and its contents without serious efforts of reason-guided self-examination and emotional adjustment.

Spinoza's account of self-awareness is directed at showing the means by which we can take our individual raw emotions and reactions, our everyday feelings, our schemes and intentions thrown up in the course of the hurly-burly of daily life and examine them in the light of reasoned understanding of the affects in general in all their complex and subtle interrelations. This should produce a clarified self-understanding that is the first step to a balanced emotional life. It could perhaps even enable a complete escape from the sway of the emotions. Spinoza believes that such reasoned abstract psychological understanding, applied to our own individual particular experience and situation, can produce in the subject a degree of resignation and thus some liberation from the power of the affects. It thereby comes as close as we are capable of coming to what men have called "freedom of the will". And it has at least a passing resemblance to the modern-day psycho-therapeutic ideal of achieving a sort of liberation by confronting what is buried in the subconscious.

What self-knowledge of the union between body and mind can we have?

As we saw in Chapter 2, Descartes says in the Sixth Meditation that he is taught by experience – by the physical appetites such as hunger and thirst and by sensations such as pain – that his mind is not lodged in his body like a pilot in a ship but rather it is mingled somehow with his whole body to form a substantial union so that, for example, he knows immediately if his body is injured without needing to exercise his external senses (AT.VII.80–81; CSM.II.56). On the other hand, he often says also that the mind or rational soul is especially united to the pineal gland in the brain through which it can influence behaviour and will free actions.

For Spinoza this Cartesian picture of the union of mind and body is largely confused, and where it is not confused it is mistaken. As has been said numerous times already, Spinoza rejects completely the view that mind and body are separate, either as substances (since neither is a substance) or as any other sort of thing. The union they enjoy is that of identity: at the ontological level there are not two things but one thing with two natures. For Spinoza the self is never the conscious mind alone as it sometimes is for Descartes but the

77

single person to whom both mental predicates and physical ones apply.[6] So self-knowledge of the union between individual mind and body is a product of all the other kinds of knowledge discussed in this section; when I know what I can learn from philosophy about the general nature of mind and body, what experience teaches about my body and likewise about my thoughts and imaginings, my passions and emotions, I have all the knowledge obtainable about my self. As Spinoza says immediately after demonstrating that "man consists of a mind and a body" we should now see "what should be understood by the union of mind and body" (E2p13cs).

In Spinoza's eyes there is not so much a "union", as if mind and body were two, intimately related things; rather, there is a single self that can be understood either as a physical entity among other bodies and governed by the laws of physical nature or as a *psyche* that has its own combination of passions, beliefs and intentions owing to its unique individual circumstances and history. Mind and body are distinct in concept but they are one and the same entity and neither can exert any sort of influence on the other. And Spinoza has this knowledge about himself, not through any sort of experience (say, of having his mind try to move his body and fail) but because his reason tells him what his mind and body are and that they are not distinct.

Some readers would say, however, that Spinoza is closer to Descartes than all this might seem to imply: Spinoza, just like Descartes, believes that human minds have knowledge of their own bodily states that is much more direct than that available to anyone else. Henry Allison finds in the admittedly obscure demonstration of Proposition 13 of Part 2 of the *Ethics* "the basic point ... that the human mind has an immediate, sensitive awareness of its own body and of its own body alone (I feel my own pain and not someone else's)".[7] As so often, Spinoza is here being more Cartesian than Descartes in regarding an individual human being as a single real thing: a genuine unity and nothing else. Spinoza thinks Descartes is mistaken in holding that reason is able sometimes to operate independently of its physical counterpart. Descartes misguidedly claims that the will can make free choices on occasion despite the fact that the body is bound inescapably by physical law. Spinoza goes beyond Descartes in regarding the union of mind and body as that of identity and thus as ruling out any possibility of free will. And this is

6. There is a noticeable resemblance here to P. F. Strawson's theory of the person; see "The First Person – and Others". In *Self-Knowledge*, Q. Cassam (ed.), 210–15 (Oxford: Oxford University Press, 1994).
7. Henry E. Allison, *Benedict de Spinoza: An Introduction* (New Haven, CT: Yale University Press, 1987), 96.

something that we know by reason but that is also confirmed by our experience of the bodily feelings.

Unfortunately for one of the positions Spinoza wishes to defend at the end of the *Ethics*, this identity between living body and conscious mind means that there is no possibility of personal – or indeed any – survival of the mind after the death of the body. It may be right to consider my mind, since it is a complex *idea*, as having an eternal aspect, like that of the idea of an isosceles triangle or Pythagoras's theorem. But just to the extent that Spinoza has convinced us that we have knowledge through reason as well as sensory experience of the identity between the mind and the body, he has left himself with a daunting uphill task if he hopes to convince us that there is any such thing as a desirable form of immortality for the self.

CHAPTER 8

The subject of thought and consciousness

What does the thinking?

Part 2 of Spinoza's *Ethics* is entitled "Of the Nature and Origin of the Mind", so it may be surprising not to find, among the definitions of "body", "idea", "'adequate idea" and so forth with which this part begins, a definition of "mind". Admittedly the definition of "idea" does say that an idea is a concept of the mind "which the mind forms because it is a thinking thing" (E2d3). Here as elsewhere throughout Part 2, and indeed the rest of the work, Spinoza says and assumes that the mind is a thing that thinks, imagines, conceives and understands. However, it is difficult to form a view on *how* he thinks the mind does this.

Of course, Spinoza explicitly rejects Descartes's (and Berkeley's) answer: that there is an immaterial substance, the rational soul, that does the thinking in each of us and makes its human possessor fully conscious and self-aware. He also criticizes Descartes for resorting to a supernatural divine agency as the immediate cause of the existence of the rational soul or mind in each human being. Spinoza cannot accept that human minds, any more than human bodies, have a source outside nature or are to be explained in non-natural terms. And, as we know, he certainly resists any suggestion that finite minds possess the features essential to being substances in their own right.

But if the human mind is neither an immaterial Cartesian rational soul nor any kind of substance in its own right, what is it? What does Spinoza take to be the *subject* of thoughts and consciousness? He says that the human mind is the complex idea of the body; is there any possibility that this formula can be construed in such a way as to give a plausible account of thinking or an answer to the modern problem of consciousness – the question what accounts for subjectivity?

One of Spinoza's commentators thinks that the key to making Spinoza's theory of mind plausible lies in paying careful attention to what Spinoza means by "idea". Far from employing this term for, or restricting it to, passively received sensory perceptions or images, on this reading Spinoza holds that ideas are "acts of conceiving or believing". So, when Spinoza says that the mind is the idea of the body he is saying that the mind is "nothing above and beyond its activity";[1] it consists of mental acts and episodes of various kinds.

This suggested interpretation has much to make it convincing. Spinoza certainly intends his individual human minds to be vital and dynamic. They are active participants in the world, striving to preserve themselves and their bodies. They are much more than simply passive receivers of sensations or inert, helpless victims of their passions. To this should be added the fact that Spinoza explicitly rejects the sort of faculty psychology subscribed to by many of his predecessors. He writes that "there is in the mind no absolute faculty of understanding, desiring, loving, etc." (E2p48s) and shortly thereafter that "the will and the intellect are nothing apart from the singular volitions and ideas themselves" (E2p49cd). So it seems right to say that, for Spinoza, human minds are essentially and exclusively their activity.

With the best will in the world, however, it is impossible not to protest that *acts need an agent*: mental acts need an actor to do the conceiving, believing, feeling, thinking and so forth. In short, episodes of thought do not "have" themselves. As we shall see in detail when looking at problems with Hume's bundle theory, acts of thought and experiences need a thinking subject. Unfortunately, we have arrived for a second time – although by a slightly different route – at the same problem as the one that afflicted the interpretation discussed earlier (Chapter 6), which took Spinoza to be saying that the mind is a (highly organized, complex and hierarchical) *bundle* of ideas. Ideas do not think themselves. They need a subject to do the thinking. Does Spinoza offer any suggestion of what (or who) could be the agent to do the thinking in the human case?

Part of the infinite intellect of God

This is the point to recall Spinoza's claim that the human mind (each human mind) is "part of the infinite intellect of God" (E2p11c). His surprising answer to the question "What does the thinking?" is that God or the one great substance is the thinking subject in each human. God is the subject whose idea of my body is my mind. This of course is not at all a comfortable answer to

---

1. Allison, *Benedict de Spinoza*, 88ff.

the question. Among other difficulties, it threatens us immediately with the problem of how to explain the relationship between the numerous individual human minds and the one great divine mind. Should we conceive individual human consciousnesses somehow as innumerable *parts*, bits of consciousness that together add up to the divine conscious subject? Or does Spinoza envisage each individual human circumscribed consciousness existing within (or possibly on another level from) a single comprehensive divine consciousness? It is very unclear how discrete self-contained consciousnesses could be individuated from one another while also being part of one big individual consciousness. Put the other way round, consciousness is not the sort of thing that can be broken down into constituent parts each of which has the same nature as the whole in the way that a cake can be cut into pieces of cake or a brick wall disassembled into individual bricks. We do not ordinarily think of consciousness in such a way as to believe that a part of a conscious subject would or could be itself a conscious subject. Alan Donagan proposes, only half jokingly, that this doctrine puts Spinoza in need of "a theory of divine multiple personality".[2]

Difficult as it is to see how each human mind could be part of the divine mind, however, a bigger difficulty with resorting to God as the conscious subject of every human mind's ideas is yet to be spelled out. It is that Spinoza appears to support the view that God's mind (God considered under the attribute of thought) is exactly like the individual human mind in being a complex collection or bundle of ideas and nothing more. God's mind is the totality of all finite modes of thought. It is no easier to see how a collection of divine ideas could be a thinker or subject of experience than it was to see the complex idea of any given individual human body as itself capable of thought. In fact, if anything, proposing the totality of all ideas as the mind that thinks in me seems even less promising than proposing the idea of my body as my mind. For we have experience to tell us that individual human beings think. We certainly have no experience of the whole of mental reality forming one thinking individual.

A materialist in spite of himself?

Ultimately, what seems insuperable in Spinoza's theory of mind (especially considered as an account of human consciousness and subjective experience)

---

2. Donagan, "Spinoza's Dualism", 100.

is his complete refusal to countenance any sort of causal connection between mind and body. Given his denial of the existence of immaterial substance it can seem that Spinoza has no alternative but to accept that mind must depend on material substance for its existence. So compelling is this line of thought that it has tempted some recent commentators – and many students – to suggest that Spinoza, notwithstanding his clear assertions to the contrary, winds up defending a view of mind and subjectivity that makes mind dependent on matter. Otherwise, how else explain passages such as this:

> [I]n proportion as a body is more capable than others of doing many things at once, or being acted on in many ways at once, so its mind is more capable than others of perceiving many things at once. And in proportion as the actions of a body depend more on itself alone, and as other bodies concur with it less in acting, so its mind is more capable of understanding distinctly.   (E2p13cs)

And again: "The idea of any thing that increases or diminishes, aids or restrains, our body's power of acting, increases or diminishes, aids or restrains, our mind's power of thinking" (E3p11). To some modern readers such passages seem to commit Spinoza to the view that physical sophistication and autonomy in an organism have a causal role in making perception, understanding, consciousness and other mental powers possible for that animal. In Allison's words, for Spinoza "mind is a function of organic complexity".[3]

Adding apparent weight to this reading is Spinoza's insistence that in order to understand the mind we must understand the body. The pages following the passage from Proposition 13 in Part 2 of the *Ethics* just quoted contain five axioms, seven lemmas and their several demonstrations with corollaries and six postulates, all designed to explain the nature of bodies, how they are individuated, what their identity over time consists in and what in particular is the nature of the *human* body. Knowing these things, Spinoza says, should help us better understand mind in general and also the union of human mind and body. But why should understanding the body be thought so beneficial for understanding the mind if the body's nature and functioning have no causal relevance to those of the mind? Is this not Spinoza's (albeit reluctant and tacit) acknowledgement that there *is* causal dependence of mind on matter after all?

---

3. Allison, *Benedict de Spinoza*, 98.

Unfortunately for friends of this reading, however, the contention that Spinoza denies mind–body interaction is too well entrenched and motivated to be refutable. Yes, he does say that degree of mental complexity and autonomy of action *covary* with degree of physical complexity and physical autonomy, but he does so without conceding that mind is causally dependent on the body.

Instead, Spinoza's explanation of this covariance is in terms of his parallelism: the whole system of physical natural law is *mirrored exactly* by the whole system of mental or psychological natural law because the modes under the attribute of thought are one and all ideas, which are identical with (alternative aspects of) the physical bodies that constitute the realm governed by physical laws. Ideas and thoughts alone appear in the chain of causation leading up to and away from any mental state or event, just as physical occurrences alone appear in the chain of causation leading up to and away from any physical state. But each physical state or event is an expression of the essence of a particular mode, which is also expressed by exactly corresponding mental states or events. It is this wholesale parallelism that enables greater understanding of the mind to be acquired through greater understanding of the corresponding human body. But covariation does not entail causal connection.

Paradoxically, it is precisely because Spinoza adheres to his own variety of strict identity theory of mind that he refuses to accept any dependence of the mental on the physical: mind and body are simply not distinct or separate in the right way to be able to interact. But Spinoza could never follow Hobbes in reducing mind to matter in motion and thought to a physical process. He strenuously opposes any theory that demotes the realm of ideas to a mere by-product of the physical. For Spinoza, mind and matter, thought and extension, are on an equal footing: all of reality is everywhere and equally characterized by both.

Despite this, or perhaps because of it, Spinoza's theory may strike present-day readers as being, nonetheless, quite reminiscent of contemporary *non-reductive materialist* theories of mind. As mentioned above, a number of differing theories fall under the general label "non-reductive materialist", but such theories are alike in the view that reality is characterized by both physical and mental properties, the latter wholly resisting reduction to the former. They also hold that mental properties only emerge from or supervene on physical beings of the right sort of complexity and sophistication, a contention that, as before, chimes in with Spinoza's claims that human minds, in order to excel as they do in perception and understanding, must be the ideas of organically complex bodies.

Notwithstanding this apparent harmony between Spinoza's theory and modern non-reductive materialisms, however, it may well be that we are left with considerable residual unease by Spinoza's refusal to countenance mind–body interaction and his view that his parallelism can hold despite lack of all such interaction. The mental causal or explanatory realm is supposed to mirror or reflect the physical causal or explanatory realm. But what are non-metaphorical "mirroring" and "reflecting" but a certain sort of *causal* interaction? And what explanation other than a real literal causal interaction could there be for Spinoza's mind–body parallelism? In the absence of immaterial minds or substances, how can consciousness be explained except as a dependence of the mental on the physical?

Panpsychism

Spinoza's theory of mind, for all its undoubted air of modernity on certain points, is not simply an early version or anticipation of a present-day theory. We should also notice that Spinoza's theory differs in a further very significant way from non-reductive materialism: non-reductive materialism, like most theories of mind, would stoutly maintain that not all bodies have minds. Indeed there is a remarkable degree of agreement across the philosophy of mind spectrum that mindedness and subjectivity are restricted to a small range of types of material objects. Even those who might be prepared to concede at least sentience to a goodly selection of fauna (and perhaps even flora!) would probably stop short of according ideas or feelings to sticks and stones, mountains and rivers, planets and stars. But Spinoza is committed to holding that every material body or mode is the material aspect of something that can equally be referred to and thought about as an idea or mode of thought and therefore as a mind: the mind of the object that the idea is the idea of.

Some early readers of Spinoza's *Ethics* were highly critical of what they saw as his panpsychism: the belief that each and every material body has a mind or soul. Allison has defended the view that Spinoza need only be taken to be subscribing to panvitalism – the view that all bodies are, in a sense, alive – and not to a view that would imply that stones have a mental life. If true, however, it is hard to see how this could help to deflect much criticism from Spinoza. That stones are alive seems every bit as heretical as the view that they are conscious, that there is something it is like to be a stone. And in any event the key passage, which says that all individual bodies "though in different degrees, are nevertheless animate" (E2p13ds) (all bodies are alive

85

because they have souls [*anima*]), comes just after Spinoza has argued that, for man, the mind is the idea of the body and nothing else and just before he goes on to say "whatever we have said of the idea of the human body must also be said of the idea of anything".

It seems clear that Spinoza accepts, and is here saying, that his account of mind must be taken to be completely general, equally applicable to all bodies. He is saying that every material object has a mind, which is the idea of that material object. It may even be that my foot and my stomach would count as distinct material bodies thus each having a mind.

Curley aims to defuse the accusation of panpsychism in a different way from Allison by offering the following reading of Spinoza's contention that every body has a corresponding idea.[4] Curley says that this is nothing more controversial than the claim that, for every material item, X, there is in God an idea of X in the sense of *a set of true propositions about* X. So, saying that a stone has a mind or that there is an idea of it in God's mind is nothing more controversial than saying that there exists a, presumably quite small and trivial, set of true propositions about that stone.

The trouble with this interpretation is that it robs Spinoza's account of a justification for attributing consciousness and capacity for thought to human beings. If my having a mind means no more than that there is somewhere a set of true propositions about my body then there is no more reason to describe me as conscious or capable of thought than there is to think this of the stone. Curley's interpretation saves Spinoza from the absurdity of "thinking stones" by making all minded beings unthinking and unconscious.

A number of commentators, including Curley, read Spinoza as hoping to escape both this absurdity and the absurdity of panpsychism by holding that those simple bodies (sticks, stones, etc.) that have very few parts and lack all internal complexity have *for that very reason* only the lowest level of mental life and nothing that could be compared to conscious experience. This interpretation may well capture something that Spinoza holds. The first difficulty with it is that, as Wilson points out,[5] there is insufficient evidence in the text of the *Ethics* to establish that he does hold it, still less to establish that what he is said to hold on this topic is consistent with the rest of his writings. True, Spinoza does say that "ideas differ among themselves, as the objects themselves do", and that one idea "is more excellent than the other and contains more reality" so that the human mind differs from the others and "surpasses them" (E2p13cs). But this falls very far short of saying – still less proving

---

4. Curley, *Spinoza's Metaphysics*, 126. See also Allison, *Benedict de Spinoza*, 96–7.
5. Wilson, "Objects, Ideas and Minds", 118.

– that human beings (and perhaps some higher animals) have consciousness and subjectivity conferred on them simply by the fact that they have more complex bodies while lesser minds lack such mental abilities simply because their bodies lack such complexity.

This shortfall persists because the interpretation under discussion goes no way at all towards explaining *why* this should be the case. What is still crucially lacking is any explanation of why a more complex body's idea should be any "more excellent" a mind than the idea of a simpler body, given that all suggestion of causal dependence of mind on body has been emphatically ruled out.

CHAPTER 9

Spinoza and mental causation

At some point in each of the preceding chapters it has been said that Spinoza's metaphysical system has no place whatever for the notion of mind–body interaction. Minds are identical with bodies. So, for Spinoza, the suggestion that a mind might be sufficiently separate from its body to exert influence on that body (or vice versa) is a nonsense. This being so, perhaps Spinoza's views on mental causation need not detain us long. The mind, for Spinoza, has *no* capacity to produce actions or to affect the body in any way.

And yet this is obviously too hasty. For a start, anyone who denies that the mind can produce or influence bodily action owes us an explanation of why human beings have such a strong pre-philosophical conviction that feelings, choices and intentions do indeed have causal power: that mental states cause their possessors to act. We are also owed some account of why, despite popular opinion, the view that mental causation of physical actions is a reality is not just unpersuasive but completely untenable. In what follows the first section will address the question whether Spinoza can successfully explain the folk-psychological belief in mental causation of physical action. The second section will examine Spinoza's case against such mental causation and the third will assess his criticisms of Descartes's account of action and free will. The fourth section will look briefly at the control Spinoza thinks each individual can exercise over his or her emotional life; this is, of course, a matter of the mind influencing the mind – the only sort of mental causation Spinoza acknowledges. It is sometimes said that Spinoza's theory of mind is a variety of epiphenomenalism. I shall end this chapter with a brief discussion of this charge.

Why do we think our actions are not exclusively determined by physical law?

For Spinoza this question reduces, for all practical purposes, to the question why philosophers and ordinary folk alike (wrongly) believe in free will. Spinoza has no patience with Descartes's view that the will is free and undetermined by external causes. The mind, Spinoza says "is determined to will this or that by a cause which is also determined by another, and this again by another, and so to infinity" (E2p48). Nor can my willing (a mental event) cause my body to do anything (a physical event). So what makes it seem to us on occasion that we are acting freely or from choice? What makes us think that some courses of action must be under the direction of the mind, and in particular the will, and could not be produced by matter alone? Spinoza gives the following explanation of why I am inclined to think that, at least some of the time, my actions are initiated and governed by my mental states rather than by my body obeying physical law. He writes: "Experience itself, no less clearly than reason, teaches that men believe themselves free because they are conscious of their own actions, and ignorant of the causes by which they are determined" (E3p2s). This is partly because each particular action, like every individual human being, is situated in a unique configuration of circumstances and at the end of numerous physical and mental causal chains, many of whose links are beyond the reach of discovery: simply "out of sight" in the present or lost from view in the past. It is also because human physiology and material science are still in their infancy. If science were complete, or much more advanced than it is at present, we could understand how astounding are the powers of matter in all its rich variety and in all the amazing array of different complex organisms and forms that it can assume. "No one has yet determined", Spinoza says, "what the body can do from the laws of Nature alone, insofar as Nature is only considered to be corporeal" (*ibid.*). Since that information is not available, and since it is much more flattering to our self-image to do so, we attribute the cause of our actions to our minds or wills rather than our bodies.

This is the principal reason why people believe the mind guides the body. But sometimes people give two further reasons. The first thing they say is that "they know by experience that unless the human mind were capable of thinking, the body would be inactive". The second is that "they know by experience, that it is in the mind's power alone both to speak and to be silent, and to do many other things which they therefore believe depend on the mind's decision" (*ibid.*). Finally, Spinoza notes that where a person does not feel impelled to act one way rather than another that individual may, as he or she might say, "simply decide" to do this rather than that and thus become persuaded that he or she has the power of unfettered choice.

These are all, to some degree, credible explanations of how we come to believe – despite its being false – that the mind can guide the body. Spinoza's position, of course, is that it *is* false and that nothing should be allowed to convince us that our beliefs, desires and so on can really have an effect on our behaviour. And this means that he presents these accounts of how people fall into error in a form that will leave that popular misconception rebuttable.

Spinoza's case against mental causation of physical action

As we know, Spinoza's whole metaphysical system rules out mind–body inter-action. So he believes that reason, informed by the arguments for monism in Part 1 of the *Ethics*, should conclude that mind cannot act on body. But he also argues that we can learn from experience as well as reason that our actions are not under the guidance of mind.

First, he says that experience teaches that it is wrong to think that conscious mental life is *necessary* for apparently intelligent action. We do not credit non-human animals with free choice (i.e. the capacity for mind-directed actions) and yet "many things are observed in the lower animals which far surpass human ingenuity" (E3p2s). Again, the often-quite-complicated actions of (unconscious) sleepwalkers rebut the claim that actions require the exercise of mental power. And Spinoza also holds that all sorts of impressive works of nature – for example, the ingenious structure of the human body – can be seen to come about without the guidance of any mind.

The fact that we often feel quite strongly that we are exercising mental power over our own actions has been said to explain why we fall into the mistake of thinking we have so-called free choice. However, this sort of experience, Spinoza argues, should be balanced against the surely more common experience of observing, say, a child, a chatterbox or a drunk whose actions are discernibly compelled by causes outside his control or knowledge, however much he may feel that his actions are guided by his own wishes, hopes and intentions. Moreover, we have all had experience of thinking we were acting as a result of free, perhaps even indifferent, choice and then discovering the true cause of that action to be something beyond our control. The feeling of control is not *sufficient* for genuine mental causation of physical action.

It is time to challenge each of these contentions in turn. That non-human animals lack minds is certainly something that would be widely denied among philosophers of mind and the general public. It is not something about which Spinoza can assume that he shares common ground with his opponents. Similarly, as was argued in Chapter 3, not everyone would agree that sleepwalkers lack every sort of mind or consciousness. Next, the fact that some amazing results are the product of evolutionary or other accident is impressive but it proves only that some surprising results lack a mental cause. It certainly does not prove that no result is ever caused by a mind.

Most importantly of all, the fact that it is sometimes possible for me to be mistaken in thinking my actions are caused by my beliefs, hopes and wishes goes no way to proving that I am *always* wrong in this way. It is beyond dispute that there may sometimes be hidden causes of our actions of which we are unaware. This does not prevent us from knowing on occasion that, without our decision or choice (mental event), we would not have done what we did (physical event). Since we are certain of the truth of this counterfactual we know that our choice was at least a part of the cause of that action, whatever hidden contributory causes might come to light. Spinoza needs to refute this argument, not just disparage it, if his opposition to mind–body interaction is to succeed. So far it seems that the verdict must be "not proven".

Spinoza's criticism of Descartes's account of free choice

In the Preface to Part 3 of the *Ethics*, Spinoza criticizes those who hold that man is somehow outside the constraints of natural law: "Indeed, they seem to conceive man in Nature as a dominion within a dominion. For they believe that man disturbs, rather than follows, the order of Nature, that he has absolute power over his actions, and that he is determined only by himself" (E3 Preface). Earlier (Chapter 1) it was argued that Descartes resorts to such a position because he thinks there is a point at which scientific explanation of human beings runs out. Since, as he believes, pure reason and moral deliberation and choice cannot be explained by natural science, he posits a rational soul in man to account for those things. The rational soul, as we have seen, is an incorporeal substance that is united to the human material body by supernatural means. As such, it can operate in the world unconstrained by natural law. To Spinoza, however, this position is culpable wishful thinking and, moreover, patently false.

Returning to this topic in his Preface to Part V, Spinoza spells out what he takes to be the errors in Descartes's attempt to put detail on the account of free will to which he is committed by his dualism. For Descartes the mind must intervene in nature in order to exercise its will and direct bodily behaviour. It does this by operating the brain mechanisms that physically control the body's actions. The mind acts on the pineal gland in particular, positioning it in different ways in order to vary the direction in which the animal spirits, the fluid in which it is suspended, circulate around the body. Depending on the speed and direction of the animal spirits, physical muscular activity of differing kinds is triggered. Descartes thinks much human activity is pre-programmed. We are born with various physical positionings of the gland already programmed so that the gland is "set" to cause specific physical activities reflexively in appropriate circumstances. We can, however, change the settings if our wills act on the positioning of the gland. Training can also alter an instinctive behaviour pattern, resetting the gland so that, for example, when threatened, the person stays to fight rather than fleeing.

Spinoza finds several crucial things wrong with this. The first is that the will on this account can be frustrated if some bodily malfunction or internal accident results in, say, the "courage setting" of the gland being physically lost so that the person flees instead of staying to fight as he had resolved to do. Spinoza also disputes the physiology of Descartes's account saying that the pineal gland is not situated as Descartes thinks in the very middle of the brain. Far more importantly, and fatally for Descartes's theory, "since there is no common measure between the will and motion, there is also no comparison between the power, or forces, of the mind and those of the body" (E5 Preface). Descartes's account of mental causation is actually completely unworkable. Mental force and physical force are of utterly different types and thus incommensurable. So mind and body can neither alter nor get any sort of grip on one another. The picture of the mind exercising even the little physical force needed to position the gland is pure fantasy.

Spinoza's criticisms of Descartes seem well founded. Descartes wants to remain a dualist but still have a mechanistic account of the springs of much human behaviour. His account of mental causation founders at the point where the subject's will must jump the metaphysical divide between incorporeal mind and physical brain.

Freedom of mind or blessedness

Spinoza's rejection of Cartesian substance dualism, and with it any meaning for the notion of mental causation of physical action or free will, might seem to imply that Spinoza can have no place in his philosophy for any sort of freedom. But Spinoza never rules out the possibility of mental causation of mental actions and states. Indeed, since mind–mind causation would simply amount to one mode of thought affecting or producing another, he can make good use of this notion in creating his account of freedom of mind or "blessedness".

For Spinoza the human mind has the power to control some of its passions by employing the understanding. As we saw in Chapter 8, Spinoza's view is, very roughly, that emotions or feelings can be made to loose their hold on their subject by being clearly understood. This understanding is a function of two things. The subject must first discover the roots and nature of human emotions and feelings in general by the conscientious application of reason. Then he or she must engage in a process of self-examination to discover what are the particular emotions whose impact needs to be minimized. In a nutshell, Spinoza's motto is "knowledge is power". To understand is to discern what could not be otherwise. A person who understands what emotional constraints are operating can make some headway in conquering them, largely by becoming resigned to what is necessary but also by replacing damaging emotions by less damaging ones. On Spinoza's view I cannot turn my head by willing or deciding to but I can turn my mind away from fruitless misery towards more joyful thoughts and feelings.

It should be said that this greater self-awareness and control of one's emotions in making choices is not all there is to the Spinozistic ideal of "blessedness". In Part 5 of the *Ethics*, Spinoza indicates that he believes that, under certain circumstances and in some mysterious way, some portion of a human mind can live eternally in the divine intellect. Unfortunately, commentators are generally agreed in finding this part of Spinoza's view extremely difficult to understand and thus, equally unfortunately, almost impossible to assess.

Epiphenomenalism

Is Spinoza an epiphenomenalist? He does not seem to be one in the usual sense of the term. The ordinary definition of epiphenomenalist is "someone who believes that the mental depends on the physical for its existence but that the physical is in no way affected by the mental". Present-day versions of epiphenomenalism would probably express this as the belief that physical processes in the brain produce and sustain mental states while these mental states have no effect on the brain processes and are impotent to cause any physical change. Spinoza certainly holds that the physical is unaffected by the mental but he also holds that the mental is not dependent on the physical or affected by it in any way. Thought and extension form utterly separate, self-contained and mutually independent systems. Or so he explicitly and repeatedly says.

However, it is possible to wonder whether Spinoza succeeds in maintaining this complete even-handedness between thought and extension. Where the human mind and body are concerned he portrays the mind (the idea of the body) as changing with changes in the body but does not describe the body changing with the mind. He says that understanding of the body is required for understanding of the mind and that the mind could not function or exist without the body. As Curley points out, "In spite of all the parallelistic talk, the order of understanding never proceeds from mind to body".[1] Once again, as we found in Chapter 8, it is very hard to resist the conclusion that Spinoza cannot escape making the mind dependent on the body.

---

1. Edwin Curley, *Behind the Geometrical Method* (Princeton, NJ: Princeton University Press, 1988), 78.

CHAPTER 10

Spinoza on representation

What is Spinoza's answer to the question how thoughts come to represent, in the mind of the person having them, the objects in the world that those thoughts are about? As we have seen, Descartes rejects the view that ideas represent by being portraits or likenesses of the external objects encountered in sense perception. In general, ideas are not images of the things that cause them. They are mental states caused by sensory interaction with physical things but also they have the phenomenal character ordained by God to represent their physical causes.

But obviously the Cartesian account of where mental representation comes from or how ideas represent their objects runs very much against the main tenets of Spinoza's metaphysical system and theory of mind. At its core, the view just sketched holds that body and mind interact in sense perception and such interaction is utterly ruled out for Spinoza. In his view no physical object could ever cause an idea. So Spinoza's efforts to improve on the Cartesian theory of representation do not involve his attempting to solve the question, which Descartes notoriously left unresolved, of how things of such utterly different natures as mind and body could interact. Rather, his own theory portrays mental representation as working in a very different way.

Improving on Descartes?

Recall that for Spinoza there is a complete parallelism between, on the one hand, ideas and on the other hand, physical events and things. As he says, "The order and connection of ideas is the same as the order and connection of things" (E2p7). Each of the infinite number of ideas or mental events that make up the great explanatory system that is the attribute of thought has a corresponding physical event or body under the attribute of extension with which it is correlated, and vice versa. Physical events and states have solely physical causes and effects. Mental states and occurrences are caused exclusively by mental causes and give rise to mental effects alone. For Spinoza, every portion of reality has its physical side and its mental side: every mental happening corresponds to a physical item and every physical item has its parallel idea.

Although we have seen above that Spinoza gives less argument than could be wished to defend the main principles of his parallelism, for present purposes let us take this parallelism as being adequately defended. Then recall also what Spinoza says about the human mind being the complex idea of the body so that each idea or episode of thought in the mind is first and foremost an idea of an organ, or limb or process or event in the body. From here it seems a natural step to think of each idea in the mind as representing (standing for or being about) the bodily item that is exactly parallel with it: what could be called its "extended correlate". Briefly put, it may even be possible to see Spinoza as thinking that ideas represent (as well as being identical with) their correlated brain states or events.

However, this tells only half the story. If what has been said so far is right, we have at this point only representations that are about our bodies. We still need to know how, if at all, Spinoza thinks human minds can think about and be aware of the world of things *beyond* the individual human body. Surely most people would say they were seldom aware of the happenings in their bodies, and never aware of the whole collection of those happenings simultaneously. Rather, most of our conscious life is passed in awareness of things external to our bodies: items in our environment including other people. And Spinoza, for his part, as we have already seen (Chapter 7), is careful to point out that while the mind may consist of ideas of the body, it does not thereby *know* the body. Spinoza does not think every one of us is an expert human physiologist. The huge store of "ideas of the body" that constitutes each of our minds must serve some function other than that of a vast horde of knowledge about our bodies.

The answer is that, for Spinoza, many of my "ideas of my body" at any given time are actually ideas of the changes that take place in various parts of my body when I use my sense organs. My optic nerves, taste buds, eardrums, nerve endings and so on are all altered in the course of seeing, tasting, hearing, touching and so forth. Such events are occurring constantly throughout my waking life. Spinoza believes that his parallelism ensures that all such bodily happenings are and must be reflected in my mind: *not* that they cause ideas in my mind and not that I am consciously aware of them *as bodily happenings*. Rather, my ideas of those bodily happenings, which are the mental sides or aspects parallel to those bodily happenings, are in part unconscious representations of those bodily changes. But they are also in part conscious perceptions or ideas of the physical causes of those bodily happenings. In so far as they are conscious perceptions those ideas represent the immediate external causes of their corresponding cerebral events: they are thus *about* the objects external to me that physically affect my body.

Take, for example, an episode where I (as I might say) look through the window at a tree. Light from the tree's surface irradiates my pupils, in turn causing other changes in my nerves and brain. The mental counterpart or ideal side of these physical changes in eye, nerves and brain is an idea that is now part of my mind. That idea is in part an unconscious idea of those bodily changes. But that idea is also in part the conscious perception or idea of the tree. The idea of those bodily changes represents them to my mind. It also represents, and involves the essence of, the tree that was the external cause of the bodily changes.[1] The unconscious part of that idea is about my body; the conscious part is about the tree.

It seems that Spinoza holds that our perceptual ideas represent what they do because they are the ideas of the causes of those exact changes in the body. To be a specific object (to be, say, a blue cube) is to be a thing that affects a human body in a specific way (through, in this case, the senses of sight and touch), producing characteristic physical changes whose mental aspects are, respectively, an idea of blue and an idea of that sort of six-sided figure.

Room for disagreement

The idea of any mode in which the human body is affected by external bodies must involve the nature of the human body and at the same time the nature of the external body.   (E2p16)

It ought to be said immediately that the interpretation given in the previous section is a reading of a small number of cryptic passages,[2] passages about

---

1. See Della Rocca, *Representation and the Mind–Body Problem*, ch. 5.
2. In addition to the quotation just given the main relevant passages are:

    The images of things are affections of the human body whose ideas represent external bodies as present to us (by IIP17S), that is (by IIP16), whose ideas involve the nature of our body and at the same time the present nature of the external body. (E3p27d)

    From this it follows, first, that the human mind perceives the nature of a great many bodies together with the nature of its own body.   (E2p16c1)

which there is wide, sometimes fierce, disagreement among Spinoza's commentators over:

- whether Spinoza's use of the phrase "idea of" is univocal or whether it has some sort of duality and, if the latter, whether this duality is intentional or inadvertent on his part;
- whether or not Spinoza really intends to say that the idea of the bodily changes *represents* those changes and, if it does represent them, whether or not it represents them in the same sense of "represent" as that in which it represents the external object that causes those changes;
- whether Spinoza would say, in the example of looking through the window at the tree, that there was just the one "idea of the tree" or two ideas, one an awareness of the tree itself and the other an awareness of the cerebral event or state that is the idea's extended counterpart; and
- how much of the ideal or mental aspect of this sensory encounter Spinoza would be prepared to describe as conscious.

A covariance theory

Rather than discuss all these disagreements and possible bones of contention in detail or attempt to resolve them where Spinoza has given little textual wherewithal to do so, I have ventured a reading that I think goes as far as a sympathetic reader *can* go in trying to produce an explicit theory of representation that Spinoza might accept as his own and which seems consistent with his other views. We can at least regard it as relatively uncontroversial that Spinoza believes we acquire ideas in sense perception that can represent in our thinking the perceived external objects that are the immediate cause of those ideas' extended counterparts. So perhaps we can cautiously describe

---

It follows, second, that the ideas which we have of external bodies indicate the condition of our own body more than the nature of the external bodies.   (E2p16c2)

[W]e clearly understand what is the difference between the idea of, say, Peter which constitutes the essence of Peter's mind, and the idea of Peter which is in another man, say in Paul. For the former directly explains the essence of Peter's body, and does not involve existence, except so long as Peter exists; but the latter indicates the condition of Paul's body more than Peter's nature, ... and therefore, while that condition of Paul's body lasts, Paul's mind will still regard Peter as present to itself, even though Peter does not exist.   (E2p17s)

Spinoza's theory of representation as what is sometimes called a covariance theory of representation.[3]

As we saw in Chapter 5, § "Misrepresentation", in such a theory my idea of X represents X if the arrival of that idea in my mind covaries with the presence of X. That is, the idea of X turns up in my mind when, only when and because I am having a sensory encounter with X. So the idea of X comes to be the symbol that represents or stands for X in my thought by being the reliable, regular, indeed invariable, mental accompaniment to X in my experience. It is very difficult to know whether Spinoza intends his account of representation to account for how the idea of X comes to represent not just the one individual X but Xs in general. If I am to think about the external world with any profit, as Locke sees so clearly, I must be able to generalize or abstract and think of kinds of things not just individuals. So, for the time being I will assume that Spinoza intends his account to cover ideas representing types of thing.

However, as we also saw in Chapter 5, covariance theories face two difficult challenges in trying to explain, as they must, both misrepresentation and the problem that some authors call "the disjunction problem". In a foggy country lane and in the presence of a large shaggy dog I may experience what I have come to call "my idea of a sheep". We might be tempted to say that this idea misrepresents the dog as a sheep. But a few more minutes' thought will show that, on the current theory, an idea cannot misrepresent. If there is no sheep there then that idea cannot represent sheep alone since the covariance theory says ideas represent what they indicate. And on this occasion my perceptual idea is not indicating – because it was not caused by – a sheep. Whatever idea is caused by what I see represents what I actually see, not what I think I see. But surely we should not accept a theory of representation that makes misrepresentation impossible.

Perhaps we should say that, in the example, my idea of a sheep really represents not just sheep but also sheepdogs. Perhaps, that is, it represents the disjunction "either a sheep or a sheepdog in certain circumstances". If that idea can sometimes be the mental accompaniment of a sheepdog instead of a sheep in my experience then its credentials as the idea in my mind that represents sheep alone is evidently compromised. For the only thing that makes it the idea that represents sheep is that, in the past, sheep alone have prompted that idea by causing characteristic changes in my sense organs and brain.

3. For more about the strengths and weaknesses of such a theory see R. Cummins, *Meaning and Mental Representation* (Cambridge, MA: MIT Press, 1989).

One response to these problems of misrepresentation is to try to build into the recipe for representation the rule that the subject must be functioning properly and that the conditions must be ideal before an idea that arises in the course of sense perception can be rightly taken to represent the external object that interacts with the perceiver's body. Roughly, the idea is that if my eyes are working as they ought and if the lighting is good I will not form what ought to count as an idea of a sheep unless what I am looking at really is a sheep. But this attempted solution immediately runs into the difficulty of specifying what constitutes proper functioning and ideal conditions. We cannot for example say that "the lighting is good" means "the lighting is adequate to tell a sheep from a sheep dog" without falling into circularity.

However, there is no suggestion that Spinoza was aware of any of these difficulties. And, in any event, other problems fatal for his notion of mental representation remain to be examined. The two crucial difficulties are well pinpointed by Wilson. She calls Spinoza's mental representation "representation" and asks first "whether 'representation' will do as an account of the sort of representation classically attributed to human minds":

> It seems obvious to me that it will not. According to Spinoza's account, my mind "represents" *every* object or physical state that causally affects my own body. So, five minutes ago my mind was "representing" a number of air molecules, the movement of Earth in space, cosmic radiation, etc. But (I would claim) none of these things were objects of my thought in the ordinary sense – even if some degree of non-conscious representation is allowed in the latter category.[4]

Worse still, as Wilson goes on to say, it is not just human minds that "represent" things on Spinoza's view. Since every physical thing's ideal side is the *mind* of that thing for Spinoza and since all bodies are in constant causal interaction with each other, bodies of all kinds must be "representing" each other incessantly. But that means that "representing" is not a sufficient condition of what we might call "real or proper representing" of the sort that conscious, thinking human minds – but not stones – constantly do. Spinoza's account of representation leaves out arguably the most important part of the phenomenon. This is the fact that representations have significance *for the mind that experiences them.*

---

4. Wilson, "Objects, Ideas, and 'Minds'", 111.

This conviction that stones do not have minds or entertain representations is not intended to challenge the view that there are physical objects such as maps or graphs that are or embody representations. But we would never think of them as having a psychology or any possibility of experiencing the representation involved. Think, for example, of a representational painting that represents its subject to a viewer. Then compare the viewer who has a representation of the painting's subject in his mind after seeing the painting. The painting contains a representation of its subject but the representation it has represents nothing *to the painting itself.* The painting has meaning or aboutness but what it represents means nothing to it.

As we saw above in Chapter 8, however, Spinoza does not (and perhaps cannot) adequately justify regarding the minds of human beings as crucially different from the non-conscious, but in his view "minded", bodies of which the rest of physical reality consists. Because this is so, Spinoza has no way of distinguishing what we might regard as "representations in the fullest sense" from the sorts of non-psychological "representations" that even a stone might have. Paintings and sculptures can be representational because we can take them to stand for or be about their subjects. Words and paintings can represent what they picture or stand for because we interpret them as such. Spinoza fails to give any account of how human minds can and do interpret representations *as* representations. His account is therefore missing what should be its most important element.

CHAPTER 11

Is the mind a substance for Leibniz?

The brief answer to the title question is that each human mind is indeed an immaterial substance for Leibniz. This might seem to threaten his theory of mind with the same stubborn problem of accounting for mind–body interaction that many have regarded as fatal for Descartes. However, Leibniz's theory of mind is very far from being just a revamped Cartesian dualism. In fact, it is not a dualism at all but rather an idealism or immaterial monism.

Or is it? Leibniz certainly also insists that material bodies such as the human body and those of other animals and physical things are not illusions. So what is a human mind for Leibniz, what is a human body and what is the relationship between the two? And what is the difference between Leibniz's metaphysical position and Descartes's dualism? In order to begin answering these questions it is necessary first to summarize what Leibniz says about what he calls "monads".

Monads

The term "monad" (from "*monas*", Greek for "unit") is used in the *Monadology* for what Leibniz, in the earlier *Discourse on Metaphysics* and other writings, had called "a simple substance". Remember that Descartes worked with an essentially Aristotelian notion of substance (or what is most fundamental in created reality) according to which a substance is ontologically independent: it depends for its existence on no other created thing. Descartes also retained the Aristotelian view that substances have *logical* priority in the sense that items in other categories – qualities, quantities and so forth – are predicable of ("said of") them whereas substances are always subjects. They are never predicated of (or "said of") anything else. Spinoza, as we have seen, took the first of these two Aristotelian–Cartesian criteria of substancehood particularly

102

seriously and it led him to conclude that there was, and could be, only one substance; namely, the whole of nature or reality.

Leibniz, likewise, is convinced that the things he calls substances depend for their existence on God alone and are completely independent of each other and everything else. But he is also very much influenced by the other strand from the Aristotelian substance tradition; for Leibniz the crucial feature of anything appropriately called a substance or monad is that it is a genuine individual. A true individual for Leibniz (as for Aristotle) has genuine unity and is a true subject of predication. A Leibnizian monad is not a collection of parts or a mere aggregate or heap. It is in no way composite and it is capable of independent existence such that it is able to retain its identity as the very individual it is through virtually all sorts of change so long as it retains its essential features. Indeed, for Leibniz there are no natural means by which individual simple substances can be destroyed (M4–6).[1] They cannot go out of existence unless they are annihilated by God.

What makes for this hardiness on the part of a monad is that it *is* a simple substance, that is, it has no parts and is utterly unitary. Since it has no parts to come apart it is indivisible, which accounts for its indestructibility. Moreover, because it is indivisible it cannot be an extended thing for every extended thing is in principle divisible into extended parts however small. But if monads are wholly unextended (i.e. not material) there is nothing else for them to be other than immaterial things or spirits.

Leibniz writes that "there must be simple substances, since there are composites; for the composite is nothing but an accumulation or *aggregate* of simples" (M2). It is possible to wonder whether this is quite right. Does the fact that some things are not simple or are only relatively simple guarantee that something somewhere is absolutely simple? However, Leibniz is convinced that there are genuine, truly simple individuals in the world because he has first-hand experience of just such an individual unity; namely, himself.

The unity of a simple substance or monad is not a contingent thing, like the union of a number of bricks joined to build a wall or two jewels set into a single ring or, again, eleven men playing together in a single football team. A monad is a unity of its very essence. Although Leibniz describes monads as

---

1. References of the form, for example, M4–6, refer to §§4–6 in the *Monadology* [M], in G. W. Leibniz, *Philosophical Texts*, R. S. Woolhouse & Richard Francks (eds & trans.) (Oxford: Oxford University Press, 1998) [WF]. Wherever possible I will give a reference to the *Monadology* by section number for a place where Leibniz uses a technical term discussed. I have not attempted the Herculean task of listing all the places in his writings where he introduces or uses these terms and notions.

"the true atoms of nature" (M3) he does not in any way think of them as tiny material building blocks of reality since, for a start, they are not material but rather are immaterial entities or souls. Indeed, he protests if he thinks anyone mistakes his monads for the atoms of the ancient atomists Democritus and Leucippus or his contemporary Gassendi. Those thinkers' atoms are material and, worse still, all alike. In contrast, Leibniz's monads are all individuals so they are substantially different each from the next. ("It is necessary that each monad be different from every other" [M9].) If there are two monads that are really two in number they *must* differ *in more than just number*. There must be some features possessed by one that are not shared by the other.

Monads have no material qualities because they are not material. But for the same reason they have the sorts of natures and qualities one would expect in immaterial or psychological entities. In particular, even though some monads are inferior in some respects to others, they *all* have perceptions. More than that, in a sense each monad *is* its perceptions. For some monads there are only unconscious perceptions. For others there are also conscious ones. The monads that will dominate an assemblage or colony of monads to compose a human being have not only the conscious perceptions that living animals possess but also reason, which is bestowed by God on each spirit or human soul at conception. In addition to perceptions, all monads also have appetites or anticipations of the events in which they will be involved: some have conscious appetites; others only unconscious ones.

By now it will be apparent that Leibniz's view of how colonies of monads compose the ordinary beings of everyday life, including human beings, is not the way any materialist or Cartesian dualist might believe to be the case. For one thing, we would ordinarily think of sense perception as being a paradigm of causal interaction between perceiving subject and object perceived. But Leibniz says very early in the *Monadology* that "Monads have no windows" (M7), that there is *no possibility of any causal interaction between monads* and that nothing can alter a monad's internal constitution from without. So monads – including human minds – have numerous, indeed unceasing, perceptions while remaining wholly unaffected by anything around them. Even where a number of monads form a composite being their cohesion as a complex entity is not a product of mutual causal interaction or influence but rather of a strong "agreement" (WF 150)[2] in their mutual perceptions.

Moreover, monads, despite their simplicity, are constantly changing. Their properties and all the qualities we might normally think of them as possessing

---

2. This is in Leibniz's "A New System of the Nature and Communication of Substances, and of the Union of the Soul and Body" (1695), para. 14 (in WF).

(including relative qualities such as being to the left of *X* or north of *Y*) come and go in their history, not because they are ever affected from without but from a dynamic principle within themselves. Leibniz describes monads as "*incorporeal automata*" (M18). Each (immaterial) monad is constantly altering and evolving spontaneously (automatically) out of its own vital force (*élan vital*).

This explains how, without causal interaction between monads, they can nonetheless have perceptions of one another. Each monad is constantly changing in its perceptions according to a programme or "detail of changes" (M12), a complete concept which includes all the alterations or developments that will occur throughout its existence, that is, all its evolving perceptions of everything else in the universe. And all monads' programmes or concepts are harmonized with each other by God at creation so that changes in each match all the changes in all the other monads. This is the famous Leibnizian doctrine of "pre-established harmony" (M78). God, at creation, chooses the reality made up of assemblages or colonies of monads that is the best reality which could be chosen. And that includes the whole of history – generations upon generations of particular human beings and other animals, geological and geographical features, even species of plants and animals and so on and so forth, which will eventually issue in our present selves and environment and, subsequently, whatever world and population ensues thereafter – right to the end of time.

Bodies

The physical world of everyday life and objects mentioned a moment ago consists, for Leibniz, of aggregates of monads composing everything from people, plants and non-human animals to clocks, houses, mountains, oceans and stars. These aggregates are more or less complex in their internal relations and are just as much a part of the real, public world as the monads that compose them. Or it might be better to say, since monads are not in any sense building blocks, that monads form the foundation or basis from which these aggregates result.

Among these aggregates or colonies of monads there are some that we would regard as lifeless material bodies: artefacts such as clocks and carriages as well as natural things such as mountains and rivers. Leibniz is not tempted to view these as more than aggregates at the metaphysical level. But he nonetheless describes them as "well-founded phenomena". This term signifies that they are, in a way, appearances (phenomena) but they have a sort of unity that results from the strength of their mutual perceptions. They are thus *real* (well-founded) and can make up a large part of the public world. At the level of physics this world is rightly seen as obeying the laws of matter in motion. However, Leibniz would not say that such corporeal bodies were substances since their unity is more a matter of how they are perceived than of the genuine unity that characterizes an indivisible simple substance or monad.

At the level of biology also, there are entities, aggregates, which are more than mere phenomena: plants, non-human animals and human beings have "organic bodies" (M64, M74, M78) that are more than just aggregates or heaps of monads. They are assemblages of monads that have a unity bestowed on them by their dominant monad, soul or (in the case of human beings) spirit. Although Leibniz was at times tempted to call these organic bodies "corporeal substances", or at least was undecided whether or not he should so call them (DM34,[3] in AG 65 n. 105), his mature writings stop short of such a commitment. The organic bodies of plants and animals are not corporeal substances but because they are structured or organized by their dominant monad they are well-founded phenomena.

So we come at last to the answer to one of the initial questions with which this chapter began. Is the human body a substance? It should by now be clear that Leibniz does not think so. He recognizes that a human animal body has a kind of permanence and unity but, at the end of the day, what matters is that that body is divisible and thus ultimately lacks the unity and simplicity that a substance "in true metaphysical rigour" (DM34) requires.

The human mind

For Leibniz a human mind (or spirit) is a special monad or simple substance. It is part of a colony or aggregation of monads and it dominates or rules those other monads which together form its organic body. It can do this because it is special even among conscious souls (which all animals have) in having reason and the ability to render what happens in the collection self-conscious. What happens in the collection is a spontaneous playing out of all the changes laid down since creation for each of the monads to undergo.

There is also complete mutual mirroring by all the members of the colony of all their perceptions. This is not, of course, *literal* mutual mirroring, which would involve literal causal interaction between the monads. Rather, there

---

3. This is in the first sentence of an early draft of Leibniz's *Discourse on Metaphysics* in his *Philosophical Essays*, Roger Ariew & Daniel Garber (eds & trans) (Indianapolis, IN: Hackett, 1989) [AG].

is the well-founded appearance of mutual interaction, which is the result of each monad's being endowed with massively comprehensive perceptions of all the others so that, as each monad alters, the others all spontaneously have a novel perception of the alteration in question.

In fact, every monad is a point of view on the whole of creation since it has or contains perceptions of absolutely every other monad. These perceptions "stretch out", so to speak, in every direction. They include perceptions of every monad in the present and every monad at every past and future stage of history. As might be expected, this profusion of monadic perceptions means that not all perceptions are equally strong or clear. So I have, as it seems to me, sharp clear perceptions of what is at present near at hand while my perceptions of past and future and the remoter parts of the universe are fainter to the point of being indecipherable. Indeed, the vast majority are simply below the threshold of consciousness.

Or rather, to put it in a more Leibnizian way, I will come to think of those things that I perceive confusedly or without clarity as spatially (and temporally) remote while I will consider those things I perceive very clearly as parts of my organic body and its immediate surroundings. Leibniz believes that spatial and temporal remoteness are themselves appearances: functions of the degree of confusedness or unclarity of my perceptions.

What relationship does Leibniz envisage between the completely individual and unitary human mind (spirit or monad) and its organic body? The mind "rules" the body; it is the "dominant monad" (M70). Leibniz thinks that it might even be right to revive the Aristotelian–Scholastic notion of a "substantial form" to describe the ruling monad in an organic body. This would imply that the dominant monad provides the organizing principle for the whole being of which it is the leading part. This seems a reasonable reading in light of Leibniz's conviction that any one of these organic bodies or "unities by aggregation" is constantly in flux (M71) so that the relation between the whole (derived) unity and the monads of which it is constituted at any moment is *not* identity. Leibniz would say that we still have the same human (or the same maple tree) after a lapse of time if there is still the same dominant monad and the same organization among the constituent monads, even though, inevitably, some matter will have been lost and replaced in the interval. What accounts for this identity over time is the dominant monad's persistence as a principle of unity and identity throughout.

In the case of human beings, however, the dominant monad is not just a sort of blueprint or structuring principle (as it would be for any member of a non-human animal or plant species). Nor is it just a conscious subject as the dominant monad in every living animal body is its conscious subject. In human beings the dominant monad is also a self-conscious spirit endowed with reason and capable of moral perception and judgement. So, as Leibniz tells us in a work contemporary with the *Monadology*, although "there is a connectedness between the perceptions of animals which has some resemblance to reason", non-human animals lack the "necessary or eternal truths like those of logic, numbers, and geometry" upon which true reasoning depends. The beings that:

> recognize such necessary truths are what are rightly called *rational animals*, and their souls are called *minds*. These souls are capable of acts of reflection, and of considering what we call myself, substance, soul, or mind: in a word, things and truths which are immaterial. And this is what renders us capable of science or demonstrable knowledge. (PNG5; WF 261)[4]

Rational animals have their reason bestowed on them by God at conception (M82). But Leibniz does not make clear what happens to that reason when the organic body dies. Monads are indestructible so the death of the human organic body does not destroy the individual mind or spirit. But without the right kind of organization of the aggregate of monads on which the conscious mind depends for its lifetime of self-consciousness and reason, it would seem that a human mind lapses back into unconsciousness. It continues to rule its body but that body diminishes, probably undergoing a metamorphosis into what Leibniz calls "another kind of animal" (M74).

It should be pointed out, however, that Leibniz does not believe in transmigration of souls (*metempsychosis* [M72]). For him, souls do not leave the body at death and indeed it would be impossible for a soul to leave its organic body at any time since its body just *is* the aggregation of monads with which it coheres or on which it is founded at any given moment. If this aggregate were to change so that some monads were lost and others acquired, the body would remain numerically one and the same throughout. Even if the mind in question lost all its subordinate monads and acquired a whole new set this would not be transmigration but assimilation of a new collection of monads into the "old" body of that individual mind.

An organic body, absent its dominant monad or spirit, is not a substance. So Leibniz is distinct from Descartes in being a monist not a dualist. For him the

---

4. G. W. Leibniz, "Principles of Nature and Grace, Based on Reason" [PNG], in *Philosophical Texts* (WF). References to PNG refer to section numbers, so, for example, PNG5 is §5. Page numbers in WF are also given.

only substances are immaterial. At the same time Leibniz recognizes the fact that our experience is unquestionably replete with re-identifiable persistent organic bodies – men, animals and plants – that seem "substantial" and independent of our perceptions of them. He accords a kind of unity and derived substancehood to these things but does not see their unity as anything like a Cartesian union of soul and body. Instead he regards the unity of such derived beings as depending wholly on the genuine unity of their dominant monad.

If we ask how the apparent *matter* of organic bodies, including those of human beings, is to be construed it may at first seem that Leibniz's position is a kind of phenomenalism. Material objects are well-founded phenomena and well-founded phenomena are not illusions but they are dependent on the mutual perceptions of an infinity of monads for their existence. So it might appear that, for Leibniz, physical objects are collections of coincident, harmonized monadic perceptions: a kind of logical construction out of actual and possible experiences. And it is only fair to say that some of Leibniz's writings support such a phenomenalist interpretation of his views.

But interpreting his position here, as elsewhere, is a difficult business. It is not made easier by the fact that Leibniz, although he wrote voluminously, did not publish very much of his thought during his lifetime. The *Theodicy* is the only one of his treatises that he saw through the press. His extensive production of essays and letters responded to the specific concerns of particular recipients, which inevitably led to fragmentary treatment and to a type of distortion or bias. And, over a long life, his thought evolved in several areas in a way that has caused unending controversy among his readers about the exact nature of his final positions, if any.

All of this makes it difficult to propose with confidence any interpretation on such a central question as what he concluded about the fundamental, metaphysical nature of material objects. However, if Leibniz is to be consistent in treating the world studied by physics as robust, independent and public he must regard physical objects as more than mere subjective experiences, however well harmonized. We have seen that he says that unities by aggregation "result from" aggregates of monads rather than being mere collections of them. If a single monad has no size or shape then it makes no sense to think that these properties would emerge simply from piling many monads together. But how exactly the monads could generate or produce material bodies is still difficult to pin down. What is certain is that Leibniz is convinced that reality – albeit not at the most fundamental level where all is immaterial – is truly correctly described by the laws of physics. Physical reality for Leibniz is as real as the genuine unities, the simple substances that underpin it.

CHAPTER 12

Self-knowledge and the monads

As we have seen, for Leibniz, the only substances are the simple monads, which are the basis of all reality. Wholly independent of all external influences, each monad is imbued with its own internal active principle or force, which means that all its actions spring from its own depths (LA 170; G 136).[1] And all substances of every grade have perceptions. Bare monads have nothing but unconscious perceptions (without memory) but non-human animals and human beings are said to have sensation as well as perception. Or rather, more precisely, Leibniz says that, because they possess sense organs that focus and concentrate their perceptions, many animals' perceptions are heightened and thus become distinct enough to be sensations. That is to say, many of the perceptions belonging to higher animal and human souls are available to what Leibniz calls "apperception" or "reflection" and are thus in some way conscious.

At the top of his hierarchy (at least among earthly beings), Leibniz's human minds differ from the dominant monads or souls of other animals and thus also from the dominant monads of plants and the bare monads constituting mere material objects. For in addition to bare perceptions and even apperceived heightened ones, human minds have mental states that are not just conscious but self-conscious.

To find what sorts of self-knowledge Leibniz thinks possible for human minds we need to try to discover what he means by "apperception" and "reflection" and how, if at all, he thinks apperception differs from perception, consciousness and memory. We also need to try to determine what relationship Leibniz sees between consciousness and self-consciousness. These tasks are perhaps not as straightforward as might be hoped: certainly commentators

---

1. G. W. Leibniz, *The Leibniz–Arnauld Correspondence*, H. T. Mason (ed. & trans.) (Manchester: Manchester University Press, 1967) [LA]. The pagination in the original German edition, *Die philosophischen Schriften*, 7 vols, vol. II, C. I. Gerhardt (ed.) (Berlin, 1875–90) [G] is also given in each reference to LA.

have disagreed strongly even about something as apparently basic as whether Leibniz does or does not think apperception and consciousness are the same thing. The rest of this chapter will concentrate on those parts of this disputed topic that concern self-knowledge, while Chapter 13 will look at Leibniz's views on the nature of consciousness.

Apperception: self-knowledge of our mental contents

"Apperception", a noun designating a mental faculty or activity, is a term invented by Leibniz and is related to the French reflexive verb "*s'apercevoir*" (present-day spelling), which means "to perceive", but it is a particular sort of perception Leibniz has in mind. The term "apperception" was to be taken up and used extensively by Immanuel Kant as his term for a special kind of self-knowledge or unity of consciousness. In Leibniz's writings it is introduced in contrast to what he calls "perception". Leibniz writes: "The transitory state which incorporates and represents a multiplicity within a unity or within a simple substance is nothing but what we call *perception* – which must be carefully distinguished from apperception or consciousness" (M14). The difference is that apperception gives the subject a second-order awareness or consciousness of what is going on in his own mind at the moment:

> Thus it is good to distinguish between *perception*, which is the internal state of the monad representing external things, and *apperception*, which is *consciousness*, or the reflective knowledge of this internal state, something not given to all souls, nor at all times to a given soul. (PNG4, AG 208)

So apperception is (at least) a kind of inner perception or reflexive awareness that gives knowledge of what is going on in the subject's mind. At any given time, for Leibniz, I *could* have self-knowledge of some of the contents of my mind. However, it is important to note that I am not necessarily aware of all my perceptions, nor am I aware of them at every moment. It takes consciousness and, at times, concerted attention to have knowledge that I am experiencing a particular perception or mental state. Apperception would seem to mean, to a first approximation, both "simple conscious awareness of my occurrent mental states" and "concentrated attention devoted to discovering what is going on in my mind".

In contrast, perception can be either unconscious – as when I am hearing, say, the noise of a machine to which I have become habituated so that I am not paying any attention to the sound – or conscious – as when I suddenly become aware of the machine noise and that it has been going on for a time unnoticed by me. What is not entirely clear is whether or not Leibniz sees any sort of difference between simple unprompted conscious perception of something external to the subject (awareness of the noise) and the simplest apperception or awareness by the subject of his present consciousness of something external (awareness of his awareness of the noise). I shall return to this distinction below.

If we recall the three usual features of self-knowledge of mental contents mentioned in the Introduction, we can ask whether Leibnizian apperception produces self-knowledge with all three features: are the deliverances of apperception authoritative, salient and immediate for their subject? I shall look in detail at all three when discussing Leibniz's views on consciousness in Chapter 13 but here is a preliminary answer. For Leibniz there can be perceptions in my mind of which I am unaware and since I do not know I have them they are not salient for me. But I *am* completely authoritative about the contents of my mind of which I *am* aware, that is, that I apperceive and which therefore are salient for me. Although it is possible for me to have perceptions, thoughts, feelings or beliefs that lie below the level of my consciousness, there is no possibility for Leibniz that I might mistakenly apperceive or think that I apperceive a certain perception as occurring in my mind when it is not really there.

This is a kind of knowledge of self that is *immediate* and does not require (nor could it be given) any further evidence or justification. So we can see that Leibniz certainly believes that apperception affords the subject *authority*. Whatever I apperceive as occurring in my mind certainly is occurring there. On the other hand this should not be counted as baseless knowledge. Leibniz would not accept that there is any mystery about the basis for such self-knowledge since it is produced by the wholly reliable faculty of apperception.

In some respects Leibniz's view of self-knowledge of my mental contents is more like the view often attributed to Descartes than the position Descartes actually held. It was argued in Chapter 2 that Descartes does not take himself to be employing any sort of *quasi-sensory faculty of inner inspection* that can be an infallible source of knowledge of my nature and essence as a mind or spirit. At the most, Descartes's supposed doctrine of the transparency of the mental only means that Descartes believes two related things: first, that I cannot be wholly unaware of my current mental operations and states; and secondly, that all my thoughts, ideas or memories – since they count as minimally conscious if they are in my mind or rational soul at all – are available to me should I decide to consider and concentrate on them. Although Descartes certainly holds that I cannot be wrong if I think that I am currently thinking x or y, he nowhere says that there is an inner private realm of my ideas and thoughts that are all equally and constantly under some sort of simultaneous introspective view.

In contrast, Leibniz does seem to regard my knowledge of my current conscious perceptions as provided by a kind of inner perception. I have only to reflect or apperceive – turn my perception back on itself – to gain a perception of my current conscious perceptions. After all, as we saw in Chapter 11, I am created with all my perceptions for all time already actually in my complete concept waiting to emerge in accordance with the pre-established harmony: so reflection or apperception is not wholly unlike inspection of an independently existing inner realm.

Such an examination may not at first blush resemble Leibniz's own notion of *sense* perception, which consists in the use of physical sense organs to focus and heighten external perceptions into conscious ones. But there are hints in some of Leibniz's writings that he does regard apperception as a sort of *internal* focusing and heightening mechanism. Nonetheless, despite all this, it would perhaps be incautious to describe Leibniz's apperception as "inner sense". It is much closer to being a kind of triggering of conscious memory of immediately previous perceptions (see Chapter 13). And, of course, Leibniz, unlike Descartes, insists that any monad – even a human mind or spirit – has many perceptions that are unconscious and destined always to remain so.

Nor should apperception be taken to be a product of reason. The relationship between apperception, reflection and reason, as Leibniz understands them, is not easy to capture but at least some of the time he appears to hold that it is the application of the faculty of apperception to the self as object that *endows* human minds with reason and renders human beings capable of science and also of a moral existence and genuine immortality. If reason emerges *from* apperception it is difficult to see how it can be either equivalent to apperception or the source of apperception.

Self-knowledge of the nature and existence of the self

Leibniz, more than any of the other philosophers discussed in this book, puts self-knowledge at the centre of his understanding of the human mind. At times, as just said, he seems to say that he regards self-knowledge or apperception as the *source* of reason in the individual human being and therefore the source of science as a collaborative human accomplishment. Again, he traces the nature of human spirits as "morally responsible individuals who can attain immortality" back to their self-knowledge acquired through reflection or apperception.

But how does Leibniz think apperception can accomplish this task: how, if it does, does apperception endow the human mind with reason, science, morality and immortality? Leibniz explains the difference between human souls (minds), which are immortal, and other substances, which do not have the possibility of our kind of immortality despite being equally imperishable. The principal difference is that the non-human souls:

> do not know what they are nor what they do, and consequently, since they do not reflect on themselves, they cannot discover necessary and universal truths. It is also because they lack reflection about themselves that they have no moral qualities ... But the intelligent soul, knowing what it is – having the ability to utter the word "I", a word so full of meaning – does not merely remain and subsist metaphysically, which it does to a greater degree than the others, but also remains the same morally and constitutes the same person. For it is memory or the knowledge of this self that renders it capable of punishment or reward.   (DM34; AG 65–6)

There is in the (slightly abbreviated) passage just quoted a single line of thought, which is highly compressed and consists of four key elements:

(i)   Leibniz begins by saying that animals do not have knowledge of (are unaware of) their own nature or actions which is to say they lack reflective knowledge of themselves.

(ii)   Because they lack reflective knowledge of themselves, they cannot discover necessary and eternal truths. For the same reason non-human animals lack moral qualities.

(iii) The self-knowledge (of their nature and actions) that human minds possess, which enables them to be intelligent or rational, is the ability to use the first-person pronoun meaningfully and to see themselves as agents of their own actions and subjects of their own experiences.

(iv)   For human minds, the ability just mentioned is what gives us moral standing or personal identity. Once aware of ourselves as subjects we can remember our actions and perceptions (mental states) as our own. "Memory" in this context is "the knowledge of this self". Thus we become appropriate objects of moral praise and blame.

This line of thought raises many questions whose consideration is vital to an understanding of Leibniz's theory of mind: *how* is self-knowledge supposed to produce reason in human minds; is the self-knowledge that renders a mind a moral subject capable of achieving immortality the same sort of self-knowledge as that which bestows reason, and if not, how are the two related; and what exactly is it that is being denied to non-human animals? Is it apperception or consciousness in the sense required to turn bare perception into sensation? If so, is Leibniz not flagrantly inconsistent, now attributing sensation to higher animals (PNG4, first para.; AG 208) and on the other hand denying animals the capacity for reflection (PNG5, last para.; AG 209) or apperception, which is precisely the capacity required if bare perceptions are to become conscious sensations?

How is self-knowledge to produce reason?
At first it may seem that Leibniz is saying that reflection on one's nature as a mind, self, I and subject of experiences somehow renders the reflecting mind an intelligent one. If he *is* saying that such exercise of self-awareness confers the ability to reason this seems frankly mystifying. And if we look at other remarks Leibniz makes about the source of reason in human minds in hopes of clarifying the matter it can seem that the sense of mystification only deepens. For example, in both "Principles of Nature and Grace" (AG 209) and the *Monadology* (M82) he says that some fortunate monads (the Elect) are "raised to the level of reason, and to the prerogative of minds", when they "achieve through an act of conception the nature of a human being". So we are left wondering: which does Leibniz think it is, reflection or physical conception as a human being, that confers reason on human minds? Or does he think that conception confers the capacity for reflection that in turn somehow makes the subject rational?

The mist may begin to clear somewhat if we look at what Leibniz says about the nature of reason and its possession. True reasoning, he writes: "depends on necessary or eternal truths, such as those of logic, numbers, and geometry, which bring about an indubitable connection of ideas and infallible consequences ... those who know these necessary truths are ... properly called *rational animals*" (PNG5; AG 209). Whatever gives us access to such necessary or eternal truths, then, gives us what we need in order to be true reasoners rather than beings, like the brutes, that cope with life's difficulties using nothing but empirical methods, that is, the accumulated memory of similar experiences or instances (i.e. induction alone).

But knowledge of necessary truths cannot be acquired inductively or in the course of experience. Necessary truths are precisely those that capture what

115

must be the case while experience shows us only what is or has been the case. And if they are not acquired in experience, necessary truths must be innate. We are capable of reason from conception onward, on Leibniz's view, because human beings have by nature innate knowledge of necessary truths.

Leibniz thinks that we need apperception to gain conscious access to, or apprehension of, these innately known truths, which are, as he says, the "inner core and mortar", the "muscles and tendons" (NE 84),[2] of our minds, enabling our activities as rational beings, as soon as we attain to any sort of reason-governed behaviour. That would explain why he says that non-human animals, "since they do not reflect on themselves … cannot discover necessary and universal truths". At conception we (unlike the brutes) are endowed with the innate knowledge of necessary truths, which is crucial for rationality, and also with the capacity for reflective *self*-knowledge, which enables us, in due course, to access that crucial innate knowledge explicitly.

Is the self-knowledge that renders a mind a moral subject the same as that which bestows reason?

The sort of self-knowledge just discussed, which I have suggested Leibniz thinks enables us to be genuine reasoners, may look very different from the self-knowledge that renders a mind a moral and thus immortal subject. Looking again at the long passage from Section 34 of *Discourse on Metaphysics* quoted above, we can read Leibniz as saying that we are given, in reflective self-consciousness or apperception, not only access to our innate knowledge but also self-awareness of our own subjectivity. In reflective self-consciousness the subject knows himself to be a substance and thus a genuine unity; the subject recognizes his own experiences and actions as his own and can call himself "I". This Leibnizian reflection, which gives us knowledge of ourselves as moral beings with personal identity and immortality, takes the self as its object rather than any set of (innate) propositions or truths. Does this make reflection after all not one faculty but two? Should we see Leibniz as saying (should Leibniz be saying) that the two objects accessed through reflective self-consciousness are so different that there must really be two sorts of reflection, one for each sort of object?

In a similar passage in the *Monadology*, Leibniz writes:

---

2. G. W. Leibniz, *New Essays on Human Understanding*, Peter Remnant & Jonathan Bennett (eds & trans) (Cambridge: Cambridge University Press, 1997) [NE]. The page references are the marginal page numbers taken from the Akademie-Verlag of Berlin edition of Leibniz's works (the Academy Edition), which are the only page numbers Remnant and Bennett use in the text.

And it is by the knowledge of necessary truths, and by the abstractions they involve, that we are raised to *acts of reflection*, which make us aware of what we call *myself* [another translation has "that which is called 'I'"; AG 217], and make us think of this or that thing as in ourselves. And in this way, by thinking of ourselves, we think of being, of substance, of simples and composites, of the immaterial – and, by realizing that what is limited in us is limitless in him, of God himself. (M30)

Here we are told that acquisition of the knowledge of necessary truths precedes and somehow enables the acts of reflection by which we each become aware of our own subjectivity and nature as a self (or "I"). So perhaps Leibniz does think there are two sorts of apperception or reflection: that which is directed on our innately known necessary truths and gives us conscious apprehension of them and that which is directed on the self and gives us knowledge of our personal identity as lasting morally responsible and culpable individuals.

On balance, though, it seems to me gratuitous to interpret Leibniz in this way as subscribing to two sorts of faculty of reflection, or as giving "reflection" and by extension "apperception" two senses, in these passages. Rather, we should try to understand how (on his view) the single faculty of apperception or reflection, once it has given the subject access to his innate knowledge of necessary and universal truths, is then enabled to give that same subject knowledge of himself as a moral subject. Leibniz sees the conscious apprehension of the principles of reason as necessary for reasoning about and gaining an understanding of subjectivity and self-hood. The self cannot be known by sense, still less by imagination: there are things that are "only *intelligible*, the *object of the understanding alone*; and such is the object of my thought when I think of myself" (AG 188).[3]

Knowledge of the self as a persistent subject requires memory and consciousness of one's perceptions as forming a sequence. But even non-human animals, which do not have reflective consciousness, have these to some extent. They have basic memory and "interconnection among [their] perceptions … which bears some resemblance to reason" (PNG5; AG 208), and this is sufficient to enable them to think empirically and adjust their present actions in the light of past experience.

---

3. This is from Leibniz's "Letter to Queen Sophie Charlotte of Prussia, On What is Independent of Sense and Matter" (1702).

Human spirits' true reasoning takes them much further, enabling them to consider "what is called 'I', substance, soul, mind – in brief, immaterial things and immaterial truths" (*ibid.*). It enables them to anticipate happenings (such as the day dawning tomorrow) not just from the accumulation of past happenings but on rational grounds (from the reasonings of astronomers). And it enables them to make reasoned and free choices and thus to choose and act morally. Bound up with this is the knowledge – conferred by knowledge of the "I" and of "immaterial things and immaterial truths" – that human souls or minds are mirrors of God. In other words, reflection and reflective acts are what enable human minds to reach a philosophical understanding of their metaphysical nature as free, unitary (and thus paradigm) substances and of their moral obligation always to act as much like "little deities" as they possibly can.

What exactly is it that is being denied to non-human animals?
As we saw above, some readers have found, in Leibniz's comparisons between human and non-human animal mental capacities, what seems to them a glaring inconsistency.[4] On the one hand he seems to say that non-human animals have sensations: in other words, conscious or apperceived perceptions. This is what distinguishes animals from bare monads. On the other hand does he not say that it is the fact that human beings alone possess reflection that distinguishes human minds or spirits from animal souls? But since Leibniz appears to treat apperception, consciousness and reflection as equivalent he would seem to be simultaneously asserting and denying that animals have sensations (conscious perceptions).

Is Leibniz merely falling into a naive self-contradiction and inconsistency on this question? It is certainly true that Leibniz can often be found disagreeing with what he took to be the Cartesian view that non-human animals are mere mechanical automata without feelings or consciousness of any kind (NE Preface, 66–7). It would be wholly insufficient for him – wishing to mark his strong dissent from this view – if he attributed nothing more than unconscious perceptions to non-human animals. It must be right to interpret Leibniz as committed to the possibility (and frequent actuality), in at least the higher animals, of conscious sensations and feelings such as pleasure and pain *of which their subjects are aware.*

---

4. Robert McRae, *Leibniz: Perception, Apperception, and Thought* (Toronto: University of Toronto Press, 1976), 30ff. See also Mark Kulstad, *Leibniz on Apperception, Consciousness and Reflection* (Munich: Philosophia, 1991).

Then again, it must also be conceded that Leibniz denies to non-human animals those reflective acts that produce true reason and moral self-awareness in human agents. Recall the passage from *Discourse on Metaphysics*: "since they do not reflect on themselves, they cannot discover necessary and universal truths. It is also because they lack reflection about themselves that they have no moral qualities" (DM34; AG 65). So if we are to rescue Leibniz from the accusation of glaring inconsistency we must concentrate on his use of the terms "apperception", "consciousness" and "reflection". Is it truly the case that he treats these as equivalent notions? And where does self-consciousness come in? Is it perhaps open to him to rebut the charge of inconsistency by claiming that animals lack one of the kinds of consciousness or reflection that human beings possess (perhaps self-consciousness) while still having perceptions and thus sensations that are truly conscious (perhaps in their own, non-human, way)? To examine this suggestion in detail and try to reach a resolution of the question whether Leibniz is guilty of the inconsistency with which he is charged, I shall now turn to an examination of Leibniz's views on consciousness.

CHAPTER 13

Leibniz on consciousness and unconscious perceptions

Because Leibniz believes that there are many perceptions in any human mind that pass unnoticed, he is often credited with introducing the notion of the unconscious into theory of mind. As we have seen, Descartes did not hold precisely the crude theory of mental transparency, according to which there is nothing in any mind that is not fully consciously apprehended by that mind. But Leibniz certainly takes Descartes to hold this, and he is convinced it is quite mistaken.

Leibniz's position is at once more subtle and more credible than Descartes's, even the more plausible interpretation suggested for Descartes in Chapters 2 and 3 above. For Leibniz there can be perceptions that come and go completely unnoticed in a subject's mind because they are too weak or too confused to be conscious. There is also the possibility of even a strong clear perception passing completely unnoticed, either because the subject is habituated to it or because it is drowned out by quantities of other perceptions or the superior distraction of some very insistent or emotionally charged perception.

The name that Leibniz gives to those perceptions which remain below the threshold of conscious experience is "*petites perceptions*". This phrase is usually translated "minute perceptions", meaning that they are low in strength or intensity. Such perceptions occur when the subject is in a dreamless sleep or has fainted. They also happen when the subject is awake and experiencing a large number of minute perceptions all at once. When I stand on the shore and hear the roar of the surf I am not aware of hearing the innumerable tiny sounds made by each individual wave, although, as Leibniz insists, I must in fact have all those minute perceptions or I would not hear the whole ("a hundred thousand nothings cannot make something" [NE Preface, 54]). So although Leibniz agrees with Descartes in saying that the mind is always active, always thinking, he does not think that each mind always notices or even could notice each of its perceptions.

Salience

How then does Leibniz think that unconscious perceptions become salient for their subject when they do? How does a mere perception get elevated to a conscious one? In Section 19 of the *Monadology*, Leibniz says first that "sensation is something more than a simple perception" and then that the only substances rightly called souls are those with sensation so that "we should only call those substances *souls* where perception is more distinct and accompanied by memory". This implies that the "something more" that sensations have which raises them above mere perceptions is distinctness together with being remembered. The point is made explicit in "Principles of Nature and Grace", where, just before drawing the distinction between perception and apperception, Leibniz writes:

> when a monad has organs that are adjusted in such a way that, through them, there is contrast and distinction among the impressions they receive, and consequently contrast and distinction in the perceptions that represent them [in the monad] (as, for example, when the rays of light are concentrated and act with greater force because of the shape of the eye's humors), then this may amount to *sensation*, that is, to a perception accompanied by *memory* – a perception of which there remains an echo long enough to make itself heard on occasion. (PNG4; AG 208)

So perceptions that are sufficiently focused representations (i.e. the ones preceded by, and thus harmonized with, sufficiently focused activity in the subject's sense organs) are perceptions that are sufficiently distinct to leave a perceptible "echo" in memory and thus they are sensations. Sensations (i.e. conscious sensory experiences) are possible for any soul with sufficiently sophisticated sensory apparatus; this means higher animals as well as human beings can and sometimes do have sensations.

Perceptions are not conscious and thus are not sensations or feelings unless the "echo" or trace of the focused perception is found in (or perhaps we should say "by") memory. This is because Leibniz, unlike Descartes, does not think that we can think of more than one thing at once or that we can reflect on a thought while we are still having it. So reflection or apperception must access a distinct perception by recalling it from the immediate past. By being thus remembered or apperceived the perception becomes a conscious thought or feeling. In *New Essays on Human Understanding*, Leibniz speaks of "a present or immediate memory, the memory of what was taking place immediately before – or in other words, the consciousness or reflection which accompanies inner activity" (NE 238). And he offers this definition: "it is *sensation* when one is aware of [apperceives] an external object" (NE 161).

It would seem that Leibniz regards reflection and consciousness (and so apperception) as equivalent to memory as well as to each other. When a perception is apperceived the subject becomes aware of the *object* of that hitherto unnoticed perception (what the perception represents, what it is a perception *of*). To become aware of an object not previously consciously attended to is not necessarily to become explicitly aware that a perception of that object is what one is having. One can perceive *x* without being conscious that one is having a perception of *x*.

Self-contradiction?

As we saw in Chapter 12, § "What exactly is it that is being denied to non-human animals?", it has seemed to a number of commentators that Leibniz contradicts himself drastically when he says that the reflection that enables human minds to reason and affords them self-consciousness is restricted to human minds, and then credits non-human animals with the sort of memory and reflective consciousness or apperception that are required to transform mere perceptions into conscious sensations. But it is possible to acknowledge that Leibniz recognizes overlaps and equivalences among these four notions without accepting that he has contradicted himself in crediting higher animals with sensations.

What needs saying in Leibniz's defence is that his sharp distinction between non-human animals and human beings (minds or spirits) is not blurred at all by crediting non-human animals with apperception, reflection and memory: this is because non-human animals have no innate knowledge of necessary and universal truths and principles to apperceive. As we have seen, these necessary truths must be accessed by their subject to render that subject rational and give him knowledge of himself, his nature as a substance, his subjectivity and personal identity. No amount of exercise of the capacity for reflection or apperception by a non-human animal can make that animal self-conscious in this way since rationality is required to make a self intelligible to itself: rationality requires innate necessary truths and non-human animals have no innate necessary truths to be revealed.

We saw in Chapter 12 that Leibniz sometimes speaks in a way that invites the interpretation that he thinks the reflection that makes a mind intelligible to itself is a special sort of reflection of which non-human animals are incapable. But his position does not require him to make a distinction between two senses of "reflection". Human subjects have a different object for their reflection from that possessed by any non-human animal. They have an intelligent persistent person to take as their object. They can thus use their capacity for reflection in self-reflection or self-consciousness.

The interpretation I am giving here says it is a mistake to think that Leibniz runs consciousness and self-consciousness together: conscious sense perception is a genuine possibility for non-human animals where self-consciousness – consciousness that involves knowledge of the "I" – is not. Although Leibniz does not go into detail or explicitly draw the obvious parallel, he is evidently here embracing one of Descartes's criteria of presence of a rational soul: he is reserving knowledge of words and meaning – particularly that of the first-person pronoun – for human minds.

Immediacy

As we have just seen, Leibniz would say that in sense experience, whether that of human beings or of non-human animals, perceptions become conscious if they are apperceived. And apperception can make a perception conscious if that perception represents an impression on its subject's sense organs that is itself sufficiently distinct. This is because only such distinct perceptions remain in memory where apperception can access them. Thus the immediacy of conscious sensations is actually the immediacy of a perceived memory of something that immediately precedes that memory rather than the immediacy of a currently occurring external perception. But Leibniz would say that the gap between the external object sensed and the conscious sensation of that object is negligible: certainly not one that could give scepticism about sensation-based knowledge a foothold.

This, of course, should not be taken as a conviction on Leibniz's part that I am and cannot but be conscious in sense experience of the way the world actually truly is. When I apperceive my perceptions gained through my senses I get infallible knowledge of how things seem, not certainty about how things are.

Leibnizian consciousness as higher-order thought

Given all that has been said so far about Leibniz's views on consciousness and apperception it is worth considering the suggestion that Leibniz's theory of consciousness is an early version of an inner monitoring or higher-order thought theory. As we saw in Chapter 3, in such a theory consciousness is explained as something that results when the mind monitors or keeps tabs on its own activities. David Rosenthal suggests that "a mental state's being conscious consists in one's having a thought that one is in that very mental state".[1] On such an account, if I am standing on a Welsh shore looking at the expanse of the sea, what makes me conscious of the blue stretching to the horizon is the fact that I am having the thought that I am now in the mental state of seeing an expanse of blue. My inner scanning mechanism (to use some of Armstrong's parlance) detects that I am in that mental state (seeing blue) and that very fact makes my mental state a conscious one and makes me conscious of my object, which is the blue of the sea.

In Chapter 3 I argued that Descartes's view of the contribution to human mental life made by the rational soul was very similar to this higher-order thought view of consciousness. Leibniz's account of consciousness in terms of awareness of *petites perceptions* via immediate memory seems very similar as well. And Leibniz shares with Descartes and Armstrong a willingness to recognize other sorts of "presence in the mind" besides full reflective consciousness. Monads have perceptions of everything in the universe and in history; even if these declaredly unconscious perceptions are faint, and even if they never ascend into full consciousness, they provide the raw material for that consciousness. In some cases they are available in the mind to be remembered and attended to. In other cases, such as the minute perceptions of the sounds of each wave, they will never be fully conscious as individuals but they club together, so to speak, to produce the roar of the surf, which can be consciously experienced. So there is some foreshadowing of what are now called "access consciousness" and "perceptual consciousness" in Leibniz's view.

What about phenomenal consciousness? Does Leibniz have any place in his theory of mind for, or any account of, the distinctive phenomenal feels, qualitative character or what-it's-like of sensory experiences? This does indeed for Leibniz come in at the level of fully conscious episodic thought or sensory perception. We have already looked at the example of the roar of the surf, which Leibniz regards as an experience whose subjective quality (as a roar) is the upshot of numerous, not consciously heard, individually faint sounds: the sounds of all of a huge multitude of waves. In another example, which Leibniz uses in several places, when I experience the distinctive expanse of

---

1. David Rosenthal, "The Independence of Consciousness and Sensory Quality", *Philosophical Issues* 1 (1991), 31.

green I see when visiting a pine forest this is actually the merging of a large number of immediate memories of many blue minute perceptions and many yellow minute perceptions, each of which is too faint, individually, to be seen consciously.

Again, in the Preface to the *New Essays on Human Understanding*, Leibniz says of the ideas of secondary qualities such as colours and warmth that the pre-established harmony ensures that these qualities that we experience in sense perception always correspond to motions in the bodies to which we attribute these qualities. This is not, as might initially be thought, because the bodies actually have motions independently of any mind. Rather, it is because we as perceiving subjects have, innately, the insensible – that is, un-experienced – perceptions of these motions, which emerge into consciousness as the qualities mentioned. For Leibniz, our conscious experiences depend for their qualitative character on the innumerable perceptions with which we are endowed by the pre-established harmony. We get those conscious experiences (as do the higher animals) by exercising our faculty of apperception.

CHAPTER 14

Leibniz and the problem of mental causation

Does Leibniz believe that my mind and my mental states have the power to move my body and to affect the course of physical events? We have seen that Descartes thinks that a human mind can move its body by force of will, just as God – although wholly immaterial – moves matter by the power of his thought alone. Spinoza disagrees, denying the possibility of causal interaction between individual minds and their bodies and, in general, between the mental realm and the physical realm. For him, all physical events have exclusively physical causes while mental happenings have none but mental causes and explanations.

Leibniz's mental causation problem

Leibniz's position on mental causation is more complex still, and perhaps also even more counter-intuitive than these. On the one hand, Leibniz describes the human mind as the dominant monad in the collection of monads making the well-founded phenomenon of a human being a genuine unity. And the dominance of the monad seems to include guiding the behaviour of the whole person or mind–body union. Moreover, Leibniz never questions (indeed he insists) that human beings are morally responsible for their acts. They are free to choose and act well or badly and therefore deserve praise and blame as appropriate.

On the other hand, he holds that monads or immaterial substances cannot be affected from without, influenced or "moved" by *anything*, even another monad. This is because monads are utterly simple and have no parts to be rearranged or removed. So no monad can affect any other. As Leibniz says, "monads have no windows" (M7). Each is a self-contained system whose every movement or alteration emerges from its "complete concept" or internal principle, that is, its "detail of changes" prescribed by the pre-established harmony.

For Leibniz, minds cannot affect bodies; bodies cannot affect minds; bodies cannot even interact with other bodies.

In Chapter 4 we saw that Descartes's problem of mental causation – the problem that critics believe he cannot solve – is that Cartesian mind and body are crucially different in a way that means they cannot interact. It seems that, on Descartes's own principles, only something capable of contact and pushing (i.e. only a material body) can move a body. This is a causation problem that does not afflict Leibniz. He is no dualist. For him the only fundamental substances or individuals are one and all of the same essential nature, which is to say immaterial. Bodies are ultimately phenomena rather than fundamental realities. So Leibniz does not have to confront the Cartesian problem that minds lack irremediably the properties that alone enable their possessors to move a body. But how then, on Leibniz's view, *does* anyone freely move his or her body and have an effect on the world?

The answer, as one might have suspected from what has come before, is that, in strictness, they do not. When I decide to pick up a glass of water and drink I may feel that my thirst and my conscious choice are motivating my body to act in this way. But strictly speaking, for Leibniz, my body moves of its own initiative and solely because it, or rather its constitutive monads, have been "programmed" (as we might now say) at creation to behave in just this way at exactly this point in history. Of course what I think of as "my action" is completely harmonized with the spontaneous occurrence of my thirst and the similarly spontaneous conjunction of glass and water in proximity to my hand. So, he writes, the:

> influence of one monad over another is only *ideal*, and it can have its effect only through the intervention of God; in the sense that in God's ideas one monad requires of God, and with reason, that he take account of it when he organizes the others at the very beginning of things. (M51)

All has been foreseen and laid down by God at creation. Each individual monad spontaneously alters in ways that chime together with the changes in all other monads to bring about the events that I would describe as "my decision motivating my movements".

This Leibnizian view is in large part the result of his conscious rejection of what he takes to be Descartes's position on how the mind moves the body and also his rejection of the occasionalists' quite different proposed solution to the mind–body problem. Leibniz is aware that Descartes maintains that the quantity of force or motion in the world always remains constant through all physical change and activity. So he takes Descartes to say that when I will my hand to move I do not actually impart some new motion to my hand. Such motion would have to come out of nothing (my immaterial mind could not supply it) and that would be impossible. Rather, Leibniz thinks Descartes's position is that I simply will a change of direction for motion that is already in my body, so that my pineal gland leans in a different direction and thus alters the bodily action that my animal spirits make my muscles perform. But Leibniz rejects this proposal since he thinks it would still require my mind to produce some (however small) quantity of motion *ex nihilo* to alter the position of my pineal gland.

Leibniz also rejects the occasionalists' proposed solution to the problem of accounting for voluntary action. Occasionalists are so called because they explain how our decisions and choices result in the movement of our bodies as follows: on each occasion when I will my body to act or move in a certain way it is actually God who steps in and makes my body move as I have willed. But, as Leibniz says in the *Discourse on Metaphysics*, "it is not rational just to fall back on the extraordinary operation of the universal cause in something which is ordinary and particular" (DM33; WF 85). The "universal cause" here is of course God, and the "*extraordinary* operation" refers to the fact that each such episode of moving a body on God's part would be a miracle. Leibniz is rejecting this proposal because he thinks it misrepresents God in several ways: God does not have to wait and see what to do as history unfolds and he would not create a world in which he was incessantly called on for miraculous acts of will. He always acts for good reasons and Leibniz is convinced the occasionalists' picture of this constant divine intervention is vastly less reasonable than the arrangement Leibniz himself suggests as an alternative.

The correspondence with Arnauld

That alternative is, of course, the pre-established harmony. As Leibniz says, "the wiser one is, the fewer separate acts of will one has" (LA 15; G 19). So God, being all-wise, presumably requires only one act of will at creation to create all the monads, which are the foundation of all of reality. In that same creative act God creates the full range of simple and complex creatures, including human beings, and endows them and all their posterity with their individual histories of change and activity. Each human mind is created complete down to the most minute detail and covering a lifetime's decisions and choices, however trivial or important. And the programmes of change and activity are all harmonized with each other so that, as in the example above, when I feel thirst my arm reaches for the water glass and I take a drink.

But surely if individual human beings only do, and cannot but do, what is foreordained in the pre-established harmony, this must mean that it is not the thoughts and choices of human minds that guide or compel the actions of those human beings. Rather, it is the creative and controlling power of God, who has created those fully "harmonized" human beings with their completely complementary histories and who thus determines the whole course of their lives and actions. As Arnauld writes, on Leibniz's theory of the pre-established harmony, "God was free to create [Adam; but] ... everything that has happened since and will ever happen to the human race was and is obliged to happen through a more than fatal necessity" (LA 9; G 15).

Arnauld's phrase "a more than fatal necessity" is his response to the idea encapsulated in a phrase of Leibniz's which he thought could not be successfully defended. Leibniz had said in the summary of the *Discourse on Metaphysics*, which he sent to Arnauld, that each person's individual concept contains:

> the reasons for the truth of each event [in his or her life], or why one event has occurred rather than another. But these truths, though certain, are nevertheless contingent, being based on the freewill of God and of creatures. It is true that there are always reasons for their choice, but *they incline without necessitating.*
>
> (LA 5; G 12; emphasis added)

Arnauld cannot see how there can be any free will for persons on Leibniz's view. He cannot see how Leibnizian reasons can "incline without necessitating". For all the actions which, as I think, I freely choose and perform because I will to do so have actually been made certain to happen by God's initial creative act at the beginning of human history. Adam's concept is complete down to the last detail of the most trivial act that he will perform. It also includes exactly the posterity which he in fact has and all of *their* actions. God chose to create that particular Adam of all the possible Adams and thus he chose and ensured that Adam's progeny would be exactly what they have been down the ages, including me and my offspring. When I act, thinking it is my choice or my decision or my will that moves my body, I am in fact predetermined to act as I do. The truth of the statement about my action "I did such-and-such" is a *necessary* truth made so by God's original and singular creative act.

Leibniz, of course, is not without a comeback. He accuses Arnauld of confusing two kinds of necessity: absolute and hypothetical. He should, as

Leibniz does, distinguish between "what God is free to do absolutely and what he has obliged himself to do by virtue of certain decisions already taken" (LA 13; G 18). God sees the whole of history in one view and creates Adam knowing that his posterity and their actions will all be thus and so. So, everything that happens in history is hypothetically necessary. But God's foreknowledge of history and exactly how it must play itself out – given his creation of exactly the world he chooses to create – does not mean that our actions are predetermined. As Leibniz retorts, "As if concepts or previsions made things necessary, and a free action could not be included in the perfect concept or view which God has of the person to whom it will belong!" (LA 12; G 17).

Arnauld is still unpersuaded, however. There are two main reasons for Arnauld's resistance. First, he cites biblical authority to the effect that God has in fact, at specific times since the creation, created particular men and also intervened in historical events with free decrees. So Leibniz appears to be going against that authority by saying God acts "once for all", so to speak, when he creates.

More significantly, Arnauld objects to what he sees as Leibniz's demolition of the distinction between necessary and contingent truth. Leibniz wants my concept to include everything that will ever happen to me, including my being here at this moment, in such a way that "my being here now" is deducible from my concept, just as "having equal radii" is deducible from the concept of the circle. But while it is an eternal and necessary truth that circles have equal radii (whether God chooses to create one or not) Arnauld wishes to say that my being here now is something that results from my free choice, so that "I am here now" is only a contingent truth or truth of fact. Of course Leibniz also wants to call this a contingent truth. He claims that truths of fact do differ from necessary truths on his system as much as on anyone's. Truths of fact for him are those that can be known (by anyone other than God) only through experience. They cannot be deduced by us *a priori*. On the other hand, necessary truths, such as the truths of geometry, can be known independently of experience to be necessarily true.

The trouble for Leibniz at this point, however, is that he is not saying merely that God knows everything that is going to happen in advance. Nor is he saying just that "truth is timeless". We could readily agree that yesterday, had I said "I will be there tomorrow at just that time", I would have said something true that an omniscient being at least could have known to be true. But Leibniz's pre-established harmony is not just "pre-known"; it is pre-*established*. God's creative act, as Leibniz construes it, surely has foreclosed all other options. If Leibniz is right about the pre-established harmony he cannot defend the claim that our reasons for our actions "incline without necessitating" those actions. Those actions inevitably occur with, in Arnauld's words, "a more than fatal necessity".

An attempt to rescue causal power for Leibnizian minds

What, on Leibniz's view, causes my body to move when I will or decide to act? Leibniz's position is that my body spontaneously acts in a fashion that appears to obey my will. But the reason why it does so is that God chose to create monads with details of changes that would harmonize in just this way. God chose to create those monads, of all possible monads, that include one with my complete concept, including willing each action I perform throughout my life. So should we say that, in a way, my willing does cause my bodily movement, through the intermediation of God's creative actions? Could it not be said that my will causes God to put "the movement of my body in just that way at just that time" into my body's "programme"? This would seem to make my mind – my mental states such as my decisions and my will – efficacious after all.

Unfortunately, this attempt to endow Leibnizian minds with causal power will not work. My present willing could not be the cause of God's former creative action unless backward causation were logically possible. On the other hand, God cannot be caused to programme a certain movement into my body's detail of changes by an act of will I am foreseen to be going to perform. He chooses just that version of me that will in fact will in just that way at just that time: God is the author of the willing as well as its fulfilment. He is not *caused* to do anything here but rather chooses both willing and bodily movement when he chooses to actualize my complete concept.

CHAPTER 15

Leibniz and representation

One of Leibniz's more striking ideas is that the model in terms of which a genuinely unitary substance should be understood is the individual conscious subject with its entirely unique point of view or perspective on reality. If we mistakenly think of individual substances as identical, minutely small, bits of matter – the building blocks of material bodies – we are bound to misunderstand them. All physical things can be divided and divided *ad infinitum*: they are all entities by aggregation with, at best, only qualified claim to genuine unity. They are thus not substances. In sharp contrast, monads or simple substances as Leibniz views them, all have the indivisibility and unity we know from our own immaterial substance. They have substantial and fundamental similarity to our minds: monads all have innumerable perceptions (or "expressions" or "representations") of the whole universe and they are all unique because each has its own distinct point of view on all the rest.

They are also all – even the barest entirely unconscious monads – moved to spontaneous activity by the force of their intrinsic unfolding appetites or desires. As we have seen in the case of the monads that are near the top of the Leibnizian hierarchy, animal and human dominant monads act through organic bodies, which result from the close correspondence existing among aggregates or clusters of more basic monads. The difference between more and less basic monads lies at least partly in the degree of confusion among a monad's perceptions. Human minds have a comparatively high degree of clarity among a relatively high proportion of their perceptions. So, as Leibniz writes, "since a monad is representative in its nature, nothing could restrict it to representing only a part of things" (M60). And he goes on: "But it is of course true that this representation of the details of the whole universe is confused, and can only be distinct with respect to a small part of things, namely those which are either closest or largest with respect to each monad" (*ibid.*).

Representation and the pre-established harmony

So Leibniz puts representation at the centre of his account of the nature of monads and thus of his metaphysics. If we ask what he has to say about the problem of where the intentionality or representativeness of our perceptions comes from, his answer is that it comes from the free creativity of God. God has created all substances, each with a complete set of representations of all the others and of all the complex structures that are founded on them or involve them. All monads, however basic, have of their very essence an infinite number of perceptions or representations of the entire universe and of all of history.

This is what Leibniz says, but can he explain what it means? In the first place it is not easy to understand straight off in what sense Leibniz takes *un*conscious perceptions to represent things. To assist with the understanding of this claim it is worth looking at Leibniz's remarks in M56 and M57:

> Now, this interconnection, or this adapting of all created things to each one, and of each one to all the others, means that each simple substance has relationships which express all the others, and that it is therefore a perpetual living mirror of the universe. (M56)

> And just as the same town when seen from different sides will seem quite different, and is as it were multiplied *perspectivally*, the same thing happens here: because of the infinite multitude of simple substances it is as if there were as many different universes; but they are all perspectives on the same one, according to the different *point of view* of each monad. (M57)

Each monad is a "perpetual living mirror of the universe". So even the barest monad, with no conscious perceptions whatever, nonetheless, like a mirror, which is not itself conscious, reflects and represents for anyone who looks into it everything within its range. Of course, for Leibniz it is the whole universe that is reflected in or expressed by each monad, even if mostly very confusedly. Bare monads are like maps or road signs, with significance for those who can read them; they are representations but they do not experience representations.

The ability to know what is represented by any monad is possessed not by the monad but by the one who looks at it; so Leibniz says "he who sees everything [i.e. God] could read off from each [monad] what is happening everywhere" (M61). A divine observer could see clearly the entire detailed universe and all of history reflected in the mirror that is even the most basic bare monad. But other minds – even human ones – cannot read off all the details of the entire universe from any monad since only a small area of any thing's perceptions is sufficiently clear to provide knowledge to a created understanding.

Again, a point of view can exist whether any conscious subject occupies it or not. Leibniz capitalizes on this fact and holds that viewpoints that are occupied only by bare monads with no consciousness are nonetheless richly endowed with a wealth of *unconscious* perceptions of every item in the universe. Whether a viewpoint is occupied by a conscious subject or not, the whole multitude of monadic viewpoints or perspectives are all mutually coordinated so that any alteration of one monad requires, and gets, a compensating adjustment in every other monad.

All done with mirrors?

We have seen that both Descartes and Spinoza believe that the intentionality or aboutness of our representational states (ideas) is bestowed by God. We can now see that for Leibniz also those perceptions that in a way define individual substances (and that higher monads capable of consciousness can and do experience in themselves) represent what they do as a result of God's will. There is no original intentionality for any human ideas or perceptions. My perceptions derive their "aboutness" or representational character directly from God as a result of the exercise of his creative will. All my unfolding perceptions – all the perceptions of each and every monad – are innate. They are selected in advance at creation when all the monads with their pre-established total mutual harmony are created.

But what sort of *derived* representational character is it that human perceptions have, on Leibniz's view? The mirror analogy may seem to suggest that he thinks perceptions represent their objects *pictorially* as images represent what they are images of. Or it may seem that Leibniz thinks perceptions represent – for the thinking subject who experiences them consciously – by *resembling* what they represent. In some ways the analogy of differing points of view on the same town might seem to encourage the same conclusion: that Leibniz sees perceptions as representing pictorially or visually, by resemblance between the perception and what it is a perception of. After all, what a viewpoint bestows on its conscious, sighted occupier is something visual, namely, a view.

But we should be careful not to build everything on one interpretative clue (the mirror analogy), especially not in isolation from another very important one. Leibniz very often says that each monad "*expresses*" all the others from its own point of view: that any single monad's entire set of perceptions is an expression of the whole universe. The words "expresses" and "expression" may suggest that monadic perceptions represent their objects as words and phrases represent what they stand for or are about and thus are conventional or arbitrary rather than natural. And indeed, when Leibniz gives examples to illustrate what he means by "the expression relationship", one thing that is certainly among them is the relationship between language and some of its objects. In a paper of 1678 entitled "What is an Idea?",[1] Leibniz gives the following examples of things that express something other than themselves and says that a monad's perceptions express the entire universe in a way analogous to all these examples:

- a model expresses the machine of which it is a model;
- a projective delineation on a plane expresses a solid;
- speech expresses thoughts and truths;
- characters express numbers; and
- an algebraic equation expresses a circle or some other figure.

What do all these examples of "expression" have in common? The answer Leibniz gives is that, in each case, relations among the elements in the expression mirror corresponding relations among the elements of the thing expressed. Immediately after giving these five examples Leibniz asserts that there is a distinction between those cases of expression that do and those that do not have "some basis in nature". In the former sorts of case the "mirroring" picks up on some kind of literal similarity between the thing expressed and the thing that gives expression to it. With the model of the machine and the projective delineation, for example, the similarity or resemblance that exists between the items expressed and the things that express them is largely that of congruence: sameness of shape or pattern, even if there is a difference in scale.

Most importantly, the similarity between a thing and its natural expression, Leibniz says, is like that "between a circle and the ellipse which represents it optically, since any point whatever on the ellipse corresponds to some point on the circle *according to a definite law*" (*ibid.*: 208, emphasis added). There is a law-governed correspondence between the representer or expresser and what is represented or expressed.

---

1. In G. W. Leibniz, *Philosophical Papers and Letters*, Leroy E. Loemker (ed. & trans.) (Dordrecht: Reidel, 1969), 208–9.

But the examples of the character that expresses a number, the equation expressing a figure and the bit of language expressing a thought or idea are all cases of "non-natural" or "arbitrary" expression. That is to say there is a conventional relationship between an expression (representation) on the one hand and what it represents or expresses on the other. The relationship is arbitrary in that it is appointed by convention but, in another sense, it is non-arbitrary since it is governed by strict laws.

Either naturally or with the aid of convention and law, it is the case that, for all five examples, we are able to learn the properties of and truths about what is modelled or expressed by examining the model, delineation, speech, character, equation or whatever that expresses it. So, too, a monad's perceptions are always a possible source of human knowledge about anything in the universe.

These facts might make it tempting to say that Leibniz regards monadic perceptions as representing the monad's surroundings by being structurally isomorphic with them. Two objects are said to be structurally isomorphic when the parts or elements of each are internally related to each other in the same way. The two objects have the same shape or pattern, even if the parts of the first object are realized in different materials or are different in colour and so forth from the parts of the other. But a monad's perceptions are not its parts. Monads, remember, have no parts and are utterly simple. Whatever the relationship of a monad's perceptions one to another, this cannot be a literal structural relationship. A monad's perceptions form a detail of changes: an abstract program something akin to a computer program. This abstract relationship internal to the set of perceptions belonging to each monad exactly parallels the abstract relationship that relates all the myriad monads of the universe to each other.

Misrepresentation for Leibniz

Could it ever occur that a monad's collection of perceptions could *mis*represent its universe? Again, could an individual conscious mind's ideas ever misrepresent the world it reflects? These questions are bound to seem odd: all of us (certainly including Leibniz) are well aware that any human mind or spirit must be able to make mistakes. Everyone has had the unfortunate experience of discovering that some of his trusted ideas are not – or at least seem not to be – accurate representations of their objects. So to be at all plausible, any account of the nature of the human mind and how it represents external reality must accommodate the truth that our ideas and perceptions at least sometimes appear to be misleading or non-veridical.

As we have seen, Leibniz holds that, for monads in general, whether bare monads or conscious spirits, the total collection of any monad's perceptions forms a detailed representation of the whole universe from its own point of view. And this total representation is such that God could read off from it every detail of the state of the entire universe. But Leibniz also says that very many of any monad's perceptions are confused. This "confusion" is contrasted with "distinctness" and explained as analogous to the lack of distinctness possessed by a visual image or perception of something spatially remote. Monads' perceptions of their "near neighbours" will be distinct compared to their perceptions of more distant things.

Looking for the raw materials to construct a Leibnizian account of misrepresentation, we might be tempted to see confused perceptions as having the potential to be Leibniz's perceptions-which-misrepresent-external-reality. But this would suggest that Leibniz thinks God creates all monads with perceptions at least some of which are *intrinsically* confused. And this seems an unlikely thing for Leibniz to hold. His view of God as a being who never acts without the best of reasons would seem to rule out God's creating imperfect, intrinsically confused things where he could have created perfect, distinct ones. What could his reason be for creating monads with misleading perceptions, perceptions that of their very nature misrepresent what is perceived? Moreover, the contention that God could read off exactly the entire detailed state of the whole universe from the perceptions of even the most basic bare monad sits uncomfortably with the view that great numbers of such monads' perceptions are intrinsically misleading.

A much better suggestion comes originally from Wilson, who offers the proposal that a perception belonging to one monad is distinct, not absolutely but only relative to a corresponding perception belonging to a second monad. And this relative distinctness obtains only if that first perception provides God's reason for his creation of the corresponding perception given to the second monad. A pinprick to my body is distinct relative to the sensation corresponding to it in my mind because God's reason for pre-establishing that I will have just that sensation at that time is that he has antecedently chosen that the "pinprick at that time" be part of my pre-established physical history.

Wilson is quick to make clear that this proposal about distinct and confused perceptions and the order of priority of God's reasons is highly schematic and, although it is supported by textual evidence, it is not something Leibniz has spelled out in any detail, let alone repeatedly. Modestly, she also emphasizes that even if her proposal catches Leibniz's position faithfully, it takes us no distance towards understanding, for example, what the states of unconscious monads are *like*. All her proposal gives us (but this is very worth having) is an alternative to an implausible view that has, despite its implausibility, attracted a number of commentators. This is the view that Leibniz wishes to identify the distinction between confused and distinct perceptions with the distinction between unconscious and conscious ones.

It is difficult to see how the claim that Leibniz identifies these two distinctions could ever have seemed convincing. Human minds often have confused perceptions that are first unconscious and later become conscious. Surely Leibniz does not mean to say that a confused perception must become distinct as soon as it is experienced consciously? Also, we are often *conscious* that our perceptions of things at a distance from us are very indistinct or confused. On these occasions our perceptions are both conscious and confused. Contrariwise, all of a bare monad's perceptions are unconscious but even bare monads are said to have some perceptions that are more distinct while some of its perceptions are much more confused than others. This last point naturally raises a further one. For Leibniz, it would seem that the distinction between conscious and unconscious perceptions is not a matter of degree: either a perception is conscious or it is not. On the other hand, perceptions can be experienced as confused to a higher or a lesser degree. They can also be very distinct or less so. Confusedness is, while consciousness is not, a matter of degree.

We can conjecture that, for Leibniz, it is not the case that monadic perceptions are ever intrinsically misleading or guilty of misrepresentation. It is our understanding or conscious apprehension, or lack of it, that some of the time leaves perceptions of external reality confused. However, Leibniz is optimistic about the possibility of each human understanding achieving considerable knowledge. This is because the difference between any of the monads that lack intelligence and a human dominant monad (intelligent substance) "is just as great as the difference between a mirror and someone who sees" (DM35). As was said earlier, we are to some extent able to discover the relationships between the elements of the things in our world by due attention to our whole array of perceptions and the relationships between them. However, our understandings are certainly not perfect and we are thus often confused where the supreme intelligence would not be. But we can and should strive to read what is reflected in the monadic perceptions to which we have access for we alone among monads are endowed with innate ideas representing the necessary truths applicable to external reality. We saw above that, once we understand those innate truths, they will lead us aright not only about external reality but also about our own nature and our place in creation as spirits and moral subjects. For human spirits there is thus the chance of approaching to the condition of little deities and thus also the possibility of genuine immortality.

CHAPTER 16

Is the mind a substance for Locke?

In earlier chapters we have seen that the question "Does this author hold that the human mind is a substance?" is by no means as easy to answer as might have been imagined. Descartes certainly, and officially, holds that the mind is an immaterial substance. But we have seen that he also holds that there are psychological features of a living human being – such as perceptual and access consciousness, experience of pleasure and pain and the passions – that can characterize a human subject in the absence of the rational soul. For Spinoza the answer to the question whether he thinks individual human minds are substances is a simple no, but the explanation of why they cannot be substances for him and of what the mind is, if not a substance, is very complex. Leibniz regards the human mind as a single, dominant monad, that is, an immaterial substance. But given that his notion of an individual substance is highly eccentric and can be understood only in the context of his whole complex metaphysical system, some time and effort are required to glean a full answer to the topic question in his case as well.

We might have hoped that the first of the classic empiricists would prove more straightforward on this subject. But there are a number of reasons why, for Locke too, it is not possible to give a simple answer to the question whether or not he thinks the human mind is a substance. First, and most significantly, there is no consensus among commentators about what Locke's account of substance (if any) is. Some of what he writes using the term "substance" in the *Essay Concerning Human Understanding* (*Essay*) (e.g. II.xxvii.1, 295) has been taken by some readers (including Leibniz [NE 218]) to offer a definition of "substance" as a quality-less "something I know not what", itself unobservable, whose role is to underpin or support the observable properties of things and account for the way simple ideas of these properties cluster together in experience. The suggestion is that reality consists of numerous discrete particulars, each of which has at its heart a portion of substance that acts as a "*substratum*" (underlying layer) for the thing's observable extension, bulk, figure and solidity plus the further sensible qualities that *these* qualities have the power to produce. If Locke thinks that all the properties of things of every kind require an appropriate sort of substance in which they can inhere then it might seem that mental states, thoughts and faculties require immaterial substance to underpin them and, thus, that Locke must think that the human mind is a single immaterial substance.

But at the opposite extreme, other commentators take Locke to be very sceptical about the notion of substance. Some even see him as condemning the very idea as absurd, much as he condemns items purportedly referred to by the technical terms of scholastic philosophy such as "intentional species" and "occult qualities". Indeed, one of the terms of philosophers' jargon about which Locke is explicitly critical is Aristotelian "prime matter" (III.x.13, 499): a supposedly quality-less, formless "stuff" with no properties of its own. So, this second interpretation asks: how could Locke reject prime matter as a nonsense and yet support the notion of quality-less *substratum* substance, which the previous interpretation says is what Locke means by "substance in general"?

Locke is certainly eager to point out early in Chapter 23 ("Of Our Simple Ideas of Substances") of Book II of the *Essay* that the contention that it is (an unknowable) substance that supports and lies beneath the observable properties of a thing goes no way towards giving any sort of working knowledge or scientific understanding of the thing or phenomenon in question. Jewellers and blacksmiths, with their hands-on experience, know much more about diamonds and iron than does any philosopher with his talk of *substratum* or substance. And if we want a scientific account of mind (or, at any rate, of self or person), references to immaterial *substratum* substance will not take us any distance at all (II.xxvii.16–17, 340–41).

In what follows I shall look first at what Locke writes about mind and immaterial substance. The points Locke makes are almost entirely negative. He thinks all we can safely say about immaterial substance is that we do not know anything about it. What Locke has to say of a positive nature about the human mind is mostly to be found in his discussion of personal identity, so that will be the topic of the second section, § "Locke on the identity of persons".

Locke and immaterial substance

Locke writes that we have "*Ideas* but of three sorts of Substances" (II.xxvii.2, 329): God (uncreated), finite intelligences (created) and bodies (also created). The human mind is certainly not identical with, nor a part of, God on Locke's view. Nor does he think the mind is a body, although he sometimes seems quite prepared to allow that God could endow matter with the ability to think (IV.iii.6, 541). But is the human mind, for Locke, a finite intelligence? And is this the same thing for him as an immaterial substance? Notice that he is here talking of *ideas* of sorts of substances. Locke often uses the term "substances" as no more than a variant on the term "things". We should not assume that Locke is here using the term as his philosophical predecessors and contemporaries might have – and as he may sometimes do himself – as a technical term for "that which is most fundamental in reality". We saw earlier that Descartes and the Cartesians all continue to present their philosophical systems in terms of the Aristotelian categories of substance and accidents. But Locke is (at least at times) trying to move away from this Rationalist–Aristotelian pattern for doing metaphysics, just as he wishes to move away from the Latinate terminology and jargon of the schools. In this context he may very well be saying simply that there are three kinds of things – God, minds and bodies – and saying nothing about their metaphysical status.

Earlier in Book II, Locke had said that "a Spirit [is] a *thing* capable of thinking" (II.xxiii.3, 297), and then gone on to suggest that, just as a material thing such as gold needs something over and above its observable qualities to which those qualities belong, so too a mind needs a substance to which its thinking, reasoning, fearing and other "Operations of the Mind" can belong (II.xxiii.5, 297–8). Unable to see how these mental properties and activities, could "subsist of themselves, nor apprehending how they can belong to Body, or be produced by it, we are apt to think these the Actions of some other *Substance*, which we call *Spirit*" (*ibid.*). In the rest of that section Locke makes very clear that he thinks we have no idea of the substance of spirit any more than we have any idea of the substance of body (material substance). The only idea of substance (of either kind) that we have is an idea of what substance *does* (II.xiii.19, 175): it supports properties or qualities.

At this point in the text Locke is principally concerned with presenting the following argument:

(i)   we have no idea of either material or immaterial substance; but
(ii) we would never think of arguing that because we have no idea of material substance, therefore bodies do not exist; so
(iii) we should not think it a good argument that, because we have no idea of immaterial substance there are no spirits.

One implication (unstated here but see II.xxiii.15, 305–6) is that experience teaches us equally that there are bodies and that there are minds but, in sharp contrast, material and immaterial substance are for some reason both beyond the reach of our experience. So we cannot have ideas of either. But that does not prove that either sort of thing does not exist.

But none of this adds up to a commitment to an immaterialist, Cartesian-dualist theory of the human mind. Locke is careful throughout to speak only of what we do or do not have *ideas* of, of what we can and cannot conceive. Sometimes, as just now, he says that we have *no* idea of either material or immaterial underlying substance. Sometimes he says that our idea of substance in general is *obscure*, suggesting at least that there is something to be known and that we can conceive, in some very broad sense, of what that something might turn out to be,[1] *if* there were such a thing at all. Mental properties are clearly not physical properties for Locke. Such property dualism, however, leaves entirely open the question whether material and immaterial *substrata* are of different ontological types or not.

Later in the chapter, Locke may seem to go further. Locke's empiricism, his commitment to the view that all our ideas come to us ultimately from experience, is very much to the fore when he writes "we are apt to think, that our Senses shew us nothing but material things" (II.xxiii.15, 306–7). But we are wrong:

> Every act of sensation, when duly considered, gives us an equal view of both parts of nature, the Corporeal and Spiritual. For whilst I know, by seeing or hearing, *etc.* that there is some Corporeal Being without me, the Object of that sensation, I do more certainly know, that there is some Spiritual Being within me, that sees and hears. This I must be convinced cannot be the action of bare insensible matter; nor ever could be without an immaterial thinking Being.
>
> (*Ibid.*)

This passage has strong echoes of Descartes's Second Meditation, which might suggest that he is here endorsing Descartes's dualism about mind. But if we look at the passage that precedes this we find that Locke is still as agnostic as he had been earlier about immaterial substance. The point he is advancing in this section is that we cannot know anything about immaterial substance except that, like material substance, we must hypothesize its existence; if it did not exist our mental properties, like our physical properties, would be unanchored things lacking a principle of unity or a metaphysical

---

1. For a consideration of this apparent tension in Locke's thought see Nicholas Jolley, *Locke: His Philosophical Thought* (Oxford: Oxford University Press, 1999), 80–99, esp. 82–3.

foundation. Thinking, understanding, willing, knowing and the power of initiating motion in a body (the distinctive features of mind) require a "thing" in which to occur as much as do "Extension, Solidity and being moved": "For our *Idea* of Substance, is equally obscure, or none at all, in both; it [underlying substance] is but a supposed, I know not what, to support those *Ideas*, we call Accidents" (*ibid.*, 305).

By now it should be fully apparent that Locke distinguishes sharply between our idea of body and our idea of material substance and again between our idea of spirit, soul or mind and our idea of immaterial substance. In the case of material and immaterial substance, as has been said repeatedly, Locke holds that we have no idea or only the most obscure idea of either. On the other hand, the idea of a body or physical object is a fairly detailed and full idea yielded unproblematically to everyone by everyday experience of things such as men, horses and swans, water, iron and gold. The idea of body is the idea of something that takes up space and has a location; that has a shape; resists pushes and pulls; can "[communicate] motion by impulse"; appears to have colour and texture; and so on. The idea of a spirit or mind is, Locke thinks, every bit as clearly conveyed to us by all waking experience: "Every one finds in himself, that his Soul can think, will, and operate on his Body [i.e. has the power of voluntary motion]" (II.xxiii.16, 17 & 20, 306–7). The ideas of body and spirit are common and familiar. The ideas of material and immaterial substance, on the contrary, are ideas of "something I know not what".

It has been suggested[2] that Locke actually holds no brief for the metaphysical notion of an underlying quality-less "naked" substance in the sense of a kind of quality-less "stuff", but rather that his term "substance in general" (which covers both "material substance" and "immaterial substance") is actually extensionally equivalent to his term "real essence". Extensionally equivalent terms are ones that, although they differ in meaning, apply to or pick out exactly the same things. On such an interpretation Locke is not guilty of the foolishness of thinking there could be something that, on the one hand, had no properties of its own but yet, on the other hand, had whatever character it takes to "sustain" or "underpin" the observable properties of things.

Instead, the job of sustaining the observable properties of gold, horses or minds is actually performed by the unobserved inner constitution or essential structure of physical things and the real, but again unknown, essence or internal constitution of spirits. Real essences for Locke consist of real structures and properties specific to the kind of thing in question, from which the

2. Michael Ayers, "The Ideas of Power and Substance in Locke's Philosophy", in *Locke on Human Understanding*, I. C. Tipton (ed.), 77–104 (Oxford: Oxford University Press, 1977).

observable properties that constitute what he calls the "nominal essence" of that kind flow. Real essences cause observable properties but are not themselves known. On the other hand, they are not mysterious quality-less stuff.

There is no room here to join the continuing debate over the rights and wrongs of this interpretation. For our purposes the important thing to realize is that Locke is equally agnostic about *substratum* substance and about real essence. Whether they are one thing or two they are equally unknown to human minds. Locke says repeatedly that we have no idea of either. It may be that he thinks that both are *in principle* unknowable.

Locke on the identity of persons

If Locke were convinced that an individual human mind is basically and essentially a single immaterial substance (or portion of immaterial substance) we would expect to find him referring to the fact when he comes to discuss personal identity over time (II.xxvii). Clearly, however, Locke does not regard substance – either material or immaterial – as important to the persistence, as the self-same individual, of any sort of created thing. Instead he sees identity as relative to the kind of thing talked about. As he says, "'Tis not ... Unity of Substance that comprehends all sorts of *Identity* ... But to conceive, and judge of it aright, we must consider what *Idea* the Word it is applied to stands for" (II.xxvii.7, 332). In general, Locke's rule for identity is "that ... that had one beginning is the same thing" (II.xxvii.1, 328). But when spotting beginnings and, again, when tracing the history of individual things over time, what matters is what sort of thing it is whose beginning, and hence identity, is in question: "It being one thing to be the same *Substance*, another the same *Man*, and a third the same *Person*, if *Person, Man*, and *Substance*, are three Names standing for three different *Ideas*; for such as is the *Idea* belonging to that *Name*, such must be the *Identity*" (II.xxvii.7, 332). Locke proceeds to say that the criterion of identity associated with the term "Man" (i.e. human animal) is – as for all plants and animals – that the human being in question is the same "living organized Body". This is true for a man even if, inevitably, much bodily matter will have been added and lost and many properties such as size, eye colour, amount of hair and so on will have changed since the man in question was born. Keeping the same portion of material substance, Locke thinks, is neither necessary nor sufficient for staying the same human animal over any stretch of time.

What about keeping the same soul or mind? Locke is sure that it is only the same animal life that makes for sameness of human animal (man) and resists the suggestion that the same mind, spirit or soul is required. He appeals to common opinion:

> whatever is talked of other definitions [for example, the traditional "rational animal"], ingenuous observation puts it past doubt, that the *Idea* in our Minds, of which the Sound *Man* in our Mouths is the Sign, is nothing else but of an Animal of such a certain Form.
>
> (II.xxvii.8, 333)

He considers the possibility that a very intelligent cat or parrot might seem to be a candidate for being a man but rejects it out of hand, not because there could not be a very intelligent parrot but simply because such a thing would be a very smart parrot, not a man: "'Tis not the *Idea* of a thinking or rational Being alone, that makes the *Idea* of a *Man* in most Peoples Sense; but of a Body so and so shaped joined to it" (*ibid.*, 335).

Locke defers discussion of the term "(immaterial) substance" and looks next at the term "person", which he later says is synonymous with "self". A person is:

> a thinking intelligent Being, that has reason and reflection, and can consider it self as it self, the same thinking thing in different times and places; which it does only by that consciousness, which is inseparable from thinking, and as it seems to me essential to it
> ...
>
> (II.xxvii.9, 335)

It is amply clear from the context that Locke is here specifying not only what we mean by "person" and "self" but equally what we mean by "mind". A human mind or self, for Locke, is a single consciousness or conscious subject: "It not being considered in this case, whether the same *self* be continued in the same, or divers Substances" (*ibid.*). Just as Locke has said that sameness of living animal body does not require numerical sameness of material substance, so he now (II.xxvii.10, 335–6) proceeds to say that sameness of person or mind does not require sameness of immaterial substance.

There is, of course, an asymmetry between body and spirit here. A single human animal remains numerically the same while the same individual life continues. There are no periods in a single life when a man temporarily ceases to be alive. However, as Locke immediately notes, there are periods in the existence of every person when consciousness is interrupted by, for example, forgetfulness and periods of deep sleep. A self can persist through such periods of unconsciousness, Locke thinks, not because that person's allotment of immaterial substance remains the same through the gaps, certainly not because it persists as an *un*conscious subject, but rather because a person, mind or self is not a substance at all. It is probably what Locke would call a "mixed mode": something that may be produced by, and certainly is supported and unified by, immaterial substance (whatever that is). But like a symphony or a weekly television serial it is the sort of thing that includes temporal gaps in its concept.

For Locke, we simply have no way of knowing whether it is the same single (portion of) immaterial substance or a series of successive ones on which our minds depend throughout our lives. Someone might object that the latter suggestion cannot be correct because it opens the door to the possibility that a later person supported by one immaterial substance might think he had done something (perhaps a crime that merits punishment) that was really committed by that immaterial substance when subtending a different person at an earlier time. Locke's answer is that God would not allow the "transfer from one to another, [of] that consciousness, which draws Reward or Punishment with it" (II.xxvii.13, 338).

Locke asks his reader to judge whether we would have one person or two if the same portion of immaterial substance underpinned first Socrates' mind and then, centuries later, the mind of a contemporary. If that later person had no consciousness or memories of Socrates' life or actions, Locke says, surely we would not think the second man the same person as Socrates, any more than we would think two men born centuries apart were made the same *man* by the fact that some of the particles of matter that were once part of the earlier man were now a part of the later man's body.

A single human mind or person then, for Locke, is neither to be identified with the man whose mind it is nor with the unknown immaterial substance or substances on which it somehow depends. A single person or consciousness is a being whose identity is solely determined by its consciousness of its own contents, its thoughts and actions, projects and memories. Locke has, in a way, cut the notion of the mind free of any particular substance whether material or immaterial.

So at last we can answer the topic question: the mind is not a substance for Locke in the way that, for Descartes or for Leibniz, each human mind is a unique individual immaterial substance. But the mind is, for Locke, realized in or by immaterial substance, which, in his parlance, is an unknown thing that at any particular moment thinks in, and unifies, a particular human being, realizing or making possible a particular consciousness or person. Person, immaterial substance and human being are ordinarily coincident so that we are apt to think of them as one thing. But Locke is persuaded that these three are by no means literally identical. So, in principle, a single person could be associated with different human animals and/or different portions of immaterial substance in different times and places. Likewise, different persons could successively make use of the same portion of immaterial substance to attain consciousness in the same human being. How immaterial substance realizes consciousness, however, is something of which we remain wholly ignorant.

CHAPTER 17

Locke's views on self-knowledge

Locke's conviction that human minds are not furnished with any innate knowledge but that all our ideas come from sensation and reflection alone was noted in Chapter 16. Now we need to ask what impact this empiricism has on Locke's views about the knowledge we have of ourselves. From sensation we mostly obtain ideas about the world outside ourselves, although we clearly also gain some ideas about our bodies, particularly the extremities, from our external senses. (Think, for example, of discovering that you have a rash on your hand by seeing it before you feel it.) But when it comes to learning about our own minds, Locke, like Leibniz and Berkeley, thinks that we rely on reflection – a kind of turning inwards of the mind on itself – as a dedicated source of information about our mental life and inner, subjective self. In this chapter I shall look at the two sorts of knowledge of self we might hope to have from reflection: first, knowledge of our existence and essential nature as minds or spirits; and, secondly, knowledge of what is going on in our minds. In the last section I shall look at Locke's rejection of the Cartesian doctrine that the mind is always thinking and then, in Chapter 18, I shall go on to discuss Locke's views on the nature of human consciousness and subjectivity.

Does Locke think I can have knowledge of my own existence and nature?

My existence
Unlike Descartes, Locke does not feel the need to begin his work by proving that he exists. Indeed, when he comes eventually to consider the question, he asserts that we perceive our own existence "so plainly, and so certainly, that it neither needs, nor is capable of any proof. For nothing can be more evident to us, than our own Existence" (IV.ix.2–3, 618–19). Nor does he think that anyone could seriously doubt his or her own existence. "Really to doubt of it" he says, "is manifestly impossible" (IV.x.2, 620).

On the other hand, it is difficult to understand how he can legitimately call our feelings of certainty about our existence "knowledge". For according to the account of knowledge that he gives early in Book IV, his criterion for knowledge as opposed to mere belief or well-supported opinion is as follows: we have knowledge when we have *"perception of the connexion and agreement, or disagreement and repugnancy of any of our Ideas"* (IV.i.2, 525). If we see that two ideas "agree",[1] then the proposition linking them (predicating one of the other, say) is seen to be true and thus known. If this agreement of ideas is not perceived, whatever firm belief we may form and whatever the evidence we muster for it, it ought not to count as knowledge.

In other words, although Locke is clearly an empiricist about ideas he is (officially at any rate) a rationalist about knowledge. On such a view, knowledge is paradigmatically of universal necessary truths such as those of geometry or logic. Yes, for Locke, all our *ideas* are either given in experience or derived from what is given in experience. But his standard of what counts as *knowledge* is very high and does not bring in experience but relies on attending to one's ideas alone. To have knowledge is to perceive the conceptual connections between ideas. So effectively knowledge is, or ought to be, confined to what can be known – once we have the required ideas – independently of experience. No contingent proposition such as "I exist" should be knowable.

Many commentators have believed that Locke's own principles should have made him deny the title of knowledge to claims about real existence. He has been read as making one or the other of two possible mistakes when he says we have knowledge of the existence of the things we sense, of God and of ourselves: either he is abandoning his definition of knowledge in the case of existence claims and comparing, for example, my idea of myself with myself actually existing rather than with a second idea; or he *is* comparing two ideas but should realize that there is and could be no conceptual interconnection between my idea of myself and my idea of real existence. Either he is unwittingly abandoning his rationalism about knowledge in mid-account because of his overall empirical sympathies, or he is sticking to his epistemological rationalism at the cost of making many of his knowledge claims incredible given his definition of knowledge as restricted to the perception of agreement between ideas.

---

1. For brevity, from now on I follow the standard practice of speaking only about "perception of agreement" of ideas rather than "perception of connexion and agreement or disagreement and repugnancy".

Locke's austere definition of what constitutes knowledge certainly comes as a surprise; whatever way the differences sketched in the preceding paragraph are settled Locke's definition of knowledge sits uncomfortably with the spirit of the earlier books of the *Essay*, where he is clearly drawn to the position that we have knowledge whenever we have beliefs that are sufficiently strongly confirmed by experience. And as we have just seen, it is also hard to square with the passages later in Book IV where (as in IV.ix.2, cited above) Locke explicitly and emphatically credits us with intuitive knowledge of our own existence and, also, knowledge by sensation of things external to ourselves.

This is not the place for a lengthy consideration of Locke's theory of knowledge or an attempt to show it coherent despite the stresses and apparent contradictions that have been mentioned. All we can really do is note that Locke is perfectly well aware that not all truths can be truths of reason and much of the time seems perfectly at home with the thought that we do get hold of, and rely on as if they were known, many truths that are not supported by reason or reason alone. Locke is officially agnostic (that is, he says we do not have knowledge) about many things. But it seems fair to say that his agnosticism varies in intensity over a wide range: from outright agnosticism, for example, about substance in general to the merest hint of a sort of formal scepticism about well-confirmed beliefs about matters of fact. We can know nothing at all of substance in general. But we can be certain of (have "an assurance that *deserves the name of Knowledge*" [IV.xi.3, 631]) of many propositions about the material world and about the operations of our own minds.

My nature

When we turn to the question how much of our essential nature Locke thinks each of us can know, the wide range of shades of agnosticism just outlined is very apparent. On the strict and negative side, near the end of his chapter on substances Locke tells us that we certainly do not know the essence of God, not because of God's undoubted uniqueness and immensity, but for the simple reason that *we do not know the real essence of anything*: "a Peble, or a Fly, or our own selves" (II.xxiii.35, 315).

This declaration of our ignorance of our real essence is reminiscent of what he has said about our ignorance of the substance of our own minds (II.xxiii.5, 297). This is one of the passages where Locke ironically observes that we have no better knowledge of material substance (construed as the mysterious support of sensible properties) than we have of the immaterial substance in which we suppose that "*Thinking, Knowing, Doubting* and a power of Moving, etc. do subsist" (*ibid.*). The moral here, as noted in Chapter 16, is that the fact that we actually have no idea whatever of immaterial *substratum* cannot constitute a reason for denying the existence of mind or spirit since we know equally little (i.e. nothing at all) of material *substratum* and yet we do not see this ignorance as a reason to deny matter exists.

So, I do not have any ideas or knowledge of my real essence or (supposing this is different) of my spiritual *substratum* on Locke's view. I have no idea *how* my essence or substance supports and unifies my various mental activities and makes them possible. However, this is a good point to recall Locke's distinction between immaterial substance, on the one hand, and spirit, on the other. He is very confident that I do have ideas of, and a good understanding of, what a spirit is because I have direct experience of what a spirit can and does *do*. I know – simply because I have done so on innumerable occasions – that I am able to reflect, know things, doubt, will and initiate motion simply by thinking (II.xxiii.15, 305). I am right to be confident about this picture of myself, which unending experience conveys. These faculties and capacities are the very core of what being a mind consists in. Locke is saying that we all have fully justified opinions, and cannot help having them, about what it is to be a mind or human spirit.

It makes little difference to my self-understanding or self-awareness that I do not have knowledge of my immaterial *substratum* or my real essence. What matters is the understanding I do have of the activities and fundamental character or nature (even if it is not called the "essence") of my mind. Locke feels that our lack of knowledge of immaterial substance and real essence is more than compensated for by the extensive understanding of our nature and functioning as spirits, which we are given by reflection.

Does Locke think I can have knowledge of the activities and contents of my mind?

As we have just seen, when it comes to self-knowledge of what is going on in my mind Locke has no hesitation in crediting each human mind with complete authority about its own ideas and activities. At times he is even prepared to say that I know nothing more surely than I know that I feel pain, doubt, perceive my own existence and so on (IV.ix.3, 618). Having proved to his own satisfaction in Book I that we are not born with any ideas, Locke designates sensation as the source of our ideas of external objects and then introduces reflection: "The other Fountain from which Experience furnisheth the Understanding *with Ideas* is the *Perception of the Operations of our own Minds* within us" (II.i.4, 105). When the mind reflects on these mental operations, Locke tells us, it gets the ideas of "*Perception, Thinking, Doubting, Believing, Reasoning, Knowing, Willing*, and all the different actings of our own Minds", ideas that we could not get "from things without" (*ibid.*).

The perception of these ideas of our mental operations constitutes immediate self-knowledge. The operations of our minds are experienced as they happen. That awareness is unmediated and authoritative. If we ask Locke how it is that our certainty about the operations of our minds needs no grounding in evidence, no justification beyond our say-so, his reply is that what reflection gives us is precisely direct access to the goings on in our own minds. This direct intuitive knowledge is more certain than anything that I or anyone else could bring to buttress or justify it. And it is, of course, a private source of knowledge no one else can have. Locke is very dismissive of any person, any – as he derisively says – "notable Diviner of Thoughts" who might purport to know better than I do what and whether I am thinking (II. i.19, 115).

Reflection, for Locke, is decidedly inner sense, which he does not distinguish from introspection. In introducing the term, he emphasizes the sensory character of this second "Fountain of knowledge": "This Source of *Ideas*, every Man has wholly in himself: And though it be not Sense, as having nothing to do with external Objects; yet it is very like it, and might properly enough be call'd internal Sense" (II.i.4, 105). With (external) sensation there is always the possibility that I might be wrong in judging that what I think I sense is actually there or that it really is as it seems to me to be. But in reflection or internal sense this possibility does not exist: it cannot be the case that reflection tells me I am doubting or reasoning or entertaining a particular idea when in fact I am not doing so.

On the other hand, something that *can* happen is that I can fail to have clear and distinct ideas of the operations of my mind, just as I can fail to form a clear and distinct idea of a landscape, a picture or a clock – even ones I pass every day – if I do not "turn [my] Thoughts that way, and consider them *attentively*" (II.i.7, 107). Concerted attention is required if I am to have the full, detailed ideas of the operations of my mind that reflection makes possible for all human minds.

Is the mind always thinking?

Locke is firmly persuaded that Descartes and his followers are mistaken in holding that the mind is always thinking. With typical Lockean irony he writes:

> I confess my self, to have one of those dull Souls, that doth not perceive it self, always to contemplate *Ideas*, nor can conceive it any more necessary for the *Soul always to think*, than for the body always to move; the perception of *Ideas* being (as I conceive) to the Soul, what motion is to the Body, not its Essence, but one of its Operations.
>
> (II.i.10, 108)

He sets about casting doubt on the Cartesian thesis of perpetual thought by a number of different means. On the one hand he suggests that his opponents may think that they are presenting an *a priori* truth but, if so then they are begging the question when they say that "actual thinking [as opposed to the potential for thinking] is essential to the Soul" (*ibid.*, 109). They are only entitled to argue from their conception of what is involved in the essence of the human mind if they have an independent proof that their conception of that essence is correct. But no such proof has been presented.

"The mind always thinks" is not a self-evident truth. If, on the other hand, the Cartesians think that it is a matter of empirical fact, they owe us a plausible explanation of why all of us have experiences that seem best described as "gaps in our thought". We all sleep regularly, often dreamlessly. People woken from sound sleep and asked if they were, just seconds before, thinking or dreaming often say no. Surely these facts tend to undermine the thesis that thought never stops.

Of course, Locke is aware of the likely response to these points about dreamless sleep and subjects woken from sleep to be quizzed about whether they were dreaming: the Cartesian could simply counter that "the *Soul thinks*, even *in* the soundest *Sleep, but the Memory retains it not*" (II.i.14, 111). Locke's reaction to this is to say that the burden is on the Cartesian to produce something more convincing in support of this claim than "a bare assertion". Usually we can remember our thoughts of only a few seconds ago, so why not the thoughts we supposedly have when we are asleep? Anyway, nature does not make "excellent things, for mean or no uses" (II.i.15, 113). The excellent faculty of thought that each of us enjoys would be employed to absolutely no purpose in devoting the hours of sleep to thinking thoughts of which no trace ever remained in memory. In Locke's view it is a powerful consideration that God would never contrive things so that such a vast amount of human thought was squandered in such a profitless fashion. It is hard for any twenty-first-century reader not to smile ruefully at Locke's complete innocence of any idea of the work modern psychologists would say is done by unconscious mental activity – particularly during sleep – whether remembered or not.

Earlier it was said that, for Locke, the human mind has from reflection private, immediate and thus authoritative certainties about its nature and operations and about its contents. It should also be said that Locke thinks the ideas that I get in reflection are one and all salient for me. As we shall see in the next chapter, Locke strongly resists the suggestion that we might have any ideas or thoughts of which we are not conscious.

CHAPTER 18

Locke on consciousness

In the second book of the *Essay*, Locke introduces ideas as the "atoms" of mental life. Exhilarated by his, as he thinks, comprehensive trouncing of the theory of innate propositions and ideas, he declares his empiricist credo that all ideas come from experience, either sensation or reflection. In a very upbeat spirit he turns almost immediately to address the Cartesian claim that the mind is always thinking. He offers the arguments summarized in the previous chapter, each of which flows from his conviction that "thinking consists in being conscious that one thinks" (II.i.19, 115). He also defines "thinking" as "that sort of operation of the Mind about its *Ideas*, wherein the Mind is active; where it with some degree of voluntary attention, considers any thing" (II.ix.1, 143). And he defines "idea" as "whatsoever is the Object of the Understanding when a Man thinks" (I.i.8, 47). If this is what thinking and ideas are, how could we possibly think or have ideas without being conscious of that very activity?

Transparency, salience, memory and being in the mind

Before very long, however, he begins to realize that this position is certainly not tenable as it stands. It is not that he hesitates about the doctrine of perpetual thought. He remains convinced that there are periods of deep sleep when I am not conscious of being engaged in any mental activity and that I cannot be actively thinking (entertaining any ideas) without being conscious to some degree that I am doing so. But the question arises how could ideas, whose whole being apparently consists in being thought of, be in the mind when *not* being thought about? Like Descartes, Locke subscribes to a version of the theory that the mind is transparent to itself. But, also like Descartes, he admits, and must accommodate in his theory: first, that there are many ideas in my mind that I am not currently thinking of; and secondly, that ideas can come into my consciousness unheralded, which seem to have been in my mind prior to that arrival. Given Locke's equation of "thinking" with "consciousness that one is thinking" and his definition of "ideas" as things that are brought into and sustained in existence by thought, how can he account for the possibility of each of these features of mental life?

There are many ideas in my mind of which I am not currently thinking
The view that the mind is transparent to itself is seen by its harshest critics as maintaining wholly implausibly and indefensibly that each human subject has the capacity to turn inwards towards all of his or her ideas and "inspect" them, and that this introspection is not only automatic, irresistible and total but also confers on the subject complete and infallible knowledge of the mind's objects. Locke rejects the charge that what I have called "his version of the transparency theory" involves the claim that introspection is total, if by that is meant that we are conscious of all our mental contents at the same time (II.x.9, 154). In fact, he explicitly denies that we can think of more than one thing at a time. For Locke, we need not, and indeed could not, be always surveying or even noticing all of our ideas (IV.i.8, 528); still less are we under an irresistible compulsion to do so.

This being so, however, he owes us an account of memory: of how ideas can be "in the mind" but not consciously so and yet accessible (as he claims they are) to introspection and recollection should the occasion arise. Locke's explicit treatment of memory is to be found in Book II, Chapter X, "Of Retention". Here Locke says that it is the mental faculty of retention that has the business of keeping or retaining the simple ideas received from sensation and reflection. Retention accomplishes its task, Locke tells us, either by keeping the idea "actually in view" or by its "Power to revive again in our Minds those *Ideas*, which after imprinting have disappeared, or have been as it were laid aside out of Sight" (II.x.2, 149).

The first of these is called *"Contemplation"* (II.x.1, 149). An idea that is being contemplated is in the mind consciously since Locke defines consciousness as "the perception of what passes in a Man's own mind" (II.i.19, 115), and an idea that is actually in view ("being viewed") will be perceived as part of the mind's perception or consciousness of this mental viewing. The second "way of Retention" is *"Memory"* (II.x.2, 150), which Locke proceeds to describe first in terms of a storehouse or repository where ideas are laid up or retained and then in terms of powers to revive perceptions, bring ideas in sight and paint ideas anew on the mind "without the help of those sensible Qualities, which first imprinted them there" (*ibid.*).

We could be forgiven for thinking that Locke is either being less than straight with his readers or floundering in this chapter. On the one hand, he resorts repeatedly throughout the ten sections of the chapter to similes and metaphors of laying aside in storehouses and repositories; lodging and hiding in the memory; dormant pictures; images that have been imprinted, drawn and painted; footprints; print or characters; inscriptions and images engraved in marble – all this to capture the way *ideas* can remain in the mind in all their varying strengths of memory. On the other hand, he says that:

> our *Ideas* being nothing, but actual Perceptions in the Mind, which cease to be any thing, when there is no perception of them, this *laying up* of our *Ideas* in the Repository of the Memory, signifies no more but this, that the Mind has a Power, in many cases to revive Perceptions, which it has once had, with this additional Perception annexed to them, that it has had them before.   (*Ibid.*)

So all these similes and metaphors and the language of visual encounter with what has been imprinted and engraved do nothing whatever to tell us *how* the memory works to retain ideas once they are in the mind or understanding but are no longer under "the Eye of the Soul". Indeed, by Locke's own admission, these figures of speech are completely misleading. For Locke there is no mental equivalent of an image, impress or picture "hidden" in the mind and waiting to be rediscovered. The only account Locke gives us of how ideas can be in the mind after they are no longer actually in contemplation is to say that the mind has a power to revive those vanished impressions. Despite the similes and the title of the chapter, his is a theory of memory as replay or revival not as retention.

"Sometimes too [ideas] spring up of their own accord"

Asserting that the mind has the power to revive ideas after they have left conscious contemplation is one thing: explaining how this revival (sometimes called "searching out") is to be accomplished is another. As Leibniz points out (NE 140), Locke has left this matter as mysterious as are the "faculties" and "bare powers" that Locke refuses to accept from the scholastic philosophers. He should realize that he has declared (II.i.1, 104) ideas to be "the inner objects of thoughts" and that as such "they can persist": "If nothing were left of past thoughts the moment we ceased to think of them, it would be impossible to explain how we could keep the memory of them" (NE 140). Leibniz concludes: "to resort to a bare faculty to do the work is to talk unintelligibly" (*ibid.*).

Leibniz's point seems well taken. If, as Locke says, passions and emotions can stimulate the recurrence of an idea it would seem that there must be something left of the original idea to be aroused by those feelings and to make the current idea a recurrence of that particular past idea rather than any other. And if, as he also says, ideas that I have had previously sometimes "spring up of their own accord and offer themselves to the Understanding", it is hard to see how this could happen unless there were some concrete vestiges or traces of those same past ideas somehow retained in my memory to account for their sudden renewal or "replay" in conscious thought. For there to be a replaying there must be something to replay. A picture that has faded away *completely* cannot be revived; it must be replaced. A revival requires a corpse to be revitalized; a visual image requires a template to guide its reproduction.

Of course, Leibniz's solution to the puzzle of "ideas retained but not in consciousness" is to say that there must be and are, in any mind, numerous ideas or perceptions that are *un*conscious. But Locke emphatically rejects the possibility of unconscious ideas. For him, allowing unconscious ideas would reintroduce the twin spectres of innate ideas and perpetual thought.

Unfortunately, however, Locke has given himself no escape route from his predicament. He has no account of how ideas that are nothing at all if they are not "actual Perceptions in the Mind" can somehow be powers on the part of the mind to reinvent those very ideas anew without new experience of the sort that gave rise to the original ideas. It helps not at all to be told that ideas which spring into the mind are memories if and only if they have "this additional Perception annexed to them, that [the mind] has had them before" (II.x.2, 150). For one thing, it seems plainly false to suggest that thoughts that are in fact memories always feel familiar (always come with this "additional Perception"). And, contrariwise, it is quite possible to have an idea that is in fact new or original and yet wonder whether it is a memory or not because it has a feeling of familiarity.

A leaning towards materialism?

In places, Locke flirts with the notion that bodily impressions are necessary to underpin ideas retained in the mind in memory. Of course, it is impressions on sense organs that produce ideas of sensation, unless the mind is "retired as it were out of [their] reach" (II.xix.1, 228) in sleep. And occasionally Locke even suggests in a very roundabout way that it may be the body "upon the right Constitution of whose Organs its Memory should depend" (II.xxvii.27, 347).

In Book II, Chapter X, "Of Retention", Locke mentions as a topic of enquiry for another time "the Temper of the Brain" and how "the Characters drawn on it" may vary in permanence from person to person. Then, in the same sentence, he notes that "we oftentimes find a Disease quite strip the Mind of all its *Ideas*", which suggests to him that it is "probable, that the Constitution of the Body does sometimes influence the Memory" (II.x.5, 152). Later in the same sentence, it is difficult for the reader to conclude whether he is talking of ideas in the mind or characters in the brain when he says that "the flames of a Fever" can swiftly "calcine all those Images to dust and confusion, which seem'd to be as lasting, as if graved in Marble". And all these remarks come only a few lines after Locke famously says of human memory "*The Pictures drawn in our Minds, are laid in fading Colours*".

Clearly Locke is aware that he cannot account for how ideas of which I am not conscious can be in any sense at all "in my mind" unless he finds somewhere (and the body is the only place left) for memory traces to reside. Unfortunately, what emerges here and elsewhere in the *Essay* are the merest hints that Locke might look with favour and relief at an account of how memory is served by the brain as a retainer of physical traces of impressions on sense organs that earlier produced changes in the brain, which in their turn produced ideas of sensation. However, even if Locke developed this notion of brain traces further this would still leave him without even the beginning of an account of the mind's capacity to remember ideas of reflection – ideas of its own operations – once these have passed out of contemplation.

Locke has stranded himself: for him, having an idea just is thinking. And thinking consists of consciousness that one is thinking. So you *cannot* have an idea you are not aware of. And yet he wants to say we can and do have lots of them: in memory. He credits the mind with the power to re-run or re-play ideas without the sensible qualities that produced those ideas in the first place. But he has no explanation of how that power works. So he cannot jettison all the metaphors of "storehouses inspected by the eye of the soul", "engraved and painted images", "footsteps" and so forth because he has nothing explanatory with which to replace them. As Leibniz says, Locke needs his ideas to persist (unconsciously) in memory. But he is not prepared to tolerate their doing so.

Consciousness as higher-order thought?

Locke's definition of "consciousness" as "the perception of what passes in a Man's own mind" (II.i.19, 115), like Leibniz's account of conscious perception in terms of awareness of *petites perceptions* gained via immediate memory, sounds very like another early version of a higher-order thought theory of the nature of consciousness. For Locke, perceiving what goes on in your own mind (consciousness) is becoming aware of your ideas both of sensation and of reflection, which is in turn, in the case of sensations, becoming aware or conscious of the external world. So Locke would say that, for example, when I open my eyes in bright sunshine looking out to sea, my eyes are affected by light reflected off the waves and this in turn produces an idea in my mind that my mind is aware of. Consciousness of the blue of the sea just *is* this consciousness that I am having a sensation or idea of blue.

Locke gives a detailed inventory of what he regards as the different modes of thinking, from sensation through remembrance, recollection and contemplation to attention and study or intention (II.xix). He follows this with a discussion of the degrees of attention from "earnest study" to "very near minding nothing at all". The conclusion of this chapter is that human thinking can range from intent and concentrated attention to almost (but not quite) total lack of awareness. Locke wants to make as persuasive as possible his claim (with which the chapter ends) that conscious awareness and thought – since they admit of such wide and subtle variation – are the central capabilities of the mind *but not its essence*. Something's essence, Locke thinks, is precisely something that cannot vary or diminish.

Earlier I argued that Descartes has a way of avoiding being accused of self-contradiction or incoherence when he says that there are some ideas that have been "long present within" him although he has "never turned [his] mental gaze on them before" (AT.VII.64; CSM.II.44). There are grounds for holding that Descartes allows that there are different types or levels of consciousness so that "falling under the gaze of the mind" might mean "being the object of a higher-order thought". On this view, memories, innate ideas and some perceptual ideas can be in the mind in a way that we might call "minimally conscious", "access conscious" or "perceptually conscious" at a time when they are not receiving the focused attention of the rational soul acting as an inner scanner, which can make them conscious in a different sense again. Any such ideas that are not currently "under the gaze of the mind" would, for Descartes, be transparent to the mind in the sense that they would be conscious in such a way as to be accessible to higher-order thought.

Could Locke's "very near minding nothing at all" (which looks at first like a species of minimal consciousness) when contrasted with "earnest study" (obviously a very concentrated conscious attention) possibly provide Locke with a similar way of avoiding the imputation that he has no explanation of how ideas could be in the mind in my memory when I am not conscious of them? Unfortunately, Locke's notion of consciousness does not seem to admit of this possibility. Whereas Descartes distinguishes between those forms of awareness (such as reasoning and exercise of moral judgement) that require the rational soul and those (such as sense perception) that can take place absent the rational soul (in sleepwalkers, for example), Locke's different "degrees of attention" all require the conscious mind equally although, as the term implies, attention can vary from detailed and focused to very casual and inattentive.

Locke recognizes different degrees of attention but not different types or degrees of consciousness. Unfortunately, consciousness for Locke seems to be very much an "all or nothing" thing. Withdrawal of the last vestige of attention – as Locke himself insists repeatedly – is fatal to any idea since an idea's whole being consists in being consciously perceived (however inattentively). And indeed it would seem that Locke's consciousness should probably not be regarded as even an early evolutionary ancestor of what a higher-order thought theory will take consciousness to be. For on such a theory it is possible for mental states to exist as such independently of being illuminated by the introspective gaze or higher-order thought that Armstrong, for example, regards as the only kind of consciousness worthy of the name. Locke, on the other hand, has only mental states (ideas) whose existence consists wholly in being thought, which in turn consists wholly in their being conscious. Locke remains convinced, as he argued against Cartesian perpetual thought, that having an idea is like being hungry: something that for him cannot occur independently of the subject's awareness of it.

Consciousness as the principle of identity for persons

Locke may give us a wholly inadequate and baffling account of how ideas that are no longer held in consciousness can survive as powers of the mind. And he may tease us with suggestions about the role of brain traces in memory, which he then fails to pursue. Again, he certainly exasperates dualists and materialists alike by championing the possibility that mere matter *might* be capable of thinking but only as a result of divine intervention or "superaddition" (IV.iii.6, 540–41) *not* because matter is naturally capable of thought. But arguably he greatly compensates for these deficiencies by proposing unity of consciousness rather than sameness of either material or immaterial substance as the criterion of identity over time for persons and, indeed, by elaborating his view of consciousness as the crucial feature of personhood.

When he is contesting the doctrines of innate ideas and perpetual thought Locke equates consciousness with all of mentality. So, as we have seen, he there seems to have a very one-dimensional view of consciousness. But his understanding of consciousness in the sense of subjective self-awareness seems to blossom when he comes to contrast the identity of persons or selves

161

with the nature and identity of both human animal bodies and portions of (unknown) immaterial substance. This is because, like Leibniz after him, he takes the most important thing about the human mind or self to be its nature as a conscience, a moral individual responsible for its own actions. In so far as I can recall my past actions as my own and remember my performing them "from within", so to speak, I am that person who made those choices and did those things. Also, in so far as I am concerned in past and future actions, projects and situations – in the pleasure or pain, happiness or misery attendant on those actions and situations – so far I am the subject, self or person, the individual consciousness whose agency and circumstances they are.

Locke does not retreat from his agnosticism about material substance and immaterial substance when proposing consciousness as the criterion of personal identity. Instead he asserts that the fact that we do not and perhaps cannot know anything whatever about either of these substances means that they are irrelevant to the question what makes one individual spirit or subject the single persisting individual it is. We do not know what dependency the mind may have on single or successive substances, whether immaterial or even material. We *do* know, about our selves, which moral subjects we are and whose welfare we are vitally interested in. And these things we know by immediate, infallible self-consciousness.

If we press Locke for some sort of explanation or account of how consciousness comes of its basis, whatever that is – that is, if we ask for an answer to the puzzle that nowadays is called the puzzle or mystery of "the explanatory gap" – his answer is that a divine act alone can produce consciousness or mindedness. Whether each human mind is the result of God's giving all the "Systems of Matter fitly disposed, a power to perceive and think" or it is the result of God's joining "to matter so disposed, a thinking immaterial Substance" in either case it is "the Bounty of the Creator" alone that accounts for the existence of each human consciousness (IV.iii.6, 541). Natural science could never explain how thought and consciousness are caused in any individual because divine causes are wholly beyond the reach of natural science.

CHAPTER 19

Locke on mental causation

Near the end of the last chapter it was said that Locke believes that a crucial feature of a human person or consciousness is the fact that each of us is a moral agent with a conscience. Like all our philosophers from Descartes to Hume, Locke clearly thinks that human persons are capable of actions and behaviour that issue from moral choices and decisions, and for which, on Locke's view, the agents will be answerable on the day of judgement. But it might seem that it is only fair to make someone answerable, to praise or blame, punish or reward someone (now or in the afterlife), if it is the case that that person's choices and decisions really do produce the behaviour in question. So we would expect Locke to hold that minds and mental states have genuine causal power.

And, indeed, it appears that this is exactly what he does believe. When he is talking about minds or spirits and what distinguishes them from bodies (in "Of our Complex Ideas of Substances"), he says that "*The* Ideas *we have* belonging, and *peculiar to Spirit, are Thinking, and Will,* or a power of putting Body into motion by Thought" (II.xxiii.18, 306), and again "we find by Experience, that barely by willing it, barely by a thought of the Mind, we can move the parts of our Bodies, which were before at rest" (II.xxi.4, 235). And, he says, "all our voluntary Motions ... are produced in us only by the free Action or Thought of our own Minds" (IV.x.19, 629). So, like Descartes, Locke believes that he has the evidence of everyday experience that mental states, in particular acts of will, cause our actions.

A possible response to Elisabeth's objection: a first approach

Locke's position is well captured by the answer he gives to what can be seen as in effect a version of the objection Princess Elisabeth addressed to Descartes. Recall that Elisabeth's objection to Descartes's claim that my mind interacts causally with body is that matter is the kind of thing that could only be moved by something extended and capable of contact or "pushing", neither of which is a feature possessed by any thought or mind. In other words, given what we know about the nature of matter and what it takes to move it and what we know about the (wholly unextended) mind it is impossible to see *how* an act of will (or any mental state) could do the job of initiating bodily movement.

Locke's response to this challenge appears as part of his answer to the religious sceptic who thinks that there could be no such thing as "creation out of nothing" because he (the sceptic) cannot conceive how such creation could be done. Addressing the sceptic, Locke draws an analogy between "creation *ex nihilo* accomplished by God's will" and "body being moved by a created mind". Of course, we have no experience of *ex nihilo* creation, Locke says, but we have constant experience of mind moving body in the innumerable voluntary actions we accomplish daily. And he is perfectly ready to confess that we have no idea how it is that the mind moves the body; nor can we even begin to understand how it is done. But it would obviously be foolish to try to convince anyone that *because* we cannot conceive of how mind could cause bodily movement *therefore* there can be no such causation. This is causation we all have immediate knowledge of from our daily experience. Of course it is possible: it actually happens!

So, in general, it would be "overvaluing ourselves" and our cognitive capacities to declare *any* effects – even creation *ex nihilo* – "impossible to be done" on the grounds that our comprehension does not stretch to conceiving how those effects are produced (IV.x.19, 629–30). Locke's sensible conclusion is that saying that I cannot conceive how such a thing could be achieved is never a good way of arguing that a particular sort of action or occurrence is impossible.

The trouble with this line of thought as a defence of the proposition that it is my choices, decisions and other such mental states that are causally responsible for my actions is that it rests on the assumption that my experiential certainty that this is the case is adequate evidence that the proposition is true. But, as we saw Spinoza observing earlier, no matter how strongly I *feel* that I am making my body move by willing it to do so this is no proof that it is my will that does the moving. No matter how sure I am that what I do is caused by my mental states it is always possible that I am mistaken or under an illusion.

An alternative approach

What I have been calling "Elisabeth's objection" relies on the conviction that physical movement and body–body causal interaction are well understood in stark contrast to our complete ignorance of how mind could possibly move body. So the other approach available to Locke, if he were mounting a response to this objection, would be to endeavour to remove the contrast by trying to undermine our confidence that we know what is required to move a body. And Locke does in fact urge his readers to address their minds to this question and ask themselves whether they have any idea at all of how body initiates movement in a body.

This is one of the first issues Locke raises early in Book II, Chapter XXI, the very long chapter devoted to what Locke calls "power". All power relates to action, Locke tells us, and there are only two sorts of action, "Thinking and Motion" (II.xxi.4, 235). We cannot fail to be aware that we have the active power to think and this awareness we get by thinking itself: in reflection. But if we look for the same sort of knowledge about motion in bodies we find that experience supplies continual examples of passive power – body's capacity to *be* moved or acted on – but experience does not give us any idea of how bodies *initiate* motion: "A Body at rest affords us no *Idea* of any *active Power* to move; and when it is set in motion it self, that Motion is rather a Passion, than an Action in it. For when the Ball obeys the stroke of a Billiard-stick, it is not any action of the Ball, but bare passion" (*ibid.*). The ball is nothing but passive when receiving the transfer of motion from the stick. It does not initiate its own movement. And if the first ball strikes a second the second ball will move only because motion has been transferred to it from the first. This gives us only "a very obscure *Idea* of an *active Power* of moving in Body" since we observe only transfer, not production of motion. But it is only "a very obscure *Idea* of *Power*, which reaches not the Production of the Action" (*ibid.*).

So we should not be impressed when anyone tries to argue that we understand physical motion but not how our will moves our body. Actually, quite the reverse, the only idea we have of "the beginning of motion" comes from "reflection on what passes in our selves, where we find by Experience, that barely by willing it, barely by a thought of the Mind, we can move the parts of our Bodies, which were before at rest" (*ibid.*).

Thus Locke tries to erode our confidence in our knowledge of the capacities of unaided matter while building up our certainty about our own abilities as minds. In particular, Locke hopes to persuade his fellow scientists that they are overconfident in believing that they know all about, and can explain all natural phenomena in terms of, matter in motion.

Is this enough to banish objections such as that of Princess Elisabeth to the view that acts of will do in fact cause our bodily movements? Unfortunately it looks as if neither approach to answering the objection that Locke's position is able to offer would altogether remove the worry raised earlier. We may feel certain that volitions alone are all it takes to move our bodies (and that matter cannot initiate movement for itself) but this does not prove that our feeling is justified. It is always possible that we are under a systematic illusion that our mental states can and do make a causal difference to any part of the material world.

Volitions alone?

It is probably worth remarking that Locke does not think that bodily move-ment can be caused by any and every sort of thought or idea. Desiring or choosing – what Locke calls "preferring" – can certainly occur in the absence of any sort of fulfilment or achievement of what is preferred. For a start, as Locke says, "though a Man would preferr flying to walking" that preference will not issue in my taking to the air unaided since this is obviously beyond my, or any human being's, physical capacities (II.xxi.15). But even actions of which I am certainly physically capable, such as taking a glass of water, will not flow from my desire or preference for a drink so long as all I do is prefer or wish for it. And this is true however strong my wish or desire.

On the other hand, Locke is well aware that one thought or mental state can determine or cause another. My desires and preferences, like my choices and beliefs, can certainly cause my will to operate and to do so one way rather than another. Beliefs, desires, choices and preferences, then, on Locke's view, can all issue, indirectly through the intermediary of willing, in actions for which I am morally responsible.

The physical exclusion problem

It may be thought that Locke's position, although it is vulnerable to the sort of extreme scepticism mooted at the end of § "A possible response to Elisabeth's objection: a first approach", above, has the hallmark of robust common sense. It is hard not to feel that Locke must be right in his staunch and unwavering conviction that we continually perform voluntary actions that are made so because our volitions directly and unmediatedly cause our bodies to move. However, whatever success Locke might have in trying to persuade his readers of the certainty of psychophysical causation and the corresponding weakness of objections along the lines of Elisabeth's objec-tion, it has to be admitted that he has few resources with which to defend his positive position about mental causation from the modern-day "physical exclusion problem".

The physical exclusion argument is one that has been addressed principally to holders of a non-reductive materialism such as the anomalous monism of Donald Davidson. This argument takes as its central premise the "causal closure of the physical", that is, the principle that every physical occurrence is perfectly accounted for causally by its physical antecedents. It argues from the contention that the *physical* properties of any particular occurrent mental event (i.e. the physical properties of the token brain event with which that token mental event is identical) are by themselves sufficient to account for all that event's effects. Thus, it is concluded, physical properties exclude the causal claims of mental properties: events such as acts of will are impotent as *mental* acts to move anything in the – causally closed – physical world.

Now, whatever Locke's unofficial materialist leanings, he certainly does not hold any variety of identity theory about ideas and physical states. For him, acts of will are acts of my mind that have no physical properties. Yes, he does sometimes contend that brain states may have some influence on memories and even that God could if he wished enable "Matter fitly disposed" to think (IV.iii.6, 540). But he never suggests that any idea or thought that I am experiencing has a material side or realization or depends for its existence on matter.

Notwithstanding this utterly fundamental metaphysical difference between his views and those of any non-reductive materialist philosopher of mind, however, Locke is every bit as vulnerable as the monistic materialist to the causal exclusion argument. If the physical realm is causally closed, if every physical event has a physical cause wholly sufficient to account for its occurrence, then there is no way a mental cause *as such* could be inserted into a physical causal chain. If my body moves, this must be because some physical cause moves it (or "transfers motion to it", as Locke would say). However strongly I feel that it is my mind that initiates action in or by my body, this must be an illusion. The causal exclusion argument leads irresistibly to epiphenomenalism: the view that mental events, states and processes are epiphenomena – phenomena that may be caused by or emerge from the physical but "float impotently above" their physical causal basis and have no power to intervene in physical causal chains or influence the material world in any way.

In the end Locke can only offer the intuition that "his [non-physical] Soul can think, will, and operate on his Body" (II.xxiii.20, 307): in present-day parlance, that his own and others' mental states make a clear causal difference to the world. His resistance to epiphenomenalism is supported by the strength of that intuition alone. If the supporters of the physical exclusion argument can establish the thesis that the physical world is causally closed, it would seem that Locke's intuition of mental causation would be comprehensively defeated.

CHAPTER 20

Locke on representation

Locke's position with respect to ideas and our experience of the external world is sometimes labelled "representative realist" to indicate Locke's belief that our ideas represent their causes (hence "representative") and that those ideas are faithful representatives that give us pictures which are as accurate as they can be – and as we need them to be – of the way the world really is (hence "realist"). Some commentators think that this rough sketch of Locke's position, when suitably refined and qualified, is reasonably correct. Others think it is, in differing ways, very far wide of the mark.

Rather than try to adjudicate in detail among the rivals, in what follows I shall try to give a survey of the main different readings and their supporting considerations. It may be that the best conclusion is that Locke, like many innovators, was better at starting promising new lines of approach than seeing and bearing in mind incompatibilities among those approaches. At any rate there is general agreement that Locke thinks ideas represent things in thought. But what are the things they represent, what does the representing and how is the representation accomplished?

We have seen that Descartes holds that his three kinds of ideas – innate, invented and adventitious – represent, respectively, (a) principles of reason and metaphysical truths, (b) imaginary items and fictions and (c) external sensible objects. And we have also seen that these three sorts of representation are all accomplished by what is the ultimate cause of each, namely God. For Spinoza, too, our ideas' power of representing things is ultimately ascribable to God, although, since Spinoza's God is not a transcendent creator, this is certainly not something accomplished by a divine agent or decree. Each bodily change, including alterations to the sense organs, has a strictly corresponding idea in the mind that stands for the object that causes that bodily change. Again, Leibniz ascribes to God's wishes and agency the capacity each monad's perceptions have to represent the entire creation and all of history from the monad's own point of view. So the "aboutness" or representational character of human ideas is for all the rationalists not "original" but "derived" intentionality. It is a product of divine creative power and intentions: God makes our ideas stand for or represent to us what it suits the divine purpose that they should represent in our thinking. Somehow, for the rationalists, human minds are, from their creation, possessed of ideas that are already representative of their objects, or fully apt to represent things encountered in experience. And, for both Spinoza and Leibniz, even the most basic object or monad has a rich representational side independently of the apprehension of it by any created mind.

Locke therefore makes a sharp departure from the Cartesian tradition. As we know, he believes that ideas in human minds are never in any sense inborn or innate. They are, one and all, "furnished by experience" (II.i.2, 104). And their capacity to represent things, whether outside the mind or in it, is also conferred on them by, or acquired somehow in the course of, experience. Or so Locke initially and mostly appears to believe. Book I of the *Essay* is given over to his numerous arguments against the existence, first, of innate *principles* of logic or morality and, then, consequently, of any sorts of *ideas* that are inborn or native to the human understanding. Having thus cleared the decks, in Book II Locke turns to the question: given that there are no innate ideas, where do ideas of different kinds come from?

Rival views

In earlier chapters we have seen repeatedly that there are numerous ways in which one thing can represent another. Portraits and representational paintings represent their subjects by looking like them. Caricatures and cartoons capture and exaggerate certain key features so that there is a different sort of resemblance between the thing that represents and the thing represented. Symptoms and other effects represent their causes, which they may or may not resemble. Words and sentences represent without resembling what they refer to and what they mean. Some representatives (such as members of parliament, lawyers and lobbyists) stand in or go proxy for their constituents or clients. And there is another sense of "represent" in which "to represent" is "to present a case or articulate a particular interest".

There are broadly two views as to what Locke means by "represent" in the phrase "ideas represent their objects". On one (the majority) interpretation, Locke sees ideas as stand-ins for the objects in the world that cause those ideas to arise in sense perception. For example, my ideas of white colour, rectangular shape and shiny surface stand for the colour, shape and shininess of the snow covering the bird table in my garden. On this interpretation, those ideas are completely distinct from the object they represent. I can use them as a rough guide to what the properties of that patch of snow are.

I say "rough" because two of those ideas are ideas of secondary qualities. I shall say more about secondary qualities and Locke's views on them below but for the present the important feature of these qualities is that each is perceivable only via one sense and thus cannot be confirmed by using another sense in the way that the rectangular shape I see can be confirmed by touch. More importantly, in addition it has to be taken on trust that ideas conceived as distinct separate entities represent the objects they stand in for with any degree of accuracy. There is no vantage point from which one could observe and establish that an idea in the mind did in fact correctly represent or match what it is an idea of.

Here is the main rival[1] to the interpretation just outlined: on this alternative view Locke is said to mean by "representation" the sort of representing that a lawyer does for his client's case. Locke's ideas, it is said, present objects in the world (and thoughts in the mind) to their human subject in the same way that a lawyer's speeches in court represent (or perhaps better "present") his client's position to a judge and jury. Ideas are not proxies or surrogates. Nor are they distinct from the things they represent. Instead – or so this rival interpretation has it – Locke thinks ideas are the very things those ideas represent *as they appear in the mind.*

One large difference between these two rival interpretations has already been touched on: it lies in the fact that the first can seem far more open than the second to a particular form of epistemological scepticism. On the first view our ideas are numerically distinct from their objects and stand between our minds and those objects. Since they are positioned in this way, they might – for all we know – be nothing like the objects or qualities they exist to stand in for in the mind. Indeed, they might constitute some sort of barrier or veil, obscuring rather than revealing what things external to us are like. For all we know, there might be no material things lying behind the veil of perception.

On the alternative interpretation, ideas in the mind give direct, immediate access to external reality. Ideas gained in experience are not distinct existences that could stand between the mind and the world; rather, they are appearances that the understanding can interpret and which are, in fact, simply the

1. See John W. Yolton, "Ideas and Knowledge in Seventeenth Century Philosophy", *Journal of the History of Philosophy* **13** (1975), 373–88, and Thomas M. Lennon, "Locke on Ideas and Representation", in *The Cambridge Companion to Locke's Essay Concerning Human Understanding*, Lex Newman (ed.), 231–57 (Cambridge: Cambridge University Press, 2007).

things presented (or represented), without any intermediary, as they appear in the mind.

Each of these rival interpretations has something to recommend it. The first (long-standard) interpretation, which takes ideas to be intermediaries or stand-ins, seems the natural, perhaps the only way, to read statements such as "'Tis evident, the Mind knows not Things immediately, but only by the intervention of the *Ideas* it has of them" (IV.iv.3, 563). Viewing ideas as stand-ins also seems to go along with the (again long-standard) interpretation that sees Locke's ideas as *images* in the mind and Lockean representation as essentially pictorial, relying on resemblance between ideas and the objects in the external world for which they stand.

In earlier sections we have seen how, again and again, Locke uses pictorial language to refer to ideas and their relation to the mind. In addition to all the talk of "pictures in the mind's storehouse" in the chapter on memory (Book II, Chapter X, "On Retention"), the following are just a few of the further places where Locke speaks of ideas as "painted" (II.i.2, 104) and "imprinted" (II.i.6, 106) on the mind. Ideas and visible images are clearly identified with each other when Locke compares the mind to a mirror that cannot help receiving the "Images or *Ideas*" caused by "the Objects set before it" (II.i.25, 118). Again, an idea is said to be a unitary idea if "it be considered as one Representation, or Picture, though made up of never so many Particulars" (II.xxiv.1, 318). Even ideas of mental operations are described as "floating visions" (II.i.8, 107). It is easy to see why critics for many centuries have read Locke as equating ideas with images acting as intermediaries between mind and world.

But the alternative, "presentation" reading declares itself able to show a number of advantages over its "surrogate" or "stand-in" rival. For one thing, if Locke sees his ideas as ontologically distinct intermediaries, it is difficult to understand why he should be as unperturbed as he evidently is about the threat that a veil of perception consisting of ideas might block off our access to those very external things that ideas are supposed to make accessible to the mind.

Moreover, Locke is quite clear that our ideas come not only from sensible objects outside us but also from reflection on the operations of our minds. But it is very hard to see how ideas of reflection could be *images* of the things they are said to stand-in for in our thinking or indeed how they could *picture* or *resemble* in any significant respects those mental operations or occurrences.

And the notion that Locke takes ideas to be appearances that present their objects, direct and unmediated, to the mind is certainly appealing since it rightly portrays Locke as confident in his faith in the informative capacity of experience. And anyway, on further thought there does not seem to be any bar to the presentation view's regarding an idea – that is, the way in which a thing appears in the mind – as an image that represents the thing it is an idea *of* by resembling it. Just because an appearance is not a distinct entity over and above the thing it represents (the thing whose appearance it is) that does not preclude it from being an image or from its having a stronger or weaker resemblance to the reality it presents to the mind.

Resemblance

The intended suggestion of the previous paragraphs is that there is something to be said for each of the rival interpretations introduced in the previous section. It is also clear that each has some difficulties to address and in some cases the same difficulty afflicts both. It could well be that Locke, if he distinguishes between the two positions, does not think it particularly important for his purposes which way ideas are regarded. Or rather, it might be better to say that he is content for an ambiguity to persist, thinking each view captures something of the way ideas function to represent their objects.

Moreover, if an idea is a thing distinct from both the thing it represents and the mind it is in, this need not automatically mean that it is an obscuring veil or barrier: surely Locke's chosen metaphor would be that ideas are windows or lenses that can give the mind a clear view of what they represent.[2] On the other hand, appearances in the mind, however faithfully they represent the reality they present, cannot present that reality in all possible detail, so appearances – just as much as any sort of stand-in – can sometimes mislead about the exact character of reality because – just as much as any ontologically distinct intermediary – they are qualitatively distinct from the reality they present. In other words, choosing the "immediate presentation" reading would not banish the sceptic's bogey: both idea-proxies and presented appearances have the potential to mislead the mind about what lies in the world external to it. Locke certainly does not think that the judgements we make about reality based on our ideas are infallible.

It is time to ask whether Locke does in fact think that ideas represent what they are ideas of *because* they resemble those objects. Is resemblance the *source* of the "aboutness" or "intentionality" of ideas for Locke? We might expect to get some help with answering this question from discussions of the

---

2. A similar point about choice of appropriate metaphor is well made by E. J. Lowe in *Locke on Human Understanding* (London: Routledge, 1995), 45.

related question whether Locke does in fact (as alluded to above) hold that all ideas are images in the sense of pictures of their objects. But there is need for caution here: Michael Ayers tells us that it is undoubtedly right to label Locke an "imagist" but goes on to explain that this is because Locke sided with the "imagists" against the "intellectualists" in an ongoing dispute over whether or not "thought can be explained adequately in terms of the imagination without recourse to a faculty of pure intellect".[3] It may be that the equation of ideas with images that Locke at times makes is not so much an expression of his thinking that all ideas are little pictures in the head as his not wishing his ideas to be regarded as excessively intellectual items: products of a pure intellect purged of all reference to the sensory. It is certainly true that Locke often talks as if ideas are simply pictures of what they represent. But arguably much of this is just unguarded metaphor or simile: it is worth reminding ourselves that on a number of occasions he asks explicitly that they be read figuratively, not taken literally.

A powerful disincentive to adopting the view that Locke thinks ideas derive their power to represent their objects from resemblance must be the fact that there are significant categories of Lockean ideas that simply do not and perhaps could not resemble their objects pictorially. The whole category of ideas of reflection has already been noted as one where pictorial resemblance seems ruled out. More importantly, Locke himself famously points to another of these categories when he talks of "the *Ideas of secondary Qualities*", such as the ideas of the blue colour and characteristic sweet scent of violets. Of such colours, smells, "*and other the like sensible Qualities*" such as tastes and sounds he says that "there is nothing like our *Ideas* [of them], existing in the Bodies themselves ... only a Power to produce those Sensations in us: And what is Sweet, Blue, or Warm in *Idea*, is but the certain Bulk, Figure, and Motion of the insensible Parts in the Bodies themselves, which we call so" (II.viii.13–15, 136–7). The flower we refer to as blue is not itself characterized by blue since this is a subjective feeling: the idea of blue is the idea of a felt or experienced sensory quality or characteristic, something that has no resemblance to the bulk, figure and motion – the physical (primary) qualities – of the body we describe as "blue".

It has been suggested[4] that, since Locke certainly still takes the idea of blue to be representational despite the fact that he explicitly denies that there is

---

3. Ayers, *Locke*, 47. For a detailed account of the whole dispute and Ayers's interpretation of Locke's position see the surrounding pages.
4. Richard Watson, *Representational Ideas from Plato to Patricia Churchland* (Dordrecht: Kluwer, 1995), 68.

any resemblance between secondary ideas and the sensible qualities of their objects, it must be some *other* sort of resemblance that underwrites the representative nature of secondary ideas. The other sort of resemblance suggested is "structural isomorphism" ("isomorphism" is literally "sameness of shape or pattern" [see Chapter 15, § "All done with mirrors?"]). The thought is that secondary ideas may mimic, translate or transmute some pattern or arrangement in the primary qualities: perhaps the pattern that confers on them the power to arouse secondary ideas in observers' minds. But this seems an almost perverse suggestion since it insists there is a kind of similarity exactly where Locke denies finding any himself. In so doing it turns away from what seems the obvious alternative, which is to conclude that in Locke's view resemblance is not what underwrites mental representation.

As we have seen in earlier chapters, the idea that resemblance is what accounts for representation (even pictorial representation) is in general very difficult to defend. Partly this is because everything resembles everything else in some respect or other. The fact that I resemble my daughter does not mean that I am a representation of her or she of me. Resemblance is not *sufficient* by itself to make something a representation of what it resembles. Moreover, even though, as I just said, it is a matter of fact that everything resembles everything else in some respect or other it does not automatically follow that x's resembling y in whatever way it does is a *necessary* condition of x's representing y. The question is whether, and if so how, resemblance to what it represents could (a) bring it about that a particular thing represents another and/or (b) enable that representation to carry out its task of representing its object.

On reflection it is difficult to see what tempts some thinkers to believe that resemblance alone could ever account for one thing's coming to represent another, even pictorially. On the one hand, it is always possible that the most striking similarity where it occurs is accidental. So the line of the rocky cliff top may look like an eagle's profile but it does not thereby *represent* an eagle. On the other hand, the resemblance to its object that an actual representation possesses is seldom enough to persuade anyone that this alone accounts for its being a representation. Think, for example, of a cubist painting of the artist's model where the resemblance between the painting and the model herself may well be very modest indeed. Surely it is something else – the artist's intentions and skill in executing it, perhaps – which makes such a painting a representation of its subject.

So, does Locke think that resemblance to their objects is what makes ideas representations of those objects in thought? Does he think that it is by resembling what they are ideas of that they are able to perform their task as representations? Locke addresses these questions (II.viii.7, 134), and his answer is no. He has been defending his claim that simple ideas are all positive as ideas, even those that represent deficiencies, absences and the non-existent: things that his contemporary philosophers would have called "privations". The ideas of, for example, cold (absence of heat), black (absence of colour) and the shadow of a man (absence of light) are, he thinks, as much positive ideas as are the ideas of heat, white and the man himself. Now Locke says we must guard against thinking that the ideas in our minds are "exactly the Images and *Resemblances* of something inherent in" their objects. Most ideas of sensation in our minds are, he says, "no more the likeness of something existing without us, than the Names, that stand for them, are the likeness of our *Ideas*" (*ibid.*). As Locke tells us in Book III, ideas are natural signs of things while names or words are conventional signs of our ideas. Here he says that ideas no more resemble their objects than words resemble what they signify. For Locke it must be something other than resemblance that accounts for the representationality or "aboutness" of ideas. And this is true despite the fact that he frequently talks as if ideas are images of (and even must resemble) what they are about.

Causation

It is clear that Locke thinks his ideas represent the objects they do – in either the external world accessible to sensation or the inner realm accessible to reflection – because those objects are the original and regular causes of the ideas that represent them. My first experience of a dog causes my idea of a dog. Perhaps numerous childhood encounters give me the same idea repeatedly, thus reinforcing it. That idea is the natural sign or idea representing that dog in my thought. At some point I then form an abstract general idea of a dog by dropping away from that very idea of "that particular dog on a given occasion" all the circumstances of time and place that tie that idea to that one particular and that sensory episode (III.iii.6, 410–11). The result is that, now, when I see any such animal, I recognize it by having the abstract general idea that is the (natural) sign for such things in my mind, that is, the abstract general idea for which the word "dog" is the (conventionally appointed) word.

Locke's view of mental representation amounts to the claim that what accounts for an idea's representing a particular object (or sort of object) in thought is the fact that that object is at the initiating end of a causal chain, the other end of which is the idea of that thing (or the general idea of such things) in my mind. Ideas are the effects of the objects that those ideas thus come to represent.

176

The main difficulty with this is that very obviously not all effects represent their causes. The fire does not represent the short circuit that caused it. So it looks as if causation cannot be *sufficient* to make an effect a representation. Moreover, it seems that ideas can be the effects of things other than the things they represent. My present idea of a house I once lived in may be called into consciousness by hearing a piece of music. Scrooge's idea of his dead partner Jacob Marley may be caused by a fragment of overdone potato.[5] These examples suggest that particular ideas experienced on particular occasions need not represent their immediate causes: that causality is not a *necessary* condition of representation either.

But Locke would doubtless want to say that all *mental* effects *do and must* represent their original causes. The ideas of Jacob Marley and of my old house are memories and we have seen (Chapter 18, § "Consciousness as the principle of identity for persons") that Locke regards memories as somehow literally the original ideas first "conveyed into the mind" (II.i.3, 105) by sensory encounters, which are then subsequently "replayed" or revived by the mind. Whether Locke thinks memory ideas are the same original token ideas or perfect copies of them is not entirely clear. But either way the important point is that memory ideas, however caused or called to mind in the present, retain their causal tie to the initial sensory encounters that originally gave rise to them. So Locke thinks causality is both necessary and sufficient for the representational character of ideas.

Is Locke's causal theory of representation a "covariance" or "reliable indication view", like those introduced in Chapter 10? On such a theory an idea represents what it is the idea of by matching percepts of such things. And a percept is a reliable indicator of such things if it appears in the mind when, only when and because a thing of that kind is present and the subject is in perceptual contact with it.[6] In the example of my old house, I (the conscious subject who has the idea of the house) cannot be in perceptual contact with it: the house is long-since demolished and so could not be perceived now. Nonetheless the present idea does "match" percepts of that house that I had in the past. If Locke were discussing this example he might regard the word "match" as something of a misnomer, since for him percepts simply *are* the ideas that arise in the

---

5. Lennon, "Locke on Ideas and Representation", 250–51. Lennon's use of an incident from Charles Dickens's *A Christmas Carol* seems not to furnish exactly the counter-example he wanted. Dickens's story has Scrooge in real sensory contact with Marley (albeit Marley's ghost) so Scrooge's idea of Marley is in fact caused at the time by what it represents, although of course Scrooge tries to convince himself otherwise.

6. Cummins, *Meaning and Mental Representation*, 37.

mind in sense perception or reflection and can be retained in memory to make later appearances as required in their subject's mental history. On the whole, however, Locke's theory has much in common with a modern-day covariance or reliable indication theory of mental representation. Is it also vulnerable to the objections that have been raised against such theories, in particular the misrepresentation problem and the disjunction problem?

Recall that the misrepresentation problem is the problem that arises because the theory says that an idea represents what it does because and only because it is caused by such things. The idea of X in my mind is a kind of symptom of the presence of Xs. But on this theory I can never have an idea that *mis*represents what causes it. If I have the X idea in the absence of Xs (it being caused on this occasion by a Y) then that idea just represents Ys on this occasion. The fact that it does so may escape my notice: I may wrongly take it to represent Xs. But that is not misrepresentation by the idea; it is misinterpretation by me. The problem is that it should be possible for an idea to misrepresent but this theory does not leave that possibility open and so should be judged wrong or inadequate as a theory of mental representation.

The disjunction problem is closely related to the misrepresentation problem. Here the difficulty arises because what causes one of my ideas may cause an idea that, as Locke would say, does not agree with that thing. I may, for example, perceive what I take to be a cat when it is dark and the creature (in fact a fox) is at the bottom of the garden half hidden in the bushes. I experience my cat-idea but what I am looking at is a fox. Since my idea on this occasion is caused by a fox, should I perhaps say that that idea is about, not just cats, but "cats or foxes-under-these-circumstances"? In other words, it might be suggested that, since both sorts of things can cause the same idea, that idea represents any member of the disjunctive class of "cats or foxes".

It may seem that Locke's views on how ideas represent their objects fall foul of both the misrepresentation problem and the disjunction problem. But Locke has an extra element additional to causation that forms a crucial if less conspicuous part of his account of mental representation and might offer some hope of helping his view avoid these two difficulties. Locke has an explanation of *why* ideas represent their causes and what ensures that they do so. Although there are hints earlier in the *Essay* (and one other summary statement [II.xxx.2, 372–3]), this explanation receives its fullest expression in Book IV, Chapter IV. It is worth quoting the passage at length:

> [S]imple *Ideas*, since the Mind, as has been shewed, can by no means make to it self, must necessarily be the product of Things operating on the Mind in a natural way, and producing therein those

Perceptions which by the Wisdom and Will of our Maker they are ordained and adapted to. From whence it follows, that *simple* Ideas *are not fictions* of our Fancies, but the natural and regular productions of Things without us really operating upon us; and so carry with them all the conformity which is intended; or which our state requires: For they represent to us Things under those appearances which they are fitted to produce in us: whereby we are enabled to distinguish the sorts of particular Substances, to discern the states they are in, and so to take them for our Necessities, and apply them to our Uses. Thus the *Idea* of Whiteness, or Bitterness, as it is in the Mind, exactly answering that Power which is in any Body to produce it there, has all the real conformity it can or ought to have, with Things without us. And this conformity between our simple *Ideas*, and the existence of Things, is sufficient for real Knowledge.

(IV.iv.4, 563–4)

Having said repeatedly that we have no inborn ideas and having also earlier proved to his satisfaction that the mind cannot create a single simple idea for itself, Locke starts off this line of thought by saying that there is only one place left for our simple ideas to come from: they must be "the product of Things operating on the Mind in a natural way". So our simple ideas are natural symbols of those things outside us that operate on our minds through our senses. God has wisely ordained that those ideas we get in sensation, which are produced by regular and stable sensory encounter with external things, will be the un-misleading regular and stable representatives in our thought representing the way those external things really are. As he puts it, our ideas are "constant Effects", which have a "steady correspondence … with the distinct Constitutions of real Beings" (II.xxx.2, 372–3).

So our simple ideas represent what they do because God wishes them to do so. God has ensured that this intention of his is fulfilled, not by giving us innate ideas already representative of external things, but rather by (a) giving us the appropriate sensory equipment and (b) placing the powers in external things to produce veridical sensations in us through those senses so that our ideas are "real" or have a "conformity" with reality. Experience thus furnishes us with ideas that represent faithfully what God intends them to represent. God has done all this so that we may control and get the things we need ("our necessities") from the environment and thereby may thrive and get on with life successfully.

Does this take care of the misrepresentation problem? I have the ideas of white and cold when I have a sensory encounter with a snowball. The purpose

179

or function of my ideas of white and cold is to help me deal with white things and cold things appropriately. And this remains the purpose of these ideas even if they come into my mind in the absence of anything white or cold. So these ideas still represent "what they should", as we might feel inclined to say, even in the absence of their proper objects. They represent their ultimate cause because at the end of the day that is the function God intended for them.

It is much more doubtful whether Locke's account can be made to yield a solution to the disjunction problem, however. What I have been calling "my cat-idea" can sometimes, by some sort of accident, be caused by a non-cat such as a fox. And it is difficult to see a way of ruling out the suggestion that perhaps that same idea is actually intended by God to have the function of representing foxes visiting the garden at night as well as the function of representing cats.

Does the introduction of God's intentions in this way at this juncture undermine Locke's empiricism about our ideas? It seems to me that it does not. Even if the sort of experience we can have is determined by God's wise arrangement of the sources of ideas available to us, the powers in things to cause those ideas in our minds and the sorts of senses and, indeed, minds that created spirits possess, it is still true that our ideas come from experience alone. It may, in a way, be correct to say that for Locke it is up to God what our ideas represent, but it is very much up to us what experiences we have and thus what and how many ideas we have about what and how many subjects, and also how clear and distinct those ideas are.

CHAPTER 21

Minds are the only substances

Berkeley's *Principles* and *Dialogues* together give us a very clear and full picture of Berkeley's metaphysics, a strict idealism, which is spelt out in explicit opposition to materialism: it puts minds and their ideas not just at the centre of its picture of reality but alone there. Minds and mind-dependent items are the only existent (real) things. All the rich variety of natural and man-made phenomena are just that: phenomena, appearances. Physical reality, for Berkeley, consists entirely in various families of ideas of sense that depend for their existence exclusively and entirely on minds. This is not to say that Berkeley does not believe there are bodies. It just means that because bodies are mind-dependent of their very nature, if there were no minds of any kind there would be no bodies either.

The phrase "of any kind" is crucial, for Berkeley recognizes two kinds of minds. His own is a created mind but there is also an eternal mind whose ideas would continue to exist even if all the created minds were expunged. The two kinds of minds differ in what they can do. Both are essentially active and their primary activity is having (or, as Berkeley puts it, "perceiving") ideas. Berkeley tells us that in the case of created minds this idea-having can take the form of willing, imagining, understanding or remembering as well as receiving ideas in sense perception. The eternal mind differs from created minds in, among other things, power of imagination: God alone can create ideas from nothing. On the other hand, God cannot have ideas of sense, at least not in anything like the way we have them.

In contrast with the sheer active nature of minds, the ideas that minds produce, reproduce and combine in all their operations are utterly inert. The causal impotence of ideas is the reason for Berkeley's view that truisms such as "fire heats" and "water cools" are strictly, literally, false. For Berkeley, minds alone have causal power. Thus the scientific study of nature is the study of the rich, vast, complex and law-governed scheme of divinely originated ideas.

Critics often complain that Berkeley's philosophy of mind is too brief or sketchy.[1] And it *is* a pity that he never produced *Principles* Part II, which was to be dedicated to spirit or mind. But it seems to me that this complaint can be exaggerated and that Berkeley's account of the human mind in the *Principles* and the *Dialogues* gives sufficient material to produce a genuine Berkeleian answer to each of the five questions on theory of mind focused on in this book. In this chapter I look first at Berkeley's account of the mind as an active principle. The second section assesses the objection that Berkeley is inconsistent in endorsing immaterial substance while rejecting material substance. The third section considers the question: does Berkeley really subscribe to immaterial substance or does he actually, perhaps secretly, hold a bundle theory of the human mind?

The mind as active principle

Berkeley's firmly stated position in his published works is that the mind, spirit or self (these terms are used interchangeably by Berkeley) is an immaterial *substance*:

> What I am my self, that which I denote by the term I, is the same with what is meant by *soul* or *spiritual substance*.　　　(P§139)[2]

> … spirit or active thinking substance …　　　(P§136)

> Philonous. … I who am a spirit or thinking substance …
> (D III, 231)

In addition to saying explicitly that created minds are substances, Berkeley also says that minds and ideas are radically different sorts of things:

> [A]ll the unthinking objects of the mind agree, in that they are entirely passive, and their existence consists only in being perceived: whereas a soul or spirit is an active being, whose exist-ence consists not in being perceived, but in perceiving ideas and

---

1.　A. C. Grayling, *Berkeley: The Central Arguments* (London: Duckworth, 1986), 155. See Tom Stoneham , *Berkeley's World: An Examination of the Three Dialogues* (Oxford: Oxford University Press, 2002), 213, for a slightly less negative and pessimistic view but on the same lines.

2　References in the style P§139 are to George Berkeley, *A Treatise Concerning the Principles of Human Knowledge*, J. Dancy (ed.) (Oxford: Oxford University Press, 1998).

thinking. It is therefore necessary, in order to prevent equivocation and confounding natures perfectly disagreeing and unlike,
that we distinguish between *spirit* and *idea*.   (P§139)

Principles §2 tells us that "mind", "spirit", "soul" and "myself" are all terms
applicable to the same "perceiving, active being" whose operations or activities include knowing, perceiving, willing, imagining and remembering. We
are also told that the terms "mind", "spirit" and so on "do not denote any
one of my ideas, but a thing entirely distinct from them". Already from §1
we know that the mind has passions and operations to which it can attend,
that human minds have knowledge *inter alia* of ideas gained in sense perception and that the mind is capable of forming novel ideas by compounding,
dividing and representing ideas already in its possession. In the ensuing two
dozen sections of the *Principles* Berkeley spells out many of the operations of
which the mind is capable: having notions and impressions; detecting truths;
conceiving what is possible.

We also learn of constraints the mind is under. It can only conceive likenesses between one idea and another (P§8). Also, its power of abstracting
is strictly limited: only things that *can* "really exist or be actually perceived
asunder" can be conceived of or imagined distinct from each other (P§5).
On the other hand, the mind's contents and operations are, for Berkeley as
for Descartes, Locke and Hume, transparent to the mind that experiences
them. There are no hidden areas in the mind and no ideas (or states) that
the subject has without being able to be aware of them fully (P§7). Berkeley
writes that "since they [our ideas] … exist only in the mind, it follows that
there is nothing in them but what is perceived" (P§25).

The experiential history or "continual succession of ideas" (P§26) of which
I am aware tells me that there is "some cause of these ideas whereon they
depend, and which produces and changes them. That this cause cannot be
any quality or idea or combination of ideas, is clear" from what he has said in
P§25; namely, that "All our ideas, sensations, or the things which we perceive,
by whatsoever names they may be distinguished, are visibly inactive, there is
nothing of power or agency included in them".

Berkeley concludes that since the cause of our ideas "whereon they depend"
is not any quality or idea or combination of ideas, the only remaining possibility
is that they depend causally on *substance*. Since Berkeley takes himself to have
shown that "there is no corporeal or material substance: it remains therefore
that the cause of ideas is an incorporeal active substance or spirit" (P§26).

Berkeley resists any suggestion that incorporeal substance is a complex
consisting of distinct *faculties* such as understanding, will, sense perception

and so forth. For Berkeley, the mind is a single active indivisible substance, now active in this way, now in that: "A spirit is one simple, undivided, active being: as it perceives ideas it is called the *understanding*, and as it produces or otherwise operates about them, it is called the *will*" (P§27). This is in sharp contrast to the nature of the mind's ideas, which possess only an accidental, "bundle" unity and which are "*inert, fleeting, dependent beings*, which subsist not by themselves" (P§89).

Is Berkeley inconsistent?

Throughout the *Principles* and the *Dialogues* Berkeley mounts a relentless attack on the notion of material substance or *substratum*. As we have seen, writers in the early modern period were increasingly sceptical about the notion of substance. But whereas Locke was ironic but ultimately agnostic about the "something I know not what" – whether material or immaterial – Berkeley vehemently denounces the very idea of a material *substratum*. So it seems a natural question to ask whether the arguments that persuade Berkeley that there is no such thing as material substance could not be equally effectively deployed against immaterial substance. Indeed, is Berkeley not being inconsistent in condemning matter while endorsing spirit? Berkeley should be even-handed: a true opponent of material substance would not countenance "spirit stuff" any more than he would tolerate "mind-independent matter".

Berkeley is well aware of this possible line of criticism, however, and has several solid responses to different strands of it. Overall his reply is that the arguments he has raised against material *substratum* will not work against immaterial substance. In the Third Dialogue he pictures Hylas challenging Philonous with this version of the charge of inconsistency:

> You admit … that there is spiritual substance, although you have no idea of it; while you deny there can be such a thing as material substance, because you have no notion or idea of it. Is this fair dealing? To act consistently you must either admit matter or reject spirit. (D III, 232)

Philonous gives a robust reply rooted firmly in the central tenets of Berkeley's idealism. He has five counter-arguments to Hylas's challenge. First, he denies that he has rejected material substance "merely because I have no notion of it". This is true. Berkeley's arguments against matter – or, in the *Dialogues*,

Philonous's versions of them – amount to much more than simply saying that there is no idea of such a thing. Not only could there not be an idea of such a thing (since it is said by friend and foe alike to be imperceptible), but he denies that there could even be a notion or conception of such a thing. For something to be material *substratum* substance it would have to meet incompatible conditions. It would have to support extension without being itself extended. And it would have to *have* sensible qualities (ideas) and yet not be a haver-of-ideas (a perceiver). This is what makes Philonous say of "material substance" that "it is repugnant that there should be such a notion".

As Philonous says: "Many things, for ought I know, may exist, whereof neither I nor any other man hath or can have any idea or notion whatsoever. But then those things must be *possible*, that is, nothing inconsistent must be included in their definition" (D III, 232). And a little later: "In the very notion or definition of material substance there is included a manifest repugnance and inconsistency. … That ideas should exist in what doth not perceive, or be produced by what doth not act, is repugnant" (*ibid.*, 233).

In the second part of his response to Hylas's charge of inconsistency, Berkeley/Philonous holds that lack of a good reason to believe in the existence of a particular sort of thing is itself reason enough to *dis*believe in such entities. And there is no good reason to believe in a material *substratum*: "I have no immediate intuition thereof: neither can I mediately from my sensations, ideas, notions, actions or passions, infer an unthinking, unperceiving inactive substance, either by probable deduction or necessary consequence" (*ibid.*). If intuition, sense experience or inference gave me the idea of a material substance that would be a good reason to believe in such things, but they do not.

Berkeley's third point is that the materialists' assertion that matter must exist because the qualities of physical, sensible objects "cannot be conceived to exist without a support" (D I, 197) is too mysterious. The word "support" here cannot be taken anything like literally, at any rate not without risking a plunge into vicious regress. A pillar may literally "stand under" a part of a building to support it but matter would have to be itself extended in order *literally* to underpin the quality of extension and thus matter's extension would have to have its own *substratum*, which would have to have *its* own *substratum*, and so on (see P§§16–17 and D I, 198).

Fourthly, I may feel I am proving that matter exists if I proceed as follows: (i) I note that ideas turn up in my mind unbidden in sense perception; (ii) I infer from this to the necessity of some *cause* for those ideas outside my mind; (iii) I choose to call that cause – whatever it is – "matter" or "material substance". But this gives us neither a demonstration that the cause of sensory ideas could be a mind-independent thing nor a reason to believe in such an entity.

185

In sharp contrast, "the being of my self, that is my own soul, mind, or thinking principle, I evidently know by reflexion" (D III, 233). Since I have this immediate reflexive knowledge of my own existence and nature, I have the best of reasons for believing in the existence of spirit or immaterial substance.

The fifth answer Philonous offers to the charge of being inconsistent in rejecting material substance while retaining immaterial substance is to point to the contrast between the derisory amount of evidence we have for the existence of unthinking matter and the large support we have for the existence of created minds other than our own. Even granting that "we have neither an immediate evidence nor a demonstrative knowledge of the existence of other finite spirits", nonetheless there is no inconsistency in the notion of another mind as there is in the supposed notion of an unthinking haver-of-ideas. Moreover, experience furnishes a good argument for the probability of other minds where there is no comparable inference in favour of unthinking matter: "we see signs and effects indicating distinct finite agents like our selves, and see no sign or symptom whatever that leads to a rational belief of matter" (*ibid.*).

A bundle theory of mind?

It is not uncommon for students to think that Berkeley ought to conclude (or even that he does conclude) that his mind is a collection of ideas: that Berkeley's notion of the self is similar to the "bundle theory" associated with Hume. After all, Berkeley is at pains to persuade us (for example at P§§25–33) that real things are collections of ideas. And he certainly believes that the individual created mind is a real thing. Also Berkeley's idealist ontology might seem too austere to permit anything other than assemblages (in Berkeley's word, "congeries") of ideas.

Some commentators also feel that it is so obvious that Berkeley should have jettisoned immaterial substance and adopted the bundle theory that he must, despite numerous passages to the contrary in his texts, really (secretly or unofficially) have held a bundle view of the created mind. They question Berkeley's sincerity in embracing the mental dualism of ideas and mental substances in his publications when he seems to have entertained a bundle theory in his private philosophical notebooks. So we need to ask whether Berkeley has really rejected the bundle-of-ideas theory in favour of mental substance. Or is he perhaps hiding his real theory in obedience to some ulterior motive?

Some version of a "secret doctrine" interpretation has been maintained by a surprising number of Berkeley's commentators: surprising because Berkeley's firmly stated position in his published works is that the mind, spirit or self is an immaterial *substance*. Indeed, he says repeatedly that mind is the *only* kind of substance there is:

> From what has been said, it follows, there is not any other substance than *spirit*, or that which perceives ...   (P§7)

> Hylas. ... I freely own there is no other substance in a strict sense, than *spirit* ...   (D III, 262; see also D III, 231)

Nor is there anything that looks like an explicit endorsement of a "bundle of ideas" theory of the mind or self in either the *Principles* or the *Dialogues*. Instead, as we have seen, Berkeley forthrightly presents the "active principle" view in those works. Moreover, he has an answer if asked why he rejects the bundle theory. He says that his knowledge that he *cannot* be simply a bundle of ideas or perceptions comes from careful attention to the difference between perceptions and perceiving. No single thing could both be perceived – that is, be inert and fleeting – and also be capable of perceiving – that is, be able to be the active perceiver in sense perception. No item equipped to fulfil the first role could fulfil the second and vice versa.

If a created mind were nothing over and above its collected ideas then that would leave nothing but, say, sounds and colours to perceive the colours and sounds in the world outside that mind. So when Hylas says: "in consequence of your own principles, it should follow that you are only a system of floating ideas, without any substance to support them" (D III, 233), Philonous replies smartly that he knows "that a colour cannot perceive a sound, nor a sound a colour ... that I am therefore one individual general principle, distinct from colour and sound, and, for the same reason, from all other sensible things and inert ideas" (*ibid.*, 234). A congeries of perceptions is precisely something that is incapable of perceiving. Berkeley is saying that to *be* an idea is to be a kind of thing that cannot *have* an idea.

But what of Berkeley's famous equation of "real things" with "collections of ideas": the student view that minds, being real things, *must* be collections of ideas and nothing else? Well, as soon as we look at the passages of Berkeley's two texts where this equation is made and explained (P§§25–33 and D III, 227–31), it becomes apparent that he is *not* arguing that *all the real things that exist* are collections of ideas. Rather, his position is that sensible objects – the physical bodies, including our own, that make up the public world – are one and all collections of ideas. But he does not say they are the *only* real things.

Contrariwise, Berkeley often seems to warn his readers away from the bundle-of-ideas theory while nonetheless proclaiming that minds are certainly real things. For example, at the beginning of the Third Dialogue, after trying lengthily to persuade Hylas that real sensible things (stones, pens, paper) are nothing over and above the sensations or sensible ideas we actually experience when we encounter them, Philonous says:

> The mind, spirit or soul, is that indivisible unextended thing, which thinks, acts, and perceives. I say *indivisible,* because unextended; and *unextended,* because extended, figured, moveable things, are ideas; and that which perceives ideas, which thinks and wills, is plainly it self no idea, nor like an idea. Ideas are things inactive, and perceived; and spirits a sort of beings altogether different from them. I do not therefore say my soul is an idea, or like an idea.
>
> (D III, 231)

It is difficult to read this as anything other than the straightforward declaration that individual created minds are not ideas or idea-collections but rather perceiving (willing, thinking) active beings, wholly unlike any ideas or idea sets. If this is not his real view then Berkeley is either seriously confused or lying to his readers. My own view is that neither of these verdicts can be made credible.

But of course someone could disagree: some commentators are reluctant to accept Berkeley's explicit declarations on this subject because it appears Berkeley himself was, at one time prior to the publication of the *Principles*, tempted by the picture of the individual created mind as a collection of ideas very like a Humean bundle-self. The following two passages come from Berkeley's philosophical notebooks, in which he made cryptic notes and tried out philosophical ideas:

> Mind is a congeries of Perceptions. Take
> away Perceptions & you take away the Mind
> put the Perceptions & you put the mind.   [580]

> Say you the Mind is not the Perceptions. but
> that thing which perceives. I answer you are
> abused by the words that & thing these are
> vague empty words without a meaning.   [581][3]

---

3. The philosophical notebooks are published as *Philosophical Commentaries*, in George Berkeley, *Philosophical Works including the Works on Vision*, M. Ayers (ed.) (London: Everyman, 1975), 375.

Berkeley did not intend or prepare these notebooks for publication and it is difficult to know which of the entries (if any) express his settled conclusions. Naturally they are of interest to scholars tracing the development of his thought and commentators looking for help interpreting the published works. On the present topic, however, there is such a contradiction between notebooks and publications that the cautious choice seems the only respectable interpretative option. Berkeley's rough and private jottings are mysterious and enticing. But we ought to trust as his real and settled view what he committed to the press.

We should also remember that, although he never produced Part II of the *Principles*, Berkeley did prepare a second edition of Part I, in which – far from resuscitating an early "bundle of ideas" theory or inserting pointers to a hidden one – he strengthened both the immaterial substance view and his defences of it from the charge of inconsistency. Surely, if his real view was the bundle theory he would have dropped some hints, not added support for the "active principle" view.

But perhaps he was hiding his real view of mind out of some ulterior motive? The thought here is that, as a young cleric with high ambitions in the church, Berkeley suppressed his (supposed) disbelief in immaterial substances or souls.[4] However, this suggestion is difficult to take seriously. It portrays Berkeley as afraid to express the eccentric and possibly heretical view that there are no substantial souls, yet prepared to publish, twice in quick succession, detailed accounts of the creator's sensible world as immaterial and wholly lacking in causal power. Had Berkeley feared that unorthodoxy or eccentricity would block his professional advancement, and had that advancement been his first priority, he would never have published his *Principles* or *Dialogues* at all.

The picture of Berkeley as presenting an immaterial substance account of minds in his published works, all the while disguising actual allegiance to a bundle theory, not only libels him as dishonest and deceptive, but also badly distorts his position. Berkeley sees created minds as the sole created *agents*. Ideas, as all of us know from our own experience, are dependent things. They come into, and are sustained in existence only by, the consciousness that has them. In Berkeley's famous phrase, "Their *esse* is *percipi*" ("their being is to

---

4. Robert G. Muehlmann, "The Substance of Berkeley's Philosophy", in his *Berkeley's Metaphysics: Structural, Interpretive, and Critical Essays*, 89–106 (University Park, PA: Penn State University Press, 1995). See also his *Berkeley's Ontology* (Indianapolis, IN: Hackett, 1992), ch. 6. For an opposing view see William H. Beardsley, "Berkeley on Spirit and its Unity", *History of Philosophy Quarterly* 18 (2001), 259–77.

be perceived, to be thought of or thought up"). So the created minds Berkeley recognizes must be entities capable of active agency and their nature must be as far as possible from that of mind-dependent inactive ideas.

Postscript: is "mental substance" just a figure of speech?

Finally, it is sometimes suggested that Berkeley does not intend us to take his active principle view *literally*. Perhaps he means his readers to regard the terms "immaterial substance" or "spirit" metaphorically, like "attraction" in physics or "grace" in theology. Or perhaps he regards them as non-observational or theoretical terms: terms that do not denote anything that can be encountered in experience but are given meaning by the scientific theory in which they are embedded.

Although these are interesting suggestions, considerations of space mean that I shall merely mention them here[5] and say that I do not feel that either offers convincing reasons to think that Berkeley was not a realist about immaterial substance. As we shall see in the next chapter, Berkeley regards his stated view that created minds are immaterial substances as the unambiguous product of the self-knowledge gained inescapably in all our conscious experience.

---

5. But see James W. Cornman, "A Reconstruction of Berkeley: Minds and Physical Objects as Theoretical Entities", *Ratio* 13 (1971), 76–87.

CHAPTER 22

What do we know about our own minds or selves?

This chapter defends the view that – in the case of at least one substance, namely his own – Berkeley believes he has direct immediate knowledge that that immaterial substance exists and what it is like as the support and cause of (his) ideas and perceptions. He would have rejected emphatically Hume's sceptical contention that introspection reveals only the perceptions currently occurring in the mind, never a persisting self that has those perceptions (see e.g. P§137). But this interpretation of Berkeley as a firm believer in self-knowledge derived from immediate experience of the self in reflection has been challenged. George Pitcher, for example, argues that Berkeley thinks we have no direct self-knowledge and that we know immediately about ourselves only that "a persistent subject of mental activities and haver of ideas is a demand of reason".[1] To assess Pitcher's position I shall try to discover what exactly Berkeley means by "reflection". But first I want to look at Berkeley's view that we have no *idea* of immaterial substance.

We have no idea of immaterial substance

It might be thought – indeed, Hylas is portrayed as thinking it – that Berkeley/Philonous is in no position to claim knowledge of immaterial substance since he admits he has *no idea* of it. In fact, he does not just admit, but says categorically, that the contrast between minds and ideas is so sharp that there can be no idea of mind or incorporeal substance. This is because an idea, for Berkeley, is an "image or likeness" of the thing of which it is an idea. And no wholly inert, inactive thing can be the image or likeness of (and thus represent) a wholly active one (P§27).

---

1. George Pitcher, *Berkeley* (London: Routledge, 1977), 221 (and see 211–24).

However, although Berkeley never considers for a moment that there could be an *idea* of mind, nor does he concede that lack of an idea of mental substance is any impediment to knowledge of it. When Hylas suggests that lack of an idea of God may be an insuperable obstacle to knowledge of God, Philonous makes this forthright response:

> I own I have properly no idea, either of God or any other spirit;
> for these being active, cannot be represented by things perfectly
> inert, as our ideas are. I do nevertheless know, that I who am a
> spirit or thinking substance, exist as certainly, as I know my ideas
> exist. Further, I know what I mean by the terms *I* and *myself*; and
> I know this immediately, or intuitively, though I do not perceive
> it as I perceive a triangle, a colour, or a sound. The mind, spirit or
> soul, is that indivisible, unextended thing, which thinks, acts and
> perceives.   (D III, 231)

Berkeley has already insisted in the Introduction to the *Principles* that "he that knows names do not always stand for ideas will spare himself the labour of looking for ideas, where there are none to be had" (P Introduction §24; see also P§89). Here he prudently heads off both the suggestion that if he has no idea of his mind it follows that he cannot have knowledge of it and the possible complaint that if there is no idea of mind the terms "mind", "spirit" and the rest cannot have any meaning. Neither for understanding the words "spirit", "mind", "incorporeal substance" and so on, nor for having knowledge of the thing signified by those words, do we need – nor could we obtain – an *idea* of mind.

Moreover, we do not gain our self-knowledge in the way in which ideas are acquired:

> [O]ur souls are not to be known in the same manner as senseless
> inactive objects, or by way of *idea* ... We may not ... have an idea
> of an active being, or of an action, although we may be said to have
> a notion of them. I have some knowledge or notion of my mind,
> and its acts about ideas, inasmuch as I know or understand what is
> meant by those words. What I know, that I have some notion of.
>   (P§142)

To have knowledge or a notion of something other than "by way of idea" is, at a minimum, to know the meanings of the words that denote the thing in question. But it is much more in the case of mind or spirit: within the first few pages of the *Principles* Berkeley has credited created minds with capacities for upwards of twenty types of mental activities of which he has empirical knowledge simply by being conscious of his own mental operations and experiences. Four of these types of mental activity are mentioned in the Third Dialogue, where Philonous says "I know or am conscious of my own being; and that I myself am ... a thinking active principle that perceives, knows, wills, and operates about ideas" (D III, 233).

Berkeley, like Descartes, thinks we can know *a priori* "that the soul always thinks" (P§98), that perpetual actual occurrent thought (rather than simply the capacity to think) is the essence of mind. As we know, Descartes says that matter's essence is obviously actual extension and, by the same token, mind's essence is thinking: it makes no sense to talk of the rational soul existing but with no mental activity. For Berkeley too, mind is wholly and perpetually active. He concludes with heavy irony: "in truth, whoever shall go about to divide in his thought, or abstract the *existence* of a spirit from its *cogitation*, will, I believe, find it no easy task" (P§98).

But if our self-knowledge of spirit does not consist of ideas and is not acquired in the way ideas are acquired how *do* we come to have this knowledge? Berkeley says: "We comprehend our own existence by inward feeling or reflexion, and that of other spirits by reason. We may be said to have some knowledge or notion of our own minds ... whereof in a strict sense we have not ideas" (P§89). And "the being of my self, that is, my own soul, mind, or thinking principle, I evidently know by reflexion" (D III, 233). These passages, and several others in a similar vein, were added to the 1734 editions of the *Principles* and *Dialogues* to reinforce less explicit remarks and to amplify and clarify where perhaps the earlier editions had courted misunderstanding by being too sketchy or tentative. In the first edition of the *Principles*, for example, Berkeley had mentioned reflection in connection with the absolute impossibility of having any idea of the soul or spirit (§27). But reflection is brought in there only in a negative and roundabout way. Reflection will show any reader that an idea of spirit is impossible to form:

> [L]et him but reflect and try if he can frame the idea of any power or active being; and whether he hath ideas of two principal powers, marked by the names *will* and *understanding*, distinct from each other as well as from a third idea of substance or being in general, with a relative notion of its supporting or being the subject of the aforesaid powers, which is signified by the name *soul* or *spirit*.
>
> (*Ibid.*)

This too is ironic: Berkeley is sure reflection will reveal that we could not possibly frame an *idea* of agency, power, activity, understanding, will or substance: all parts of the signification of the terms "spirit", "mind" and so on.

This is because ideas are all inert and passive; no idea could stand as an image or likeness of an agent. Berkeley is as certain as Hume will be that sense experience can furnish us with no impression or idea of power, agency or necessary connection. But unlike Hume, Berkeley does not think agency an illusion or fiction. He concludes instead that agency is definitely real and that our knowledge of both its reality and its nature is provided, not by sensation ("I do not perceive it as I perceive a triangle, a colour, or a sound" [P§89]), nor by reason ("that of *other* spirits [I know] by reason" [*ibid.*, emphasis added]), but by reflection: that kind of inward consciousness that can be used to discover whether we can frame this or that idea or not and what particular mental capacity we are exercising.

Reflection and self-knowledge

What has been said so far is bound to seem insufficient. To get a fuller picture of what Berkeley means when he says he knows himself through reflection or a reflex act this section will look at the following questions: Is reflection: a kind of inner sense that furnishes us with notions instead of ideas; a sort of reasoning that allows us to infer the existence of spirit from the knowledge that we have ideas which require a mind's support in order to exist; intuition that furnishes the subject with knowledge of the self-evident truth that he exists and is a mind or spirit; a kind of "unmediated knowledge by acquaintance"?

Is reflection inner sense?
There is a view held by a number of commentators[2] that Berkeley (whether knowingly or not) employs the term "reflection" in two distinct senses. In the first suggested sense, reflection is introspection whose objects are one's passions (roughly, emotions) and mental operations. It is passive and involuntary like the outer senses and it yields knowledge that the reflecting subject cannot fail to know. In the second sense, reflection is an active operation of

---

2. S. C. Brown, "Berkeley on the Unity of the Self", in *Reason and Reality*, Royal Institute of Philosophy Lectures, Volume 5, 1970–71, G. N. A. Vesey (ed.), 64–87 (London: Macmillan, 1972), and Pitcher, *Berkeley*, 212ff.

the mind, which is thus subject to the will. It yields knowledge that is non-inferential: intuitive certainties that, nonetheless, a subject can fail to appreciate until such time as he attends properly to their certainty. And we can find passages in which Berkeley appears to use the vocabulary of "reflecting" and "reflection" in each of these two putative senses. Reflection as a kind of passive operation might seem to be what is referred to when Philonous talks of the possibility of getting an idea by reflection or reason if not by sense (D I, 197). Also, in the *Principles*, Berkeley mentions "ideas, whether of sense or reflexion" (P§25). Reflection in this sense would be a source, like the outer senses, of *ideas* (see also P§§13 & 35).

Reflection in the second, active, sense seems to come in two types. The first, for example, occurs when Philonous says that Hylas knows himself "by a reflex act" (D III, 232) and when Berkeley says both that we "comprehend our own existence by … reflexion" (P§89) and also that this knowledge of the existence and nature of an active principle or spirit is knowledge of a *notion* not an idea. Then there is a *second* sort of active reflection when it is used as a philosophical tool. For example, Berkeley concludes his argument that bodies "have not any subsistence without the mind" by urging that the reader "to be convinced of which … need only reflect and try to separate in his own thoughts the being of a sensible thing from its being perceived" (P§6). Active reflection, then, yields either knowledge of one's own existence and nature, or knowledge of what ideas are possible and what genuine (coherent) conceptions can be formed.

It might be thought that the appropriate name for at least the first of these suggested Berkeleian senses of "reflection" (or "introspection") would be "inner sense" by which the subject examines his mind and what goes on there. But we should be extremely wary of assimilating reflection – certainly where the two second sorts of reflection are concerned – to inner sense. This is for the very good reason that Berkeley considers this very thought and rejects it: "It will perhaps be said, that we want a sense (as some have imagined) proper to know substances withal, which if we had, we might know our own soul, as we do a triangle" (P§136). Here Berkeley explicitly considers the suggestion that, if only we had the right sensory apparatus for detecting and examining them, we would not be ignorant of our own souls as people commonly think we are.

But any such new sense, Berkeley then says, would only give us "new sensations or ideas of sense" just as the old senses do. And, as we have seen, he is fully convinced that there can be no idea of an immaterial substance or mind. So no new (or quasi-) sense could give us immediate self-knowledge. No idea could "be the image or likeness of" a spirit, so such a new sense could not even give us indirect or "mediate" knowledge of our selves. No idea, however novel its sensory provenance, could stand for a spirit or mind.

195

So "inner sense", since it carries just the implication of *sensory encounter with its object* that Berkeley here rejects, cannot be the correct term for the kind of Berkeleian "reflex act" that provides direct, immediate knowledge of the existence and nature of our own minds. Moreover, the putative second sort of reflection – whether pure self-awareness or the sort of philosophical activity whereby I attend to my thoughts and passions and learn which ideas and mental operations are possible – is clearly regarded by Berkeley as a voluntary mental *activity*.

What about the so-called first sense of "reflection"? Does Berkeley really recognize – in addition to the two sorts of active reflection just outlined – a passive reflection that furnishes ideas rather than notions? Those passages cited above in which Berkeley mentions ideas "whether of sensation or reflection" recall Locke in the *Essay* talking about ideas acquired when the mind "turns its view inward upon it self and observes its own Actions about those *Ideas*" (*Essay* II.vi.1 & II.vii [title], 127–8). These few Lockeian passages in Berkeley seem mysteriously out of kilter with the emerging picture of reflection as a source not of ideas but of notions: not passive but active. And when we look carefully it becomes apparent that these places where Berkeley might seem to consider reflection as a possible idea source are all ones where he is rejecting some position of Locke's: when he is arguing that no such idea could be acquired by either sensation or reflection. That Berkeley asserts that the equally despised "abstract idea of unity" and "idea of material *substratum*" cannot be obtained by reflection is no evidence that Berkeley thinks reflection a source of ideas. He is precisely saying that these are bogus ideas unobtainable from any source.

I would say that Berkeley does employ the term "reflection" in two senses but these are the two sorts of active, notion-furnishing reflection distinguished above. Occasional Lockeian language notwithstanding, Berkeley does not think that self-awareness is ever a source of ideas. Reflection is in no way a passive, sensory source of knowledge. Rather, it is either some sort of non-sensory immediate contact with oneself or an active attending to and reasoning about the mind's passions and operations.

Is self-knowledge the product of inference?
There comes a point in the Third Dialogue where Philonous takes himself to have succeeded in disproving scepticism about the external world of sensible things:

> What a jest is it for a philosopher to question the existence of
> sensible things, til he have it proved to him from the veracity of

> God; or to pretend our knowledge in this point falls short of intuition or demonstration? I might as well doubt of my own being, as of the being of those things I actually see and feel.   (D III, 230)

Berkeley is saying through his spokesman that Descartes and Locke are both wrong about our belief in the external world of sensible things. Descartes is wrong to think we need be certain that there is an undeceiving God before that belief can be known to be true. Locke is wrong to assert that that belief falls forever short of both intuitive and demonstrative knowledge. Belief in the existence of sensible things is as certain as the most certain knowledge there is: the knowledge of "my own being".

From this we *also* know that Berkeley thinks the certainty of his own existence is so secure that for it, too, it would be absurd to suggest that it must wait on a successful proof of God's existence (or anything else). That certainty is as immediate and trustworthy as any intuition or demonstration on offer. It follows that Berkeley feels under no requirement to prove his own existence. As he says "I ... know, that I who am a spirit or thinking substance, exist as certainly, as I know my ideas exist" (*ibid.*, 231).

That said it seems evident that Berkeley's thought here shares much with Descartes's *cogito*. His certainty that he exists is based on his immediate awareness of his ideas. Now if there are going to be *ideas* to be aware of (Descartes would add, "even self-doubts"), there must be a thing of the sort that can bring ideas into being: that is, a mind. And for there to be an *awareness* of ideas there must be a thing of the sort that can receive or be aware of ideas: that is, a mind. Moreover, if the awareness of ideas that I am sure exists is *mine* then the mind on which both awareness and ideas depend is obviously me. So Berkeley can, without further ado, simply assert that he knows that he – an immaterial substance – exists:

> [B]esides all that endless variety of ideas or objects of knowledge, there is likewise something which knows or perceives them, and exercises divers operations, as willing, imagining, remembering about them. This perceiving, active being is what I call *mind, spirit, soul* or *my self.*   (P§2)

Later, in both the *Principles* and the *Dialogues*, Berkeley will say that this self-knowledge of his own existence as an active principle is given him by reflection or "a reflex act". So it might seem very plausible to conclude that self-knowledge through reflection is, for Berkeley, an inference from the existence of ideas and perceptions, via the major premise that ideas depend for their existence on minds, to the existence of the mind or perceiver required to sustain those ideas in existence.

However, Berkeley also says a number of things that undermine the view that reflection is for him some kind of inference. So, for example, the passage from the *Dialogues* continues: "Farther, I know what I mean by the terms *I* and *myself*; and I know this immediately, or intuitively, though I do not perceive it as I perceive a triangle, a colour, or a sound" (D III, 231).

And a little later Philonous says, "My own mind and my own ideas I have an immediate knowledge of" (*ibid.*, 232). Something known "immediately" and "intuitively" would seem a very inappropriate candidate to be inferential knowledge.

This tension between an "intuition interpretation" and an "inference interpretation" may feel familiar. It is very reminiscent of the tension between the view that Descartes's *cogito* is an intuition and the view that it is a product of inference. Descartes staunchly maintains that *cogito ergo sum* is no inference but something known intuitively, something the mind can grasp in a single mental grasp. He defends his position by saying that the proposition "in order to think a thing must be" is a truth that provides part of the ground for "I think therefore I am" but is not a premise in a deduction. I do not think of that proposition when I rehearse the *cogito*. Berkeley, likewise, regards his foundational truth ("sensible ideas need a mind to support them") as something on which his knowledge of his own existence rests in some way; but that way is not as a premise from which the conclusion that he exists is inferred.

Is reflection a kind of intuition that furnishes self-evident truths?
When Berkeley has Philonous say "My own mind and my own ideas I have an immediate knowledge of" (D III, 232), we might naturally think this says that each individual mind has immediate awareness of itself and its ideas. Pitcher urges us to read it differently as saying only that: "[Berkeley] has an immediate knowledge of *the fact* that his mind and its ideas exist, or an immediate knowledge of *the truth* of the proposition that his mind and its ideas exist".[3] To support his reading, Pitcher cites the Third Dialogue (*ibid.*) where Berkeley says that knowledge gained from discursive reasoning such as inference is "mediate". He argues that this implies that "immediate knowledge" must mean for Berkeley "knowledge gained without recourse to inference or any other kind of discursive reasoning". And such knowledge, Pitcher concludes, "must be obviously or self-evidently true". Why? Because know-

---

3. Pitcher, *Berkeley*, 215, emphasis added.

ledge must be either the product of reasoning such as inference or else self-evident: that exhausts the possibilities.

But this holds only if the knowledge in question is knowledge of propositions. And nothing compels us to view Berkeley's self-knowledge gained through reflection as propositional. A "reflex act" is a turning back on oneself, a kind of self-encounter. It is more likely that he regards it as a species of what might be called "knowledge-by-acquaintance" rather than a species of "knowledge that". In which case, we would not expect the immediacy involved to be that which is opposed to the mediacy of inference. Rather, we would expect it to be the immediacy of unimpeded contact.

Pitcher thinks Berkeley has specifically excluded the mind from his "survey of the objects of human knowledge" (P§1) at the beginning of the *Principles*, when he says, "besides all that endless variety of ideas or objects of knowledge, there is likewise something which knows or perceives them … This perceiving, active being is what I call … *my self*" (P§2). To Pitcher this suggests that Berkeley divides reality into two *mutually exclusive* categories: "objects of direct awareness" and "something which knows or perceives them", that is, the mind.[4] But is it likely that Berkeley, if he had set up such a dichotomy and denied that minds can be the objects even of their own direct awareness, would then have said, in the 1734 edition of the *Dialogues*, "I know or am conscious of my own being" (D III, 233), and in the 1734 edition of the *Principles*, "We comprehend our own existence by inward feeling" (P§89)?

And, anyway, if Berkeley intended to make a division of reality into two mutually exclusive categories in Section 2 of the *Principles*, these would surely have to be minds or knowers and objects of knowledge, not just objects of direct awareness. But this would mean that nothing whatever can be known of minds; they are simply not objects of knowledge. But Pitcher is (rightly) committed to the view that Berkeley thinks we *do* have propositional knowledge about our minds. If he is right in this then he is wrong in his interpretation of Section 2 of the *Principles*.

Reflection as unmediated knowledge-by-acquaintance of the self
If Berkeley's self-knowledge is not restricted to intuition of self-evident truths about minds or to propositions produced by inference, what *does* Berkeley mean when he says I know myself "by a reflex act"? Philonous tells Hylas that he knows his own nature by reflection and that that known self is a spiritual substance: "How often must I repeat, that I know or am conscious of

---

4. *Ibid.*, 219.

my own being; and that I my self am not my ideas, but somewhat else, a thinking, active principle that perceives, knows, wills and operates about ideas …" (D III, 233). Here he says explicitly that the self-knowledge delivered by reflection is "conscious[ness] of my own being". This consciousness, in other words, furnishes him with direct intuition or knowledge of himself, not just knowledge of propositions that must be true of him. A page earlier, Berkeley had Philonous say: "all the notion I have of God, is obtained by reflecting on my own soul heightening its powers, and removing its imperfections". And, again, "My own mind and my own ideas I have an immediate knowledge of" (*ibid.*, 232).

In these lines Berkeley/Philonous says that reflection gives access to the self, soul or mind, which is adequate to make the subject aware of its own powers and imperfections. This access is also there described as "immediate" or "intuitive". So here we have the final answer to the question: does Berkeley's reflection furnish a kind of intuition? The answer is that it does furnish an intuition, one that has something in common with Descartes's "single mental grasp" intuition of the *cogito*. But this intuitive self-knowledge is not Pitcher's "intuitive knowledge of self-evident truths". Rather, it is the immediate or intuitive grasp of the nature of an individual encountered *without any intermediary*.

In the First Dialogue, Philonous explains to Hylas what "immediately sensed" means. It is what is sensed "without the intervention" of other things. An author makes the reader aware of his subject matter by means of intermediaries: letters on the page. In sensation there is no intermediary. The senses give unmediated access to the sensible objects known as ideas (D I, 174). Of course, we have already ruled out that reflection is any sort of inner sensation for Berkeley. But reflection is *analogous to* sensation in being a kind of access where no intermediary is involved. I know my mind and its activities by a reflex act, an episode of consciousness in which no intermediary stands between me and myself.

It is the absence of any kind of intermediary between me as object of knowledge and myself as self-knower that Berkeley wants to stress when he declares the inadequacy of ideas to represent minds. Closer still than the best imaginable close observation, the self-knowledge gained by self-consciousness has the immediacy of *participation*. This reflexive self-awareness has not even the slight distancing that a knower has from the certainty of a known self-evident, obvious proposition. It has the even greater immediacy of a person's knowledge that he is having the experiences that he is having and exercising the mental powers he is exercising. Berkeleian self-knowledge is thus something built into the conscious life of every conscious subject and, as such, available to be appreciated at any moment at which it is consciously adverted to.

A spirit's self-knowledge is something unique. Only a mind can be both knower and its own object. If Berkeley fails to mention the mind on his list of the objects of knowledge in Section 1 of the *Principles*, this could simply be because he wants first to make a sharp split between inert ideas and the active minds in which those ideas appear. Only after his readers have adjusted their thinking to Berkeley's matterless world, where nothing exists except minds and their contents, will Berkeley explicitly remind us of what we knew all along: that we know not only what is going on in our minds but the self whose goings-on they are, in each of our conscious experiences.

CHAPTER 23

What is the nature of consciousness for Berkeley?

I concluded in the previous chapter that Berkeley means by "reflection" a kind of acquaintance or contact that is neither a species of inner *sense* nor any sort of inference nor the intuition of self-evident truths. This reflection gives intuitive knowledge of the self or mind in both broad senses outlined in the Introduction: it gives us knowledge of our own existence as minds, as supporters of ideas and thoughts, by giving us direct knowledge of our own, individual mental operations. I have, in reflection, awareness of the existence of the individual doing the reflecting (myself) and also awareness of the activity of reflection among the many other mental activities happening simultaneously in the same subject.

In reflection, as Philonous says, I am conscious of my own being: as a single, active principle, constantly acting. So, if we want to see what conscious experience is for Berkeley and how he might have addressed recent modern problems about consciousness we should continue to look at the role of reflection in his account of mind and the self. Arguably (and less cautiously), Berkeley's "reflection" just is, or at least overlaps significantly with, "consciousness" and perhaps "a reflex act" could without distortion be paraphrased as "self-consciousness".

What accounts for the phenomenal character of experience?

At least one reason for caution here is easily explained. We have seen in previous chapters that present-day philosophy of mind boasts a wide array of different definitions of "consciousness" and different accounts of the nature of consciousness and conscious states: they range from higher-order-thought or monitoring theories through causal and phenomenal accounts to protestations of the impenetrability of the mystery of consciousness. Most, however, share a feature that Berkeley's theory of mind completely lacks. Present-day theories of mind and consciousness are predominantly materialist theories. For them, mind is nothing over and above matter. Conscious states depend wholly for their existence and entire character on the existence and nature of appropriate matter, suitably arranged. They are thus vulnerable to the threat that subjectivity can appear to pose to any materialist view of mind. The subjective or phenomenal character of experiences, the "what it's like" of, for example, tasting lemon or seeing blue, have seemed to some to elude scientific theory, to lie outside even the complete set of physical facts that would be recognized by an ideally complete science.

But, of course, Berkeley does not think that mind (spirit) depends on the physical for its existence. There could be no such thing, on Berkeley's view, as consciousness supervening on or being caused by anything physical. That he believes this is obvious from his metaphysical position in general. For him, the matter of the philosophers is a fiction. The real physical things that he readily agrees *do* exist – such as his own body and all of the natural and man-made environment around him – are, one and all, collections of ideas, thus utterly causally inert.

Berkeley denies explicitly that conscious sensory experience depends on the brain or could be explained in terms of it. He has Philonous smartly reject Hylas's suggestion that there is something "so natural and intelligible in the modern way of explaining … [and] accounting for our sensations and ideas". Asked to explain what that modern account is, Hylas answers with a quick, fairly crude version of a view that should sound familiar from the earlier discussion of Descartes's account of ideas of sensation. Hylas says:

> It is supposed the soul makes her residence in some part of the brain, from which the nerves take their rise, and are thence extended to all parts of the body: and that outward objects by the different impressions they make on the organs of sense, communicate certain vibrative motions to the nerves; and these being filled with spirits, propagate them to the brain or seat of the soul, which according to the various impressions or traces thereby made in the brain, is variously affected with ideas.   (D II, 208–9)

Philonous condenses this to a brief formula, telling Hylas that his view amounts to taking "certain traces in the brain to be the occasions and causes of our ideas", a view that Philonous immediately denies could explain anything. The brain is by common agreement a physical, sensible object. That means that it is a collection of ideas: something that exists only in the mind and cannot cause anything.

Even if Hylas reverts to his view that imperceptible material *substratum* (the matter of whatever is being sensed) is what causes the sensing subject's ideas, this will not save his theory of the origin of such ideas. For now those ideas are apparently being caused by something Hylas *imagines* to be at work, supporting the sensible qualities, namely a *substratum* substance. But, as Philonous hastens to point out, imaginary things (including the materialists' imagined *substratum*) are causally impotent just as much as any other mind-dependent ideas. Brains are ideas; sensible things are ideas. So neither can be what causes or produces ideas in a mind.

When Hylas expresses his embarrassment at having previously been taken in by this modern theory, Philonous closes that discussion as follows: "this way of explaining things ... could never have satisfied any reasonable man. What connexion is there between a motion in the nerves, and the sensations of sound or colour in the mind? or how is it possible these should be the effect of that?" (D II, 210). It might be thought that Berkeley is here offering only the old argument that mind and body are so different in nature from each other that we cannot conceive how a thing of the one sort could interact with a thing of the other sort.[1] Certainly the second question in the quote would seem to be making precisely this point.

But I wonder whether there is not, in the first query, the suggestion that Berkeley may be thinking of the question: what could possibly explain the fact (if it were a fact) that a certain "motion in the nerves" is associated with a particular experienced quality rather than any other? Indeed, Berkeley seems to me to go further here. For the question "What connexion is there between a motion in the nerves, and the sensations of sound or colour in the mind?" seems clearly a rhetorical one. Berkeley is saying there is and could be no intrinsic connection between a particular sensation with its particular specific phenomenal character and any supposed physical underpinning or cause (e.g. motion in the nerves) of that sensation. This is very reminiscent of the point made by David Chalmers, Robert Kirk and numerous others that there is an "explanatory gap" between physical states and conscious mental states that is impossible to remove.[2] Suppose that we had the most detailed

---

1. Dancy's "Notes to the Second Dialogue", in Berkeley, *Three Dialogues*, 164 n. 3.
2. Joseph Levine, "Materialism and Qualia: The Explanatory Gap", *Pacific Philosophical Quarterly* 64 (1983), 354–61; David Chalmers, *The Conscious Mind* (Oxford: Oxford University Press, 1996); Robert Kirk, *Raw Feeling: A Philosophical Account of the Essence of Consciousness* (Oxford: Oxford University Press, 1994), see esp. 4 for introduction of the term "intelligibility gap". See also David Papineau, *Thinking About Consciousness* (Oxford: Oxford University Press, 2002), ch. 5.

correct scientific account conceivable of the physical, causal mechanisms by which sights or sounds or smells are received by our bodily organs and delivered to our minds. Why should *that* physical arrangement or system go with any particular subjective experience rather than any other?

I think Berkeley is here arguing from the existence of an intelligibility or explanatory gap to the falseness of the theory that creates the gap. If, on a materialist theory of experience, there is good reason to conclude that there could never be an explanation of why one sort of brain set-up or mechanism went with hearing birdsong while another went with seeing red then, Berkeley would say, surely we should look altogether elsewhere for the causes of the ideas or sensations of birdsong, red and all the rest, in our experience. And Berkeley has a ready alternative that he thinks vastly superior. An intelligent agent who puts just those ideas with just their qualities into my mental stream is, for Berkeley, a far better explanation than the materialist's for the phenomenal character of my experiences.

Berkeley's theory is that God supplies and maintains my sensory ideas and those of every other created mind:

> The ideas of sense are more strong, lively, and distinct than those of the imagination; they have likewise a steadiness, order, and coherence, and are not excited at random, as those which are the effects of human wills often are, but in a regular train or series, the admirable connexion whereof sufficiently testifies the wisdom and benevolence of its Author. Now the set rules or established methods, wherein the mind we depend on excites in us the ideas of sense, are called *the Laws of Nature*: and these we learn by experience, which teaches us that such and such ideas are attended with such and such other ideas, in the ordinary course of things.
>
> (P§30; see also P§36)

The two cited passages make abundantly clear that Berkeley believes that the regularities that our experience – with just the phenomenal character it has – teaches us to ascribe to nature, calling them "the laws of nature", are actually properly attributable to the wisdom and omnipotence of God. There is no independent nature over and above the activities of the divine mind.

We might object (as Berkeley imagines someone objecting at P§60) that, if God is ultimately or immediately responsible for each and every one of our sense perceptions then a good deal of what we see and what happens in nature is in fact redundant. Why does God not simply give us visual ideas of plants in full flower, or alternatively laden with fruit, from time to time? Why must gardeners labour throughout the growing season? Why must plants contain their subtle (but normally invisible) internal structures? Berkeley's response is that God presents us with the whole collection of sensory ideas that will allow us to understand, predict and to some extent control, on the basis of previous experience, what experiences we will have. To be such guides our experiences must be governed by a vast complex of mutually supporting rules: the natural laws that experience tells us all phenomena obey. Likewise, there must be complex inner plant structures for the gardener to nurture and the botanist to discover with his microscope.

A more wounding objection might be that Berkeley's "divine ideas" account is far less plausible than materialism, even admitting the materialist's inability to explain why subjective experiences (the taste of lemon, the feel of cashmere) have just their characteristic phenomenal feel. For, to begin with, Berkeley's God seems very heavily burdened: providing sense experiences at every instant to every one of the innumerable created minds. Remember that Berkeley subscribes to the doctrine of "perpetual thought": the Cartesian view that the mind is literally always having ideas, the majority of which are sensory ideas.

Berkeley would agree that the image of God as "run off his feet" supplying a vast population with all their unending sense perceptions *is* ridiculous. But this is not for the objector's reason. Rather, it is absurd because it forgets that God is omnipotent. Constant "exciting" of ideas in created minds is not a burden to one capable of creating minds in the first place (see P§151–2). Robert Fogelin gives us a very good analogy when he points out, in another context, that Berkeley's God is like a cosmic internet provider.[3] Only twenty years or so ago the idea of instant simultaneous transfer of ideas and text from innumerable points on the globe to innumerable *other* points might have seemed like a wild flight of fantasy. Nowadays we take it for granted that this is occurring night and day all over the world. Berkeley would be quick to point out that "omnipotence" really means just that. There is no reason to think that an all-powerful being would lack the capacity and resources – the technology – to make light work of the task Berkeley envisages him performing.

However, someone might protest that this still does not deal with the real philosophical problem. How does even a divinely powerful mind produce ideas in another mind? We might be prepared to agree with Berkeley's view that ideas are mind-dependent entities: that it takes "being thought up by a

---

3. Robert J. Fogelin, *Berkeley and the Principles of Human Knowledge* (London: Routledge, 2001), 76.

mind" for an idea to exist. I can sustain an idea in existence just by thinking of it. But try as I might I cannot put an idea directly into another person's mind simply by willing it or concentrating really hard. So how does Berkeley think God contrives that ideas of sense perception appear in the minds of perceivers?

Commentators disagree about what (if any) answer Berkeley gives to this question. On the one hand, passages such as Section 26 of the *Principles* strongly suggest that he believes that God does in fact somehow insert ideas into our minds individually, one at a time, appropriate to every individual sensory experience of every created mind. So, many readers conclude that Berkeley's God "excites" ideas in us directly and without any intermediary. On this view it is simply a brute fact about the divine creative capacities that God is able to create, not just spirits, but their conscious sensory ideas. Recall that Berkeley says that he is aware that ideas imprinted on the senses "are not creatures of my will" (P§29). Passages such as the following undoubtedly also support this reading: "visible ideas are the language whereby the governing spirit, on whom we depend, informs us what tangible ideas he is about to imprint upon us" (P§44).

On the other hand, some readers take particular note of what Berkeley says in both the *Principles* and the *Dialogues* about the rich variety of the public, interpersonally available sensible world (e.g. D II, 210–11). These passages suggest that Berkeley need not, and perhaps does not, regard God's role in our sense perception as a piecemeal affair of individual divine fiats. Rather, he often writes as if he believes that there is a sort of divine structure of sensory ideas arranged according to the rules we call natural laws that is somehow available to created minds in sense perception in somewhat the way that the material world is thought by materialists to be.

Again, the analogy of the internet is one that might seem to shed some light on Berkeley's views for us, although, obviously, it was not available to him. Berkeley clearly does not believe that the public world, both natural and man-made, is a persisting *material* complex if by that is meant a realm of things each consisting of an unknowable *substratum* in which sensible qualities inhere, whatever that is supposed to mean. But it is possible that he believes in the public world as a complex *ideal* structure sustained in existence by the divine mind and available to all perceivers through the operation of their created minds, somewhat in the way that the internet is available to all those with the appropriate equipment for logging on.

I have just sketched two very different versions of what Berkeley may think is God's role in the sense perception enjoyed by created minds; neither, it must be said, seems sufficiently convincing or robust to put materialism, even with all its problems, conclusively into the shade. Moreover, both suggestions about the role of God in sense perception are, and can only be, offered as candidates for "best explanation" of the divine role in the origination of sensory ideas in a matter-free world. The two proposals, therefore, cannot both be correct. Is either superior to the other in its capacity to explain the origin of our sense perceptions?

Perhaps unfortunately for Berkeley, neither version seems definitively superior to its rival. The one proposal is for constant intervention by God. The other, is for an ideal immaterial structure permanently available and accessible to created minds. Each has problems to overcome. The "constant intervention" proposal, as some of Berkeley's contemporaries pointed out, may seem to show God in a poor light as unable to create an independent world where created minds can carry on their lives of sensory experience without continual massive and incessant input from the creator. The "permanent ideal structure" proposal raises worries about what this structure is. (Is it some arrangement of ideas or archetypes in God's mind?) Also there is the question how it is sustained and made available to be accessed by all created minds. (Are our ideas of sense *copies* of God's ideas? If so, how does he make them available to be copied and how do we copy them?)

Compounding the difficulties just described, there is also the problem that Berkeley sometimes says the mind is passive in sense perception whereas he also says the mind is pure activity: an "active principle" that is ceaselessly willing and understanding and wholly unlike inert impotent ideas (e.g. P§27). If sense perception is some sort of reception of divine ideas it is surely *passive*. So, just to the extent that Berkeley thinks sense perception is passive, the "constant divine intervention" account of perception may seem what he should plump for. But just to the extent that sense perception is some kind of active apprehension or copying of divine archetypes, the "permanent ideal structure" proposal may be the right interpretation. It is possible that Berkeley finds himself unable to decide between these two rival accounts. He may have hoped to produce some sort of amalgam of the two. If so, there seems little textual evidence that that hope was realized.

Is Berkeley's view of consciousness a form of "higher-order-thought" theory?

The preceding section sprang from the suggestion that the principle contrast between many present-day accounts of consciousness and Berkeley's lies in the fact that most present-day theorists do, while Berkeley decidedly does not, regard matter as the metaphysical foundation of mind and conscious experience. There may, however, be some similarity between what Berkeley says about the relationship between conscious awareness and self-consciousness and what some present-day writers have to say about that relationship. To some, it has seemed that there is a striking resemblance or overlap between contemporary "inner awareness" or "higher-order thought" views of consciousness and Berkeley's reflexive self-consciousness.

On a higher-order-thought view, remember, there is a crucial difference between mental states and activities that are, and those that are not, conscious. The conscious ones are the mental states of which I am aware in self-consciousness. So seeing red is a conscious state of mine if – when I look into my own mind to see what activities are taking place there – I am aware that one of my present mental activities is seeing red, having a red sensation. If I have (or could have) the thought "I am seeing red" or "It is red that I am seeing" then my sensation of red is a conscious sensation. Such a thought, displaying as it does both self-awareness and understanding of the concept of red, is a thought of a "higher order" than the mere sensation of red, which becomes conscious only when I am aware of it in self-consciousness.

This very brief summary reminder of a "higher-order-thought" or "inner-monitoring" view of what makes a mental state conscious might seem to have much in common with Berkeley's view that individual minds can know themselves by a reflex act and also that the self that is known in reflection is an active agent experiencing an endless flow of ideas, perceptions and notions. I said earlier that Berkeley's self-knowledge gained in reflective self-awareness has the immediacy of *participation*. I know what I am seeing and hearing, feeling, willing, understanding, remembering, imagining, thinking and so on simply by realizing or focusing attention on what is going on in my mind, what mental activities I find myself actively engaged in.

But those activities are the (already, in themselves) conscious ones of seeing, hearing, feeling, willing, understanding and so forth. Berkeley has no inkling of the view that there might be ideas of any kind that are in a mind but not consciously so. In fact, quite the contrary: just like Descartes and Locke he believes that there is no such thing as unconscious or non-conscious thought, perception or feeling. The mind is always thinking and there is nothing in the mind of which the mind is not aware.

So, to return to the example of seeing or sensing red, we should ask: is it, for Berkeley, my reflexive awareness of what mental activities I am actively engaged in that makes those mental activities conscious ones? Once the question is formulated, however, it seems plain that the answer is no and that Berkeley does not have a higher-order-thought theory of consciousness. For

Berkeley nowhere says or implies that it is my reflective self-awareness that *makes* the sensations and ideas I find myself having into conscious ones. Rather, having ideas or mental contents is "all one as to perceive" (P§7). In reflection I discover certain already conscious sensations and ideas. When I reflect, I cannot avoid the knowledge that this or that conscious sensing, feeling, remembering, imagining and so on is taking place in me.

Someone might well object that – whatever he may wish – Berkeley cannot have both the truth of the doctrine of mental transparency (the view just mentioned that there is nothing in the mind of which I am not conscious) and also the truth of the view that reflection can help me to *discover* which ideas are, and which ideas are not, possible for me. Either there is mental transparency or there is not. Surely for Berkeley there should not be any such thing as *discovering* in reflection that certain ideas I thought were in my mind (such as the idea of *substratum* substance, say) are not there after all.

Berkeley would say that despite appearances his position is actually consistent. At any time, any idea, notion, thought or emotion I have is conscious. However, at any given moment we are also involved in experiencing some or all of the following: sense perceptions across the full range of sensory modalities; emotive reactions to what we sense; endless acts of will; understandings; memories; imaginings; numerous other conscious activities.

So reflection meaning something like "discriminative attention" may be needed for the subject to home in on a particular conscious idea or notion in the whole field of mental activity available to reflective self-awareness. And possibly the same directed attention may be needed, in the hurly-burly of daily conscious experience, to experiment and conclude that a certain idea does not, or could not possibly, appear in the mind. The point of all this is that, while Berkeley insists that all ideas in the mind are perceived and thus in some way conscious or available to their subject, some ideas are more "visible" than others to the spirit having them.

When he asks us to "reflect and see ..." whether or not we can form this or that idea or conception he is asking us to apply our discriminative attention to our ongoing mental activities and also to govern them or intervene to the extent that we can. He is sure we can direct the mind to produce ideas of certain things, always assuming such ideas or concepts are genuinely possible (i.e. coherent) ones. We know we can do some such directing and intervening because we have memory and imagination each of which is an ability to "replay" ideas, or at least to produce ideas that represent the ideas which sensation has furnished in the past (P§1).

So, in a way reminiscent of Descartes, Berkeley holds that some of our conscious perceptions and ideas are very much at the forefront of consciousness and others need to be highlighted before we are fully aware of them. Then again some putative ideas require to be looked for before we can assure ourselves of their – as it turns out – inevitable absence. There are no hidden corners in the mind where wholly unconscious ideas could be hiding but that does not mean that all corners are equally illuminated all the time.

CHAPTER 24

Berkeley's problem of mental causation

This chapter considers the possibility that Berkeley is trapped in an acute problem of mental causation that results from the fact that God is the source of all sensory ideas, a problem that initially seems strongly analogous to the intransigent "physical exclusion problem" discussed in earlier chapters. Before turning to this uniquely Berkeleian problem, I shall look briefly at Berkeley's way of dealing with more familiar versions of the question whether mental states or events can have physical effects.

Causation across the metaphysical divide

We have seen that, at first approach, the problem of mental causation can seem just another form of the dualists' heterogeneity problem. How could two utterly metaphysically heterogeneous things such as a mind and a body interact causally? In particular, how could a non-physical thing cross the metaphysical divide and exert a physical force or produce a physical effect? How could a mental item such as being thirsty, regarded as a state or event in a Cartesian immaterial mind, possibly move a subject's physical body?

Now Berkeley's created minds certainly share many features with Cartesian immaterial minds. But Berkeley is no dualist. He does not think that a metaphysical divide separates created mind and body. If I am thirsty and move my hand to pick up a glass this is not to be construed as something mental (my thirst) causing something non-mental (my hand moving). So Berkeley is unencumbered by the traditional dualists' problem of mind–body interaction. Indeed, he boasts that one of the great advantages of adopting his immaterialism is that to do so is to escape the "difficulties … and endless disquisitions" of trying to explain "the manner how two independent substances, so widely different as *spirit* and *matter*, should mutually operate on each other" (D III, 258).

212

Berkeley can also readily dispatch Elisabeth's problem. Recall that this is the question how matter (e.g. my body) can be moved by a cause lacking extension and the ability to push. Berkeley would say that this is a problem only if my body is something extended and material. But there is no such thing as material substance. My body is not material: it is a collection of ideas. And what better than a mind to move and manipulate ideas?

The physical exclusion problem

Alas, even where dualism is rejected and there is no metaphysical divide between mind and body the physical exclusion problem still needs to be addressed. Present-day philosophers of mind who worry about mental causation are predominantly monistic materialists. But their conviction that reality is of only one metaphysical type does not relieve them of the desire or the obligation to explain how mental states and events can be efficacious as such, given the causal closure of the physical. Dualists and convinced materialists alike feel uncomfortable at the suggestion that the brain state that initiates a particular physical movement does so entirely in virtue of its physical properties and not in virtue of any of its mental ones. Surely it is common sense that it is my thirst – in so far as it is just that *feeling* – that causes me to drink, or again that it is my *beliefs* that make me vote as I do. Surely mental items as such can and do cause actions.

It might seem that the physical exclusion problem poses less of a threat for a Berkeleian idealist than for a monistic materialist. After all, Berkeley, like Leibniz, holds that there is no such thing as real causal interaction between *bodies*. For him, bodies, although real, are collections of ideas, and ideas are, as he says, inert: "the very being of an idea implies passiveness and inertness … it is impossible for an idea to do any thing, or, strictly speaking, to be the cause of any thing" (P§25). It follows that the only kind of cause that exists, is mind or spirit (D II, 102; P§102).

So surely Berkeley does not believe in or feel threatened by the causal closure of the physical realm? For him, no body (= collection of ideas) is ever moved by another body (= another collection of inert ideas). Far from there being a complete physical cause of any piece of my behaviour that would exclude the causal agency of my mind, my behaviour has *no* physical causes whatever.

On Berkeley's view, I reach for the glass of water when I am thirsty *because* I will to do so. The mental cause producing my behaviour is my will. And I will to do so because I am thirsty. Nor does this mean that my will is determined by the feeling of thirst (which is an inert idea). Rather, my willing in this way is the result of my understanding my needs and wants and choosing to satisfy them. For Berkeley, "will" and "understanding" are just two names for the same thing: mind, spirit, soul or self. In the created world, wills or understandings are the only active causes or agents. Or, rather, they are the only agents other than God.

So why does God create a phenomenal world, a complex natural world, which appears governed by scientific, causal laws? When it appears to us that physical bodies interact with each other or that a physical thing causes, via a sense organ, a sensation in a created mind this "connection of ideas does not imply the relation of *cause* and *effect*" but rather the relation of sign to thing signified: "The fire which I see is not the cause of the pain I suffer upon my approaching it, but the mark that forewarns me of it" (P§65; see also P§32).

These apparently causal regularities enable us to understand and control our world. So they help us to thrive. But they also have the ultimate purpose of "convincing our reason of [God's] attributes by the works of Nature" (P§63). God would rather, Berkeley says, that we understood God's wisdom by appreciating the order, end-directedness and wise contrivance of the world presented by the senses than try to "astonish us" into an appreciation of him by means of frequent miracles interrupting "the ordinary series of things".

So actually Berkeley does (again like Leibniz) believe in the completeness of science and a sort of apparently causal closure of the bodily creation. For God to have and sustain this natural law-governed order in existence, he must and does bind himself to sustain the entire fabric of all created minds' sensible ideas in a perfect meshing structure of what we might be tempted to call a "virtual reality" governed by scientific laws. The whole of what each of us perceives must be *as if* there were a material world of interacting bodies governed by scientific law and affecting our sense organs to produce our sensory experience. This apparent law-governed natural world is God's way of giving created minds a realm in and on which their own understandings, wills and creative powers can operate.

Berkeley's problem of mental causation

But this is where the threat of a Berkeleian version of the problem of mental causation arises. For Berkeley, if I am thirsty and decide to drink what actually happens first is that, in response to my will, my hand reaches for the glass. Strictly and in more detail, this means that I cause, by willing, a change in the cluster of ideas constituting my hand. The ideas of my fingers are rearranged so as to shape them to grasp the glass. Those sensory ideas also change position in my visual field relative to the ideas of my arm, the rest of my body, the surrounding furniture and the glass of water. And, of course, the ideas in the sensory fields of all created minds observing must alter appropriately. Now, ordinarily, when I voluntarily lift a glass I would not say that I am aware of accomplishing this by consciously willing changes among my sensory states, still less by willing the alteration of my watching friend's sense perceptions. What I will is the movement of hand, arm, glass and contents. How could a mental act of mine literally cause a change in another created mind's ideas? But Berkeley would say that, of course, my act of will does not, nor could it, bring about a change in the observer's ideas directly, by some sort of telepathic control. Instead Berkeley thinks that I bring about changes in the ideas in others' minds by willing my body to move in ways that result in changes in the public world available to others' sense organs.

To many readers it has seemed that this is the point where Berkeley unwittingly creates his own inescapable immaterialist version of the mental causation problem: for how *can* my act of will move my body? Berkeley draws a sharp distinction between ideas that are, and those that are not, creatures of my will:

> I find I can excite ideas in my mind at pleasure, and vary and shift the scene as oft as I think fit. It is no more than willing, and straightway this or that idea arises in my fancy: and by the same power is obliterated, and makes way for another ...   (P§28)

Whereas

> I find the ideas actually perceived by sense have not a like dependence on my will.   (P§29)

Put these two pronouncements together with the following principle:

> [T]he ideas imprinted on the senses by the Author of Nature are called *real things* ...   (P§33)

and it would seem that, for Berkeley, ideas that are under the control of my will are all fancies while real things, otherwise known as sensory ideas ("the ideas actually perceived by sense"), are not under the control of my will. So it seems to follow that Berkeley must hold that all changes in my ideas that are under the control of my will are works of my imagination and thus imaginary and thus not real physical changes. On the other hand, since God ("the Author of Nature") produces the changes of ideas that occur in me when, for example, I will to lift a glass and immediately see the glass and my hand rising, it is actually God alone who does the lifting.

A number of commentators[1] have hammered home the unfortunate implication. On this account, if I will to pick up the glass I cannot get further than simply imagining doing so. If I have a perception of my hand lifting the glass this cannot be because of anything I have done (i.e. it cannot be *because* I willed to lift it). It can only be because God lifts both hand and glass, perhaps in accord with my wish.

As Ayers puts it, Berkeley offers no explanation of:

> the difference between voluntarily imagining one's leg moving and voluntarily moving a leg. Worse, no coherent explanation could be offered, since in the latter case the ideas that constitute the leg-movement would have to be both voluntary and, being real, involuntary.[2]

Tom Stoneham makes the point that there is actually no incoherency in regarding my leg movement as being constituted by both involuntary ideas (those of an observer) and voluntary ones (mine when I am willing the leg movement).[3] But, as he hastens to add, this seems not to solve the problem. If I too am perceiving my leg's movement – and how could I not be, at least through bodily feeling? – my ideas that constitute that movement are sensory ones and, as such, passive and not under the control of my will. It seems that no movement of my body perceived by me could be under the control of my will. So my mind cannot make any changes to the physical world. Voluntary action for created minds is an illusion.

---

1. J. Foster & H. Robinson (eds), *Essays on Berkeley: A Tercentennial Celebration* (Oxford: Clarendon Press, 1985), Introduction, 1, 16, 17; C. C. W. Taylor, "Action and Inaction in Berkeley", in *Essays on Berkeley*, Foster & Robinson (eds), 211–25; Ayers's Introduction to his edition of Berkeley, *Philosophical Works*. Stoneham, *Berkeley's World*, 178–200, has a convincing reply to Ayers and to Taylor.
2. Berkeley, *Philosophical Works*, Editor's Introduction, xxxi.
3. Stoneham, *Berkeley's World*, 193–4.

Power to created minds

This is obviously not the conclusion Berkeley had hoped for. It seems that I am impotent. I can only form ideas and hope that God will bring about what I have imagined. This is not because of weakness of will in any conventional sense. But just as the modern-day physicalist holds that the whole system of physical causes and effects is closed and complete so that it is difficult to see how a mental cause could intervene, so, in Berkeley's immaterialist system, the divine will – although certainly a mental cause – seems to allow of no others.

"Because it is what God wills" would seem, for Berkeley, to be the only genuine cause of every change that happens anywhere. We might christen this Berkeleian problem of mental causation "the problem of the universality of divine mental causation". How could any created spirit be the cause of any physical change when it looks as if all such changes are actually effected by God's will?

In the Third Dialogue, Hylas presses Philonous on the subject of personal responsibility: "You are not aware, Philonous, that in making God the immediate author of all the motions in Nature, you make him the author of murder, sacrilege, adultery and the like heinous sins". This produces the following two responses from Philonous:

> [S]in or moral turpitude doth not consist in the outward physical action or motion, but in the internal deviation of the will from the laws of reason and religion. This is plain, in that the killing an enemy in a battle, or putting a criminal legally to death, is not thought sinful, though the outward act be the very same with that in the case of murder. Since therefore sin doth not consist in the physical action the making God the immediate cause of all such actions is not making him the author of sin.
>
> Lastly, I have no where said that God is the only agent who produces all the motions in bodies. It is true, I have denied there are any other agents beside spirits: but this is very consistent with allowing to thinking rational beings, in the production of motions, the use of limited powers, ultimately indeed derived from God, but immediately under the direction of their own wills, which is sufficient to entitle them to all the guilt of their actions.
>
> (D III, 236–7)

Here Berkeley/Philonous offers two considerations to counter any critic who baulks at the suggestion that all physical movements are ultimately caused by God. The first is that we would have no real reason for regret if we *were* strictly impotent in the physical world. Sin never consists in "physical action". Behaviour is sinful when it is the outward sign of a sinful will. We do not punish or criticize accidents in the absence of wicked intent or culpable negligence. Only "internal deviation of the will from the laws of reason and religion" is morally deplorable and merits punishment. So our literal impotence and God's activity on our behalf would neither make God open to blame for shameful acts nor get us off the hook if it were the case that, having willed evil deeds, they were performed, not by us, but by God.

It seems to me questionable whether God could be obliged to perform heinous acts on our behalf or could be acquitted of blame if he did. But whatever its merits as a way of defending God from moral criticism, this first point would be compatible with acceptance of the view that created wills are impotent to produce their own, real changes in the physical world. At this stage Philonous might seem to be accepting that, in the end, God alone is an agent.

On the contrary, Philonous's second point is designed to show that created agents have genuine potency. Berkeley here says that God *delegates* to us some of his power to will (and thus cause) changes in the physical world. God, after all, is capable of creating not just ideas but also minds. Why should he not be able to endow those created minds with (albeit limited) power to alter the ideas that constitute the real world?

Here is one suggestion of why this might be beyond God's reach. What makes the contemporary problem of mental causation intransigent is the causal closure of the physical realm, the fact that every physical happening has a full physical causal history that appears to leave no room for the intervention of a mental cause. Just in an analogous way, someone might argue, in Berkeley's system God's will operates everywhere and at all times. Every apparent causal interaction in the physical world comes about only because of God's unbroken will to sustain obedience to the laws of nature throughout the sensible realm. Again, God alone is responsible for "exciting" all the ideas of sensible real things, or of alterations in those real sensible things, in the minds of those who perceive them. This seems to leave no room for agency or intervention by a created will.

Now one crucial feature of causes is that they are things whose non-occurrence would have prevented the happening of what was caused. Without God's willing that all sensible objects continue to appear to obey natural law, and without his activity in exciting the requisite ideas in perceivers, whatever past happening we pick as an example would not have come about. So Berkeley's God is the cause of every happening in the physical world.

218

Or so it might appear. However, there is a second crucial part to the notion of a cause. Not only is a cause something whose non-occurrence would have prevented the happening of the exact effect caused, but it is also the case that something is a cause only if, given that it is present, the effect does in fact occur. But in any particular case where a created will wills to act (say, to lift a glass) Berkeley thinks the lifting would not occur unless the created spirit willed it. God's ceaseless activity to sustain continued obedience by the sensible world to the laws of nature would *not* be *enough* to ensure that exact lifting of my glass unless God also excited the perceptual ideas of its lifting in my mind and the minds of other perceivers. But this would not happen unless I also willed it to happen.

In other words there is a crucial *dis*-analogy between the problem of mental causation generated by the causal closure of the physical realm and the "problem of universal divine mental causation". The physical exclusion argument says bodies move as a result of physical causes alone, apparently *irrespective* of subjects' thoughts, feelings, desires and beliefs. Mental items (as such) are neither necessary nor sufficient to produce any physical happening. For Berkeley, however, the unbroken activity of God's will in sustaining natural law is a necessary part but it is not sufficient for those happenings we call human actions. There is something additional that my will alone provides. If I did not will to lift the glass it would not be lifted and, given that I will to lift it, it is lifted. That is enough to make me *the* cause of that action. Indeed, it could be said that God's role here is only to provide a background condition rather than a cause.

We can now see why Berkeley/Philonous says that created spirits are entitled "to *all* the guilt of their actions" rather than saying that they share the blame with God. Some commentators, for example Jonathan Dancy, have suggested that the relationship between God and man, where voluntary action is concerned, is a kind of collaboration or joint action.[4] And if God is a collaborator or accomplice then he should share responsibility and guilt for human sins and crimes just at Hylas suggests. In any true collaboration the collaborators are agents sharing a single set of aims or will and sharing credit or blame for what they perform together. Think, for example, of workers collaborating to clear rocks from a field by dragging them using a rope. All those who pull simultaneously on the rope deserve a share of the credit for whatever success results. Other sorts of project may require different sorts of

---

4. Dancy's "Notes to the Third Dialogue", in Berkeley, *Three Dialogues*, 174 n. 24. See also Stoneham, *Berkeley's World*, 195–6.

activity from the various collaborators, each agent deserving a proportionate share of the credit (or blame) for what is accomplished.

But remember that Berkeley is suggesting in the passage above that God *delegates* power to created minds so that, as he says, "thinking rational beings, in the production of motions, [have] the use of limited powers … immediately under the direction of their own wills". On this view, God does not share power in the sense of doing part of the work. Rather, he surrenders (some of) his power for use by someone else: a created spirit. If I borrow a bulldozer the lender is not a collaborator who should share the blame for my shoddy work. His machine is under the direction of my will alone. I am wholly responsible for the results. When I act, my will moves my body and effects changes in the physical world, not with God's help but using the admittedly limited power that God has delegated to me.

But it will still be asked how exactly I can exercise that delegated power. I said above that when I will to reach for the glass I must, among much else, alter the ideas that constitute my hand. And critics are quick to point out that those constitutive ideas (of sensation) can be excited in my mind or anyone else's only by God. To the critic, it appears that if God creates or excites the sensory ideas that constitute any willed change in my body then he is actually the only agent in the case. At the least he seems to be a collaborator, not just a power delegator.

The answer to this is to repeat that the arm movement that happens when I will it has numerous background conditions, including God's activity in bringing about the change in appearances. But I would say that God is not an agent in the action of moving my arm at all. He would be an agent or a collaborator only if he willed the movement of my arm and it does not seem to me that Berkeley is committed to the view that God does so will. God does the moving only in the sense that the bulldozer does the moving. The bulldozer is not an agent. It does not will the results achieved in using it. And God is not an agent where the action that is "my moving my arm" is concerned. As I have said repeatedly, the new sensory ideas God produces when I move my arm are results of both his unvarying will to sustain the physical world's obedience to the laws of nature and his choice to put some of his power under the immediate direction of my will. He is an agent in producing these two ends but not in the action of moving my arm.

Is Berkeley's view here a variety of occasionalism? Recall that this is the view (introduced briefly in Chapter 14) that our decisions and choices result in the movement of our bodies only because, when I will my body to act or move in a certain way, God steps in and makes my body move as I have willed. It seems to me that Berkeley's position differs from occasionalism because he holds that God has granted individual human beings the limited power to move their bodies themselves. Yes, Berkeley believes that God somehow ensures that I and others will have the ideas of sense appropriate to my body's movements when I move but he is convinced that I am the one who moves my body on each occasion, not God.

It is time to look again at Ayers's worry that Berkeley offers no explanation of "the difference between voluntarily imagining one's leg moving and voluntarily moving a leg". I hope it is now apparent that Berkeley could and should reply that he never said that all real ideas are *wholly* involuntary in every respect or in exactly the same sense. Although ideas of sensation are not dependent on my will to the same extent or in the same way as the ideas of my imagination (they "have not a like dependence on my will" [PS29]), I do have indirect, conscious control of a kind over some of them. I can end my sensory ideas of this room's walls by leaving the room. I can will to move my leg and thus ensure that some of the ideas of sensation that I and my neighbour experience (passively, involuntarily in that sense) are no longer ideas of a stationary leg but new ideas of a moving one. I will my neighbour's idea of my leg moving: it is my willing my leg movement that (indirectly) results in his seeing that movement. No such sensory idea arises for him if I only *imagine* moving my leg.

It might be objected that this interpretation reduces God to the role of will-less tool or servant of human actions: a derogatory view of God alien to Berkeley's beliefs. But Berkeley's wise and benevolent God has as an overriding intention to preserve the vast scheme of ideas constituting his natural creation for the good of mankind. Also, it is God's will that created spirits be able to exercise their wills and be genuine agents in the world. So he must always continue to excite in men's minds all the ideas that constitute the sensible objects and qualities that make up his physical, natural world. And he must do so in perfect accord with both the successful acts of will of created minds and the laws of nature, which he uses to communicate with the spirits he has created. God can only achieve this end if he undertakes to be a tool of the wills of created minds in all their genuine actions. And although it is certainly the case that Berkeley thinks God would scorn to employ an instrument himself to achieve any of his ends (D II, 219), he nowhere says that it would be in any way a failing or imperfection if God, in appropriate contexts, were to offer *himself* as an instrument.

CHAPTER 25

What is Berkeley's theory of mental representation and intentionality?

Berkeley's rejection of Locke's view

It should be said at the outset that there is no evidence that Berkeley ever set out specifically to explain where intrinsic intentionality comes from. Like Locke he is sure that there are no innate ideas. But how those of our acquired ideas that represent anything come to do so is not a question Berkeley addresses as such. Still, like Locke, he has a – largely implicit – theory of what accounts for the intentionality of mental states. And that theory, like so much in Berkeley's thought, can be seen as arising as a result of his rejection of Locke's position.

For a start, Berkeley obviously rejects Locke's view that the ideas I receive in sense perception represent mind-independent material objects that cause those ideas in me. Such a view opens the possibility of perceptual error and illusions resulting from a mismatch between the perceiver's ideas and the way the objects or events that those ideas represent *really are*, independently of any mind. If the particulars that cause my ideas somehow fail to cause ideas that accurately represent the items that cause them I might be irremediably misled about the nature of extra-mental reality. Locke did not see this as a very serious problem for his position. But Berkeley and readers ever since have seen this picture of how ideas represent the world and therefore might *mis*represent it as a sceptic's charter. How can anyone claim to know with certainty anything whatever about the things our senses seem to inform us about? It is always possible that an idea given in sense experience may be a false representative. As Hume will argue in *A Treatise of Human Nature*, the idea of "knowledge of the world" becomes just a hollow one since it is *in principle impossible* ever to verify that our sense perceptions really match their supposed (mind-independent) causes. For all we know, there may not even be any mind-independent causes.

Berkeley styles himself, perfectly sincerely, the great enemy of such scepticism. So he rejects strenuously the whole philosophical position that seems to make it inescapable. He takes Locke's view to say that the ideas the senses supply are mere representatives in the sense of intermediaries or go-betweens, bearing news about the external world to the mind, which cannot ever have, for itself, unmediated contact with that world. Berkeley thinks the only way to defeat such scepticism is to deny the existence of a gulf between a world of sensible objects and a world of ideas. For Berkeley, as we have seen repeatedly, there is no such thing as a mind-independent realm. Sensible objects are constituted somehow by ideas of sense. This means that, for example, Snowdon is constituted by sensory ideas. It also means that when I view Snowdon I am having an immediate experience of that very mountain: I am not experiencing some mental representatives of that mountain.

Ideas of the imaginary and ideas of absent things

What about when I am not viewing that mountain but remembering it many miles away? Where do the ideas that represent those things I am not at present perceiving come from and how do they come to represent the absent but mind-dependent realities that Berkeley takes the physical world to consist of? If those ideas of absent things are products of my mind, how are they to be distinguished from the merely imaginary?

As we saw in Chapter 24, Berkeley certainly wishes to distinguish ideas of the imagination in the sense of "fictions" or "fancies" from ideas that occur when I am, as I would say, "sensing a real thing". Philonous tells Hylas:

> The ideas formed by imagination are faint and indistinct; they have besides an entire dependence on the will. But the ideas perceived by sense, that is, real things, are more vivid and clear, and being imprinted on the mind by a spirit distinct from us, have not a like dependence on our will. ... In short, by whatever method you distinguish *things* from *chimeras* on your own scheme, the same, it is evident, will hold also upon mine. (D III, 235)

And in the *Principles*, Berkeley replies to an imagined objector who asks:

> What must we think of houses, rivers, mountains, trees, stones; nay, even of our own bodies? Are all these but so many chimeras and illusions on the fancy? ... I answer, that by the principles premised, we are not deprived of any one thing in Nature. Whatever we see, feel, hear, or any wise conceive or understand, remains as

secure as ever, and as real as ever. ... the distinction between realities and chimeras retains its full force. (P§34)

I can test whether ideas I have are realities or not by means of two criteria:
first, lack of voluntary control by me over their arrival in my mind; and,
secondly, their vividness ("strong, lively, and distinct") and – as they appear
over a period of time – their lack of randomness as a series ("steadiness,
order, and coherence" [P§30]). In other words, if the ideas appeared in my
mind without my willing them to appear and if they have a distinctive vividness and also form an orderly series in such a way as to imply obedience to
the laws of nature, they are real things. These are ideas that are *constitutive* of,
for example, the tree I see or the birdsong I hear.

In contrast, Berkeley says that:

> I find I can excite ideas in my mind at pleasure, and vary and
> shift the scene as oft as I think fit. It is no more than willing, and
> straightway this or that idea arises in my fancy: and by the same
> power it is obliterated, and makes way for another. This making
> and unmaking of ideas doth very properly denominate the mind
> active. (P§30)

So a *test* of whether an idea is real or not is to check whether its appearance in my mind was entirely a matter of my willing it to be there. If my will
was responsible for its appearance then it is *not* a real thing. It is, of course,
a perfectly real idea. But it is not an idea that is partly constitutive of a real,
publicly accessible thing. On the other hand: "The ideas imprinted on the
senses by the Author of Nature are called *real things*; and those excited in the
imagination being less regular, vivid and constant, are more properly termed
ideas, or *images of things*, which they copy and represent" (P§33). This says
that ideas of sense are real things. It also talks about "ideas excited in the
imagination", which *copy and represent things* (the real things mentioned
earlier in the quotation).

In Sections 26–33 of the *Principles* Berkeley has been principally concerned
to head off the possible objection (discussed directly in P§34ff.) that, in
equating physical things with collections of ideas, he is obliterating the line
between the imaginary and the real and making everything imaginary. So (in
P§33) he insists that he draws that line as firmly as everyone else but between
two different sorts of ideas: those that are excited in my mind by God and
those that are excited in my imagination by an exercise of my own will. The
real things (whether or not we have a handy test to prove that this is the case!)

are the ideas caused by God. Fictions are ideas – particularly complex ideas, like that of a chimera – which we cause ourselves. Then, almost as an afterthought, Berkeley makes clear that, for him, not all the ideas in the imagination are fictions. In fact ideas used in the production of new ideas by the imagination are images of real things.

We need to pause over this point to try to understand exactly what Berkeley is saying here. For Berkeley, the ideas that are "excited in the imagination" make their appearance owing to my will. Some of them are, as we would say, ideas *of* fictions, for example, an idea of a chimera or of a dragon. Some of them are, again in common-sense terms, ideas of real things, for example, my ideas of Snowdon, my house, the Thames and the apple in my lunch box. But my will cannot create ideas "from scratch" so to speak. All the ideas that I can call up at will are copies of ideas – or made up of collections of copies of ideas – that have originally been excited in my mind in sensory experience by God. So my idea of a chimera consists of ideas such as those of a lion's head, of a goat's body, of a snake and of a tail and so on, all of which ideas come from past experience of real things, put together so as to form the idea of something never encountered in experience. When Berkeley contrasts those of my ideas that are creatures of my will with those that are not he is making a contrast between, on the one hand, my active power (whenever I like) to call up and to combine remembered ideas that have come from past experience, and, on the other hand, my comparative lack of control over the ideas that are coming to me in present, largely passive, sensory experience.

Berkeley says that the ideas in the imagination, recalled from past experience, are "copies" of sensory ideas (real things) that they "represent". It might at first be thought that the copies, although they are in a sense new ideas, are indistinguishable from the ideas of real things that they simply re-present. However, he also says that the ideas of imagination are "faint, weak, and unsteady" compared to ideas of sense, which are "more affecting, orderly, and distinct" (P§36). Are the sensory ideas and their fainter copies token instances of the same ideas or are they ideas of different types? And what does Berkeley mean by saying that these copies represent things? In particular, do they represent anything other than the ideas of sense from which they are copied?

Consider, for example, the idea of Snowdon that I use when thinking about that mountain while in London (thus not sensing it). That idea is copied from the idea (or collection of ideas) "imprinted on my senses" by God while I was viewing the mountain. It is now a memory idea that I can call up at will and it is, Berkeley would say, "fainter" or "weaker" (whatever exactly these words mean) than the one I had when viewing the mountain. But it seems likely that Berkeley thinks it nonetheless contains most or all of the same information content and significance. That is, the copy-idea can give me information about the nature of possible future sensory experiences involving that mountain. It is the image or reflection of the real thing (i.e. the God-given sensory idea I had at the time) so it represents at least that unique perceptual idea of Snowdon. It also seems likely that Berkeley thinks it *resembles* that unique perceptual idea so it would not be too risky an interpretation to say that Berkeley thinks of it as a token instance of the same idea type as the original sensory idea. But would it be right to say that Berkeley holds that it represents the mountain?

How illusions and perceptual error occur

As was noted above, Berkeley thinks his view markedly improves on Locke's. In particular, he thinks he has a better explanation of how illusions and what we might call "perceptual errors" are possible: an account that adequately explains their possibility while erecting a powerful bulwark against scepticism. Perhaps if we look at the explanation of illusions and perceptual errors that Berkeley gives we will discover the answer to the question whether ideas I produce in my imagination can represent realities outside my mind and, if so, what it is to which those ideas owe their capacity for such representation.

Since, for Berkeley, ideas that come to me in sense perception are not *representations* of real things but are *the actual real things themselves*, there is (as Berkeley intends) no gap into which a sceptic could insert doubt about the fidelity of those sensory ideas to reality. My immediate sensations, since they do not represent at all, cannot *mis*represent the world. However, I can still suffer illusions precisely because the ideas I receive in sense perception are not and could not be representations of a mind-independent external reality. They are signs given by God of what to expect from further experience of his creation, that is, the real created natural world, which depends wholly on God's mind for its existence and nature.

For example, sight of the fire warns me of the warmth and then the pain I will feel if I approach nearer and then nearer. The sound of birdsong, apparently from a nearby tree, promises sight of a particular bird if I walk, as I would say, "towards that tree". So, an illusion can occur if I read present sense experiences as signs that a certain sort of action on my part will yield a particular change in my sensory ideas and, then, instead of the expected changes, that action yields unexpected and quite different changes in my ideas. It is mistaken judgement or misinterpretation of my sensory ideas, rather than misrepresentation of reality by those ideas, which makes illusions and mistakes possible. So, to take another example, if I see a shimmering pool on the horizon after hours of waterless trudging in the desert and then form the expectation that my thirst will shortly be quenched I may be bitterly disappointed. This will not be, for Berkeley, because a sense experience or the idea copied from it misrepresented reality, but because I misinterpreted the real mirage I saw as a sign that I would soon encounter water.

It might reasonably be asked, however, how God-given sensory ideas could fail to be *infallible* signs of what to expect from future experience. Does Berkeley think that God sometimes misleads us or utters falsehoods to created minds? The answer, of course, is not that Berkeley's God can ever be a deceiver. Rather, it is that, although there is no way for sense experience to misrepresent anything, it *is* unavoidably *limited*. It is unique to the subject, time and circumstances of that experience. So perceivers can receive only hints and signs that inevitably do not give the complete picture. There is nothing false about these signs. They convey exactly how things are, at the time, with the portion of reality perceived. But human judgement is required to attempt to subsume what is sensed under appropriate, experience-taught natural laws and then, using those laws, to attempt to predict what further items lie in the future of the series of perceptions of which those hints and signs are earlier members. Since this prediction is always based on evidence that is unavoidably limited in detail and, moreover, must employ incomplete knowledge of natural law, it would be surprising if errors were not a reasonably frequent occurrence. Human judgement and interpretation are fallible. That is how it comes about that my context-and-occasion-bound sensory ideas sometimes may give the illusion of somehow misrepresenting the world.

So Berkeley's view is that sensory ideas signify what they do because God intends them to signify what they do. God excites all the ideas of sensation that turn up in created minds. Their intentionality is thus, as for all the previous philosophers examined in this book, not original intentionality after all but derived intentionality. What about the ideas I produce by copying those ideas of sensation? I believe Berkeley would say that those copy-ideas, in representing the utterly particular ideas of sensation that they copy, also represent, and thus in turn possess, the God-given intentionality or significance of those sensory ideas. So my London idea of Snowdon does represent the mountain, not by being caused directly by the mountain, but because it is made in the image of something whose intentionality was conferred by God.

Snowdon depends for its existence on the mind of its creator and also, in a different way, on being perceived by those who perceive it. It is thus a collection of ideas and therefore causally inert. The particular idea of it that I

227

form on the occasion of a single particular sensory experience is also causally inert. But that idea inherits the significance of the sensory ideas from which it is copied, and is thus a source of information about the public world and the realm of potential sense experience. Such information can be invaluable, for example, in helping the emergency services devise a rescue plan when walkers become lost on Snowdon in foul weather. The sensory ideas, each of which provides some of that vital information, are signs or, as Berkeley would say, "prognostics" of various possible mountain experiences.

The piece of the jigsaw that is still missing where this account of the intentionality of our ideas is concerned is what Berkeley has to say about how it is possible to have what might be called "general" or "universal" thought. Of course, he rejects utterly the idea of abstraction and abstract general ideas. For Berkeley, there is no Lockean abstract general idea of a triangle or an animal that could be used in thinking about animals or triangles in general. But Berkeley does think that I can and do simply let a particular idea, of, say, a particular line in a geometry diagram, stand for or represent lines in general in my thinking. I can attend to those particular features of my representative particular line that it shares with other lines however much those other lines vary from mine in their inessential features.

Presumably, I can also survey my many sightings of different particular animals or triangles or lines in order to get the best notion possible of what shared features might characterize each member of each kind. Thus, chosen particular sense ideas and their copies produced in imagination can incorporate even more information into the idea I use to represent such things to myself when thinking about the world and planning my active progress through it. Here is more derived intentionality: my occasion-bound, unique sensory idea of this line is made, by my choice, to represent all lines of the same type.

To sum up, sensory ideas, for Berkeley, do not represent things since they just are the things sensed and not their representatives. Still less are those sensory ideas the effects of the things sensed since sensible things are inert ideas and incapable of causing anything. However, ideas copied from them can, depending on my choice, represent whole classes or kinds of things in my thought. These particular copy-ideas can also represent particular individual objects or geographical features of which, inevitably, I have only limited and incomplete perceptions. These copy-ideas are produced by created spirits but their intentionality is bestowed by God via the significant sensory ideas that the copies represent and mirror.

Berkeley's notion of intentionality and its source has both a very traditional face and a very modern one. On the one hand, representations all (immediately or ultimately) derive their significance from God. On the other, representation, for Berkeley, is a matter of ideas being appointed to guide our actions and make possible for all created spirits a life that is both fruitful and safe. As Berkeley says:

> experience ... teaches us that such and such ideas are attended with such and such other ideas, in the ordinary course of things. This gives us a sort of foresight, which enables us to regulate our actions for the benefit of life. (P§§30 & 31)

Our ideas represent things for Berkeley because doing so confers a tremendous advantage that nowadays would be called "evolutionary". That word would be out of place in an interpretation of Berkeley's position but it is clear that he thinks the ideas enjoyed by created spirits have the significance they do because such significance conduces to successful actions that ensure the thriving and survival of those spirits.

CHAPTER 26

Is the mind a substance for Hume?

The Newton of the mind

David Hume, like Locke, is very sceptical about the nature of substance, whether material or immaterial. And he goes much further than Locke's agnosticism, saying that both sorts of substance are inconceivable. He thinks we cannot get beyond our impressions (roughly, our sensations) to know anything whatever about their causes. For all we know, our impressions could be caused by any of the following: material objects (whether similar to our impressions or wholly unlike them); God (as Berkeley might say); our own minds (either dreaming or hallucinating), that is, nothing at all external; an arch deceiver; any other as-yet-un-imagined cause. But knowledge of these causes is in principle impossible for us: like Berkeley, Hume holds that we only ever know or have experience of mental items. We thus have no standing to hypothesize, let alone any grounds for inferring, the existence of anything that is, as Hume says, "specifically different" (of a different species or kind) from impressions and ideas: the two sorts of mental items that are the only ones he recognizes and which he refers to in general as "perceptions" (T I.ii. vi, 67–8).

On the other hand, readers should be aware from the outset that, notwithstanding the sceptical position just outlined, Hume often writes about material objects, our relations with them and their relations with each other in ways that take those objects to be perfectly real. We shall see in Chapter 29, for example, when he is talking about cause and effect, that he never questions the existence of billiard balls and other bodies, including human ones.

In what follows I look first at Hume's argument that material substances are a wholly ungrounded supposition – and, in fact, a nonsense – and then his argument that we have no justification for positing immaterial substances either. Since Hume is also notoriously sceptical about the existence of the self and about personal persistence over time it would seem that he certainly does not think that the mind is a substance. However, none of this means that he is in any way sceptical about the existence of the human mind. Nor does it mean that he believes we can make no headway in knowing its nature, in general or in our own particular case.

Indeed, Hume has great ambitions to further our understanding of the mind by his own efforts. He has boundless admiration for the way that Isaac Newton, in astronomy and physics, has made systematic sense of the movement of the planets by discovering the "laws and forces, by which [they] are governed and directed". Hume clearly aspires to be the Newton of the mind and discover "at least in some degree, the secret springs and principles, by which the human mind is actuated in its operations" (EH I.i.9, 14).[1]

Hume begins *A Treatise of Human Nature* (*Treatise*) by declaring his belief that the mind and human nature should be the first objects of scientific study: "There is no question of importance", he says, "whose decision is not compriz'd in the science of man", which is "the only solid foundation for the other sciences". He proceeds to tell us that the *Treatise* has been born out of his sense of the urgent need for this study of the human mind, a study that is to be undertaken not using the barren methods of the rationalists, but in the modern empiricist style with "the application of experimental philosophy". "The only solid foundation we can give to this science itself must be laid on experience and observation" (T Introduction, xvi):

> For to me it seems evident, that the essence of the mind being equally unknown to us with that of external bodies, it must be equally impossible to form any notion of its powers and qualities otherwise than from careful and exact experiments, and the observation of those particular effects, which result from its different circumstances and situations ... 'tis still certain we cannot go beyond experience; and any hypothesis, that pretends to discover the ultimate original qualities of human nature, ought at first to be rejected as presumptuous and chimerical. (*Ibid.*, xvii)

Hume thinks a rationalistic faith that unaided reason can reveal the ultimate nature and essence of mind has been shown to be simply pretentious armwaving. He will follow, in his science of the mind, the method of careful exper-

---

1. David Hume, *Enquiries Concerning Human Understanding and Concerning the Principles of Morals*, L. A. Selby-Bigge (ed.), 3rd edn, P. H. Nidditch (ed.) (Oxford: Oxford University Press, 1975) [EH]. References in the form, for example, EH I.i.9, 14, refer to the First Enquiry, §i, paragraph 9, page 14.

iment and observation that has yielded such impressive results in physics and astronomy.

No material substance

Hume's argument against material substance employs a strategy that might, on analogy with Ockham's razor, be dubbed "Hume's hatchet". He uses it again and again when attacking any concept that rationalist metaphysicians have recognized but which he regards as suspect. In the very first section of Book I, Part I, Hume gives his first expression of what commentators call his "correspondence principle", which says that "every simple idea has a simple impression, which resembles it; and every simple impression a correspondent idea" (T I.i, 3). He treats this principle as a necessary truth although he introduces it as an empirical observation that he has made by conducting an introspective survey of his own mental contents and which he invites his readers to confirm with introspective surveys of their own.

Since the only contents our minds can have on his view are the impressions gained in experience and the ideas copied from them, and since the words and terms we employ are only given meaning by standing for our ideas, Hume now has a way of exposing metaphysical jargon as literally meaningless. All he has to do is convince his reader that any term that supposedly designates some item cannot designate anything real because the idea that might give that term meaning is an "impossible idea". An impossible idea is one where there is no possible impression to which that idea could correspond. This is because the correspondence principle says that there is no simple idea that lacks a correspondent simple impression. After all, ideas are just copies of impressions: so the rule is "no impression, no idea".

Now consider the metaphysicians' notion of a material substance. For there to be such things as material substances it must be the case that there is an idea of material substance to provide the term "material substance" with a meaning. But for it to be possible that there is an idea of material substance it must be possible for there to be an impression of material substance from which that idea could be copied. So Hume asks ironically whether the impression of material substance from which the idea is derived is an impression of sensation or an impression of reflection, these being the only two kinds of impression Hume recognizes. But we cannot have a sensory impression of material substance since: "if it be perceiv'd by the eyes, it must be a colour; if by the ears, a sound; if by the palate, a taste; and so of the other senses. But I believe none will assert, that substance is either a colour, or a sound, or a taste" (T I.i.vi, 15–16). On the other hand, we could not get an impression of material substance from reflection since reflection for Hume, as for Locke and Berkeley, is a turning-in of the mind on itself and material substance is thought (by those who think there is such a thing) to be something external to the mind. "We have therefore no idea of substance, distinct from that of a collection of particular qualities" (*ibid.*, 16).

This, in brief, is Hume's hatchet applied to material substance: if there is no possible impression of material substance there can be no correspondent idea of material substance. But if there is no idea of material substance the term "material substance" is literally meaningless: it cannot designate a real thing.

Commentators are divided as to whether Hume is here saying only that material substance is inconceivable (although it may exist) or that there cannot be such a thing since we could have neither an impression nor an idea of it. But the whole tone of his writing here and his use of this strategy when writing about eventless time, the vacuum (genuinely empty space), necessary connections in nature, persistent external objects and the self – to all of which he denies existence – together make clear that Hume thinks not only that Lockean material *substratum* substance is inconceivable but that no such thing exists.

No immaterial substance

In the *Treatise* Hume says that, when it comes to the existence of immaterial substance, that notion "labours under all the same difficulties" as did the notion of material substance and then is burdened with some additional ones peculiar to itself (T I.iv.v, 232). Hume attributes to other philosophers disagreement about whether our perceptions "inhere" in material substance or in immaterial substance and says that this issue cannot be settled until the meanings of "substance" and of "inhesion" have been made clear. But applying his hatchet to "immaterial substance" in the same way that we saw him apply the same strategy to "material substance" should, he believes, swiftly show us that this too is an impossible idea. Hume is ironic to the point of sarcasm:

> I desire those philosophers, who pretend that we have an idea of the substance of our minds, to point out the impression that produces it, and tell distinctly after what manner that impression operates, and from what object it is deriv'd. Is it an impression of sensation or of reflection? Is it pleasant, or painful, or indifferent?

> Does it attend us at all times, or does it only return at intervals? If
> at intervals, at what times principally does it return and by what
> causes is it produc'd. (*Ibid.*, 233)

Unable to come up with a possible impression of immaterial substance that
could be copied by the mind to give us an idea of it, we should simply accept
that immaterial substance, like material substance, is a nonsense.

Hume imagines his opponent trying to evade his challenge to produce
the impression from which the idea of immaterial substance could be copied
(an impossible task Hume thinks) by reciting the standard, philosophers'
definition of "substance" as "something that may exist by itself". Then he
responds to the offered definition with a puzzle for anyone who thinks that
that definition is adequate to let us distinguish substances from anything else.
Since

(i)   our perceptions (ideas and impressions) are clearly conceived and
      "whatever is clearly conceived, after any manner, may exist after the
      same manner"; and since
(ii) "every thing, which is different, is distinguishable, and every thing
      which is distinguishable is separable by the imagination". Then, since
(iii) all our perceptions differ and are thus distinguishable from each other
      and everything else, they can *all* exist separately without need of
      support.

This all means that

(iv) "as far as this definition explains a substance" (*ibid.*) our *perceptions* are
      substances: indeed the only things that could be substances.

Hume is, in effect, here reducing the notion of substance to what he is sure
his opponent would regard as an absurdity; to the conclusion that the only
substances are impressions and ideas. Moreover, "inhesion in something
is suppos'd to be requisite to support the existence of our perceptions" but
"nothing appears requisite to support the existence of a perception. We
have therefore no idea of inhesion" (*ibid.*, 234). Finally, therefore, in Hume's
judgement the debate between those who think mind "inheres" in material
substance and those who think it inheres in immaterial substance cannot
even get started; the key terms of the question are meaningless. The very
notion of a substance is devoid of content as is the notion of inhering in a
substance.

Scepticism about the self

Having seen Hume's treatment of the notions of material substance and immaterial substance we can be fairly sure what fate awaits the notion of the self as soon as we read Hume saying at the outset of his chapter "Of Personal Identity" that "There are some philosophers, who imagine we are every moment intimately conscious of what we call our SELF" but shortly there-after asking "from what impression cou'd this idea be deriv'd?" (T I.iv.vi, 251). Again he wields his hatchet: we must be able to produce an impression of the self "if we wou'd have the idea of the self pass for clear and intelligible". And he is confident that no one can do so since he has tried very carefully using introspection but has been unable to find such an impression in himself. So his case against the self is largely an empirical one. The evidence from reflec-tion is that we do not and cannot have an impression of the self.

But how does Hume know when he introspects that he *is not* having an impression of the self (of his own self) but just failing to recognize it for what it is? After all, he is saying that he has no idea of the self, so perhaps he is mistaken in his identification of the impressions and ideas he encounters in reflection.[2] But Hume has a criterion by which to recognize an impression of the self (should there be one), which he says he has taken from those philoso-phers mentioned earlier who are sure that we are every moment conscious of the self and "feel its existence and its continuance in existence": "If any impression gives rise to the idea of self, that impression must continue invari-ably the same, thro' the whole course of our lives; since self is suppos'd to exist after that manner. But there is no impression constant and invariable" (*ibid.*). Here Hume makes the swiftest transition yet from arguing that a certain impression does not exist to concluding that a putative entity answering to the missing impression does not exist. This is Hume's famous description of his introspective failure to find an impression of the self:

> For my part, when I enter most intimately into what I call *myself*,
> I always stumble on some particular perception or other, of heat
> or cold, light or shade, love or hatred, pain or pleasure. I never
> can catch *myself* at any time without a perception, and never can
> observe any thing but the perception.   (*Ibid.*, 252)

---

2. Sydney Shoemaker, "Introspection and the Self", in *Self-Knowledge*, Q. Cassam (ed.) (Oxford: Oxford University Press, 1994), 119.

Hume's conclusion is that if all his perceptions cease he is nothing at all. "When my perceptions are remov'd for any time, as by sound sleep; so long am I insensible of *myself*, and may truly be said not to exist" (*ibid.*). The "self" that has his perceptions is "nothing but a bundle or collection of different perceptions, which succeed each other with an inconceivable rapidity, and are in a perpetual flux and movement" (*ibid.*).

Hume makes very clear that he is not just reporting a truth about his own nature. The bundle he has just spoken of is what he takes the mind to be for all human beings. The mind is literally a bundle of perceptions. Figuratively, he says:

> The mind is a kind of theatre, where several perceptions succes- sively make their appearance; pass, re-pass, glide away, and mingle in an infinite variety of postures and situations ... [However] the comparison of the theatre must not mislead us; They are *the succes- sive perceptions only*, that constitute the mind.
>
> (*Ibid.*, 253, emphasis added)

A bundle theory of the nature of mind presents anyone who subscribes to it with a number of very difficult problems. Not least is the question what holds the bundle together: what makes just these and these (but not those and those) perceptions one individual mind. And Hume is aware that he must also address the question what makes each of us believe he or she is a persistent re-identifiable person or subject who lasts over time. There is also the question how such a thing as a bundle of perceptions could think, judge, remember, imagine and so forth.

Identity and personal identity

Hume's answer to the question what holds the bundle together is that the bundle of perceptions that constitute the mind is held together by the imagi- nation. He says that "the identity which we ascribe to the mind of man is only a fictitious one" (T I.iv.vi, 259). The difficulty with interpreting this passage is that Hume's use of the terms "fiction", "identity" and "imagination" is highly idiosyncratic so that we need to look at his whole account of the conscious operations of the mind and in particular his principle of association of ideas in order to understand what Hume means by it. We also need to examine Hume's views on identity. Chapter 28 will start with a detailed account of Hume's associationist psychological theory and the role he gives to what he terms the imagination. What follows here is a brief sketch of Hume's views about identity over time and in particular the identity of persons.

Strictly speaking, Hume thinks, there is no such thing as identity over time for *anything* including human beings. For what do those who use the term "identity" mean by it? Think of a typical statement of supposed identity in the present: "*A* is identical with itself". This statement seems to be unable to make up its mind. On the one hand it is saying that there is only the one thing, *A*, involved. But as Hume says "One single object conveys the idea of unity, not that of identity" (T I.iv.ii, 200). On the other hand, identity appears to be a relation and that suggests that there should be at least two *relata* to be related. However, a multiplicity of objects "conveys the idea" of number (again, *not* identity). As Hume concludes "Betwixt unity and number there can be no medium; no more than betwixt existence and non-existence" (*ibid.*).

What would inspire anyone to think that there might be a sort of halfway house between unity and diversity? The source of this notion of something that is beyond simple unity but which is not real plurality either is the passage of time. We form the notion of identity to capture our sense that objects remain invariable as time passes. We compare earlier and later observations in our experience and ascribe them to a single lasting object, thus combining the ideas of plurality and unity. But Hume is convinced that this is an error. On his view the only things whose existence we have any evidence for are perceptions and such things are instantaneous. When there are interruptions in the perceiving subject's experience (as there always are) we may *imagine* a persisting object lasting through the gaps in our observations but that is all we are doing: imagining that something lasts from earlier to later.

In fact Hume describes this as our propensity to *identify* the earlier with the later *perceptions*. And it is the imagination that, he says, leads us to do this. Moreover, just as the imagination leads us to identify earlier with later perceptions of (as we think them) external objects, so too our strongly resemblant earlier and later perceptions lead us to identify our earlier with our later selves. This, again, is strictly a mistake. There is no persistent self-identical subject. There are simply successive collections of perceptions that resemble each other in various ways seducing us into identifying earlier and later perceivers.

This account of human minds and the illusion we have that they last through time is so eccentric, and is so often made the target of various objections, that it is worth approaching a number of times from different directions in order to be sure that we really understand what Hume is saying. In

what follows I shall return to the subject of the mind as a bundle of perceptions that does not persist through time, first in Chapter 27, when looking at
Hume's response to the question how much self-knowledge we have, and then
in Chapter 28, when discussing the bundle theory of mind, the imagination
and Hume's doctrine of the association of ideas.

CHAPTER 27

Hume and self-knowledge

Notoriously, Hume denies that there is such a thing as the simple and unitary, persistent, unchanging, re-identifiable self recognized by other philosophers. As we have seen, he bases this denial on his own inability to find such a self in introspection. For Hume the subject of experience is, as a matter of empirical fact, never presented to the subject *in* experience. And this, for Hume means that there can be no true idea of the self since such an idea would have to be copied from or at least correspond to an impression of the self and he is convinced that no such impression ever occurs.

He also hints that it is a truth of logic that there cannot be an impression of the experiencing subject: that the notion is "a manifest contradiction and absurdity" (T I.iv.vi, 251). This is presumably because a subject cannot receive an impression of itself receiving that very impression. As Armstrong says, "A mental state cannot be aware of itself, any more than a man can eat himself up".[1] So it might be expected that this chapter, devoted to Hume's views on self-knowledge, would be very brief. If there is no self to be known there is nothing for self-knowledge to be *of*. Self-knowledge should be limited to that very fact.

But of course Hume does not recognize such a limitation on self-knowledge for two main reasons. First, he is very sure that human minds are transparent to themselves. That is to say, he is sure that he has that "particular self-knowledge", as it is sometimes called, that consists in being aware of all the sensations, beliefs, intentions, emotions and mental operations currently occurring in his mind. He is sure that he is, or at least can be, aware of everything that is going on in his mind at any given moment: that there are no perceptions hidden from his consciousness.

---

1. D. M. Armstrong, "Introspection", in *Self-Knowledge*, Cassam (ed.), 110.

Secondly, he does not deny that he has a mind, that he is a person with experiences, sense perceptions, thoughts, intentions, memories and figments of the imagination: quite the contrary. But that undeniable mind or person is for Hume neither a (material or immaterial) substance in the sense of a mysterious *substratum* with no properties of its own that somehow exists to have mental properties, nor any sort of persistent particular that somehow mysteriously remains one and the same thing "through a supposed variation of time" (T I.iv.vi, 253).

Hume's rejection of material and immaterial substance combined with his rejection of identity over time for *any* particular of any kind mean that the only notion of a mind or self left for him to embrace is the notion of the mind as a bundle of perceptions or psychological states. This is a bundle-self whose membership is constantly changing and evolving as new impressions, ideas, memories, fancies and thoughts join the bundle while old ones fade, are overlaid or drop away. And this bundle-self is something of which individual subjects can have self-knowledge. We can have knowledge also of our "natural propension" to fall into the error or accept the fiction that persons endure, one and the same, from one time to the next.

Particular self-knowledge

Let us begin with the sort of self-knowledge Hume is sure that we all have in abundance; namely, our knowledge of what is going on in our own minds at any given moment. This is Hume's version of the notion of mental transparency. Famously, Hume says "all actions and sensations of the mind … must necessarily appear in every particular what they are, and be what they appear" (T I.iv.ii, 190). This knowledge of our mental contents and activities comes to each human mind courtesy of our "most intimate" consciousness.

Hume often creates the impression that mental transparency is such that there is no possibility of our being mistaken about any aspect of our own conscious psychological states. The infallibility, incorrigibility and completeness of our self-knowledge of our mental states contrast sharply for Hume with the distinct possibility that we might be misled about the nature of external reality, judging it as we do on the basis of the perceptions "conveyed in" by the bodily senses. Indeed, he is persuaded that there are a number of errors that are almost inevitable in our judgements about what (if anything) exists outside our perceptions. But the deliverances of introspection or reflection are officially, for Hume, utterly trustworthy.

240

Introspection as a philosophical tool

In Chapter 26 we saw that Hume often uses introspection as a philosophical tool. He wants to understand the mind through empirical research by (in so far as this is possible) applying the experimental method to the investigation of the functioning and limits of the human mind. However, in the Introduction to the *Treatise* he acknowledges that the experimental method cannot be applied to minds in quite the same way as it can be applied to this or that physical body. In physics or chemistry, if I want to know "the effects of one body upon another in any situation, I need only put them in that situation, and observe what results from it" (T Introduction, xix). But such control and "premeditation" are not possible in scientific study of the mind. If I were to place myself in a particular situation in order to study my reactions I would learn little about the nature of mind in general, since the contrived nature of the case would upset the natural sequence of events and interfere with the principles guiding my actions.

Nor can we treat *other* human beings like test tubes full of chemicals, putting them in different situations and combinations in order to see how they react and are affected: "We must therefore glean up our experiments in this science from a cautious observation of human life, and take them as they appear in the common course of the world, by men's behaviour in company, in affairs, and in their pleasures" (*ibid.*). This will provide us with some scientific understanding of mind but, unfortunately, no matter how cautiously we observe others, we are not able to get access to our subjects' minds to observe what goes on there; as Hume realizes, our knowledge of others' mental contents and psychology is on a different footing from the knowledge that reflection can give about our own mental states.

But then again, this asymmetry between our knowledge of others' mental states and our knowledge of our own means that Hume has, after all, a ready and reliable source of the possible "observations of human life" that he needs in order to create his science of the human mind. He has immediate access to his own mind and all that happens there. So, although Hume's science of the mind will inevitably be characterized by a good deal of speculation and extrapolation and an equal amount of reliance on what would now be called "anecdotal evidence", his hope is that it will also have firm principles that have been discovered by introspection and thus are known infallibly and incorrigibly.

So we find him confirming, for example, his correspondence principle by "running over" and "carefully examining" his simple ideas to see whether he has in his own mind any simple impressions that lack a corresponding simple idea (or *vice versa*) and making the introspective observation that he does not

241

(T I.i.i, 3–4). He invites his readers to do their own introspective surveys on such questions and – if they are inclined to disagree with his conclusions – to "produce" if they can the perceptions that he fails to find in his own mind. It is, however, far from clear how exactly one is supposed to produce an idea or impression to counter say (to take a second example) Hume's contention that an impression "of the substance of our minds" is unobtainable (T I.iv.v, 233). It seems that Hume can be guilty of sliding away from his initial empiricism and taking his own personal observations or lack of them as sufficient confirmation of what he then treats as necessary truths about the mind.

Is introspection "inner sense" for Hume?

Does Hume regard introspection or reflection as a sort of "inner sense" or "inner perception" in the way that Locke certainly and explicitly takes his own "reflection" to be? Does he think of it on what has been called an "observational model" or "perceptual model" of introspection? Or is he, like Descartes and, even more so, Berkeley, wary of the analogy between introspection and sense perception? Hume's language when talking of his introspective search for the self is all in terms of observation of appearances and perceptions. He speaks of the successive extremely varied perceptions he always stumbles over "when I enter most intimately into what I call *myself*" (T I.iv.vi, 252), and says that he would expect to "observe" there an impression of the self if there were such a thing to be found. His description of the mind as a theatre where successive perceptions "make their appearance; pass, re-pass, glide away and mingle" (*ibid.*, 253) certainly makes reflection or introspection seem very much a matter of inner seeing or spectating for Hume, as does his saying that the great resemblance between impressions and ideas is "the first circumstance, that strikes the eye" (T I.i.i, 2) when reflecting about them.

In addition, although Hume never actually gives any explicit account of sense perception in the *Treatise* there is a clear and strong parallel between what little he tells us about what happens in (outer) sense perception and what he thinks happens in reflection or inner sensing of the contents and activities of the mind. Indeed, he says towards the end of Book I that, even when it seems that we are having sense perceptions of the "limbs and members" of our own bodies (something clearly outside the mind), "properly speaking" it is not our bodies we perceive but our sense impressions (T I.iv.ii, 191). In other words, it is impressions and ideas (mental states) that are the proper and only objects of both outer and inner sense for Hume. (See also: "nothing is ever present to the mind but perceptions" [T I.ii.vi, 67].) Experience, whether through the bodily senses or introspection, simply and equally consists in the appearing or arising of perceptions in the mind (T I.iv.ii, 189). If anything, it almost seems that Hume assimilates sense perception to introspection. (For a discussion of his tendency to assimilate *consciousness* to introspection see below, Chapter 28, § "Introspective consciousness".)

In fairness we should note that Hume does warn that the comparison of the mind with a theatre could mislead, and that "They are the successive perceptions only, that constitute the mind" (T I.iv.vi, 253). But instead of drawing out the disanalogies that exist between outer and inner sense he goes on immediately to speak of our lack of knowledge of the "place, where these [theatrical] scenes are presented", thus continuing to use spectatorial imagery when endeavouring to explain the nature of mind and introspection.

First-person authority

Since Hume treats the deliverances (at least of his own) introspection as incorrigible it is natural to wonder what accounts for this incorrigibility on his view. Hume does not offer an explanation of the trustworthiness of reflection but it seems likely that he thinks that it is our exclusive and immediate access to our own psychological states that makes us infallible about them and that, like Locke, he thinks that we have privileged access to our mental contents: I alone am able to introspect what is going on in my mind; you alone have access to your mental states and activities. I know my own psychological states immediately and non-inferentially, whereas I always need to infer from observation and evidence in order to find out what another person is thinking, feeling, even sensing.

I mentioned above that, contrary to what we might have expected, Hume at times shows himself quite well aware of this asymmetry between our knowledge of what is going on in the world, including the minds of others, and our knowledge of our own inner states and happenings. For example, he says of an imagined rival philosopher who persists in claiming that he is aware of possessing a simple and lasting self:

> If any one upon serious and unprejudic'd reflection, thinks he has a different notion of *himself*, I must confess I can reason no longer with him. All I can allow him is, that he may be in the right as well as I, and that we are essentially different in this particular. He may, perhaps, perceive something simple and continu'd, which he calls *himself*; tho' I am certain there is no such principle in me.
>
> (T I.iv.vi, 252)

Hume is here, of course, heavily ironic. He is sure that his own case is paradigmatic and provides perfectly adequate grounds for his belief that there is no such thing in any human subject as the philosophers' lasting and unitary self. But the other side of this coin is that he must avoid in any way undermining or disparaging the view that each individual subject's self-knowledge of the contents and activities currently taking place in his or her own mind is authoritative. He would agree completely with Locke in condemning as absurd anyone who might pretend to know better than I do myself what and when I am thinking and which psychological states and operations are occurring in my mind. Hume must maintain (and is happy to do so) that no one else is in a position to correct another's introspective reports about his or her own psychological states. Hume can deny with unchallengeable authority that he has a unitary and lasting self because our privileged access makes each of us the final authority on what is to be found (or not) in his or her own mind.

But it is important to note (in the quotation just given) Hume's opening qualification that he will leave off arguing with his opponent *only* at the point where the opponent has engaged in "serious and unprejudic'd reflection" and yet still sticks to his opinion. The suggestion is that concentrated attention is necessary if the deliverances of introspection are to be reliable and also that prejudice can prove a barrier to accurate introspective survey. Intentionally or not, Hume here shows that, at some level, he realizes that mental transparency cannot be as simple, straightforward and unqualified as he might have hoped. When talking of others' beliefs about their inner states he cannot always and unambiguously regard introspection as infallible or incorrigible. And although each of us has first-person authority in the sense that each of us has exclusive immediate access to his or her own psychological states, Hume cannot deny that we are not necessarily always fully accurate or comprehensive reporters or analysts of what falls under our introspective view.

No unconscious perceptions

So it is time to look again at Hume's pronouncement that "all actions and sensations of the mind ... must necessarily appear in every particular what they are, and be what they appear". This seems to say without qualification that all my current ideas and impressions and all my mental operations are equally and fully transparent: that none has any aspect that could – or even does – escape my awareness. In other words, that there are no such things as psychological states that are wholly or partly unconscious. And this quotation is not the only remark of Hume's where such unqualified transparency seems to be claimed for mental contents: for example, earlier Hume says that "all sensations are felt by the mind such as they really are" (T I.vi.ii, 189), and later he says that "the perceptions of the mind are perfectly known" (T II.ii.vi, 366). What does Hume actually mean in these and similar passages? And is he simply contradicting himself in the passage that I discussed in the previous section, when he suggests (albeit ironically) that serious reflection unimpeded by prejudice is required before the contents of the mind can be clearly perceived in introspection and thoroughly and accurately understood?

Certainly many of Hume's readers have judged that when Hume says that all actions and sensations of the mind "must necessarily appear in every particular what they are", he is offering an explanation of the asymmetry between my infallible, incorrigible knowledge of my own psychological states and my fallible knowledge of others' minds: the explanation is that all our psychological states are what present-day philosophers would call "strongly self-intimating". That is, Hume is saying that it follows necessarily from the fact that I have a particular psychological state that I am aware of having it: that it is automatically salient for me.

But Hume's words could be read as meaning something less strong. He could be saying that *if* one of my psychological states appears to me, in the sense that it turns up in my introspective field during an episode of reflection, then it cannot mislead me about its nature but will "appear in every particular what [it is]". If this is right it is still appropriate to attribute to Hume the belief that psychological states are self-intimating, but it is a weaker sort of self-intimation whereby it is up to me to engage in introspection and consider carefully whether or not I have the state in question, at which point my perceptions will not mislead me.

The trouble with this as a way of attempting to rescue Hume from the charge of self-contradiction is that it actually does little to remove the clash between Hume's belief that introspection cannot fail to give effortless, incorrigible, indeed infallible, knowledge of one's current mental states and activities and his apparent and conflicting concession that prejudice and lack of seriousness might, in the case of some individuals, prevent introspection from yielding truths about their minds. How am I to know when reflection has been careful and serious *enough* and when prejudice and bias have been sufficiently detected and rooted out or adequately compensated for? Once self-intimation is weakened so that my inner states are not deemed to be *necessarily* such that I cannot help knowing of their existence and true nature, I surely need some standard by which to judge when to trust that things introspectively "observed" really "are what they appear". Unfortunately, Hume shows no sign of appreciating this need or being aware that he has a difficulty to resolve here.

Self-knowledge of the existence and nature of the bundle-self

Unlike Descartes, Hume scorns to offer any sort of "proof" of his own existence. Perhaps he thinks, as he says of the belief in the existence of body,
that nature has deemed this belief too important to be left "to our uncer-
tain reasonings" (T I.iv.ii, 187). At any rate Hume takes his own existence
for granted and would probably consider that any enquirer can also safely
assume the existence of his or her own mind.

What about self-knowledge in the sense of knowledge of the nature and
capacities of the bundle-self? Does Hume think that such self-knowledge
is within the grasp of each human mind? In the *Abstract*[2] Hume gives the
following précis of the teaching of the *Treatise* on the nature of the mind or
soul:

> [T]he soul, as far as we can conceive it, is nothing but a system
> or train of different perceptions, those of heat and cold, love and
> anger, thoughts and sensations; all united together, but without any
> perfect simplicity or identity … it must be our several particular
> perceptions, that compose the mind. I say *compose* the mind, not
> *belong* to it. The mind is not a substance, in which the perceptions
> inhere … We know nothing but particular qualities and percep-
> tions … So our idea of any mind is only that of particular percep-
> tions, without the notion of any thing we call substance, either
> simple or compound.   (T *Abstract*, 657–8)

The individual human mind or subject of experiences is, for Hume, a bundle
or collection of mental states and each of us can get self-knowledge of our
fundamental nature as a bundle in two ways. First, we can follow Hume's
example and make an introspective survey, thus "seeing" that this is all we
are. That is, we can discover the nature of the human mind as a collection of
perceptions by empirical research. As we have just seen, Hume thinks that the
perceptions that make up the bundle are all accessible to the mind, which is
the bundle as a whole.

Secondly, we can do proper philosophy, that is, not the "deep metaphysics"
practised by the rationalists, which Hume deplores. Rather, we can read
Hume's *Treatise* and follow his arguments. There we will find that there is
no acceptable account of the mind or human nature in the works of Hume's

---

2. The *Abstract* is now always published after the Appendix in editions of the *Treatise*.

predecessors. Then, once we have seen through the theory that the mind's essence is thought-in-general (attributed to Descartes) and the notion of unknowable immaterial substance underlying all psychological states (attributed to Locke), we will realize that Hume's bundle theory is the only remaining possible theory of mind, the only one worthy of support.

In Chapter 26 we saw that Hume maintains that it is the imagination that holds together the bundle that is a particular human mind and makes us believe that our successive ideas constitute a single lasting unchanging self (T I.iv.vi, 260). Hume's notion of the "imagination" is idiosyncratic and broad. It includes, of course, the "fancy" or fiction-making faculty, but Hume starts off the *Treatise* by giving the imagination the additional large task of copying all our impressions to produce their corresponding ideas (I.i.i, 1, 6). And he assigns more and more work to the imagination as the *Treatise* goes on. The imagination is responsible (among much else): for associating ideas in thought according to the three great principles of resemblance, contiguity and cause and effect; for enabling us to recognize genuine possibilities (the imaginable is the possible); even for producing the "vivacious fiction" that is our belief in the existence and persistence of the external world, despite our lack of any rational justification for holding that belief.

And, finally, the imagination is said to be what unites or associates our numerous ideas and perceptions into the bundle-self and leads us to believe that each individual human mind lasts through time as a single persisting individual. In effect for Hume "the imagination" becomes almost another term for "the understanding". Our crucial practical beliefs, as opposed to the conclusions of the demonstrations furnished by reason, are all provided by the imagination.

So how does the imagination hoodwink us into accepting the belief that the mind is a simple subject that lasts over time, a belief that Hume takes to be an "error", a "fiction", a "confusion and mistake" and even an "absurdity" (T I.iv.vi, 254–5, esp. 253; see also 259)? It seems we are misled by the similarities between our earlier and our later perceptions into identifying the earlier perceptions with the later ones. Because we think experience teaches that the objects we perceive are sensed without any intermediary between us and them, and because we only ever perceive perceptions, we come to think that our perceptions are lasting objects. This is despite the fact that there are often gaps and interruptions in our sense experiences that should tell us that the earlier and later perceptions *cannot* be numerically identical with each other. The imagination "fills in the gaps" and imagines lasting perceptions existing during the times when we are not looking, so to speak. So I come to think that what I perceive lasts and preserves its identity as one simple thing over a period of time. At the same time as I am attributing object identity to the things I see and feel I also attribute personal identity to myself – the thing that has, or rather is, the successive related and resembling perceptions.

In Hume's eyes, then, identity over time for the perceiving mind or bundle of perceptions is literally imaginary, a creation of the imagination. Neither over time nor at a time is there any real bond holding the bundle-self together. For perceptions are one and all distinct: "'Tis still true, that every distinct perception, which enters into the composition of the mind, is a distinct existence, and is different, and distinguishable, and separable from every other perception, either contemporary or successive" (T I.iv.vi, 259). The mind we come to have self-knowledge of, if we follow Hume's arguments about the self, is a loose association of ideas mostly related by the resemblance that relates originals to memories of them.

There are numerous difficulties and objections that can be raised against Hume's bundle theory of mind. Most of these concern how it is that a bundle of perceptions could perform the functions and engage in the activities that Hume assigns to human minds.

First, there is the question how any given mind is to distinguish those of its perceptions that are the objects it contemplates (i.e. the things in its environment) from those of its perceptions that constitute itself. For according to Hume's account my imagination is being misled into both running together perceptions to form ideas of persistent external objects and running together perceptions into a persistent me. So how does my mind distinguish itself from its world?

Secondly, how are persons to be individuated on a bundle theory? That is, how can one bundle be distinguished from another (even by itself) if the patterns of association and the resemblances among perceptions happen to be similar? How can I distinguish myself from you, or you from me?

Thirdly, is Hume's refusal to accept that any object lasts through change not just counter-intuitive but just plain wrong? Surely a human body, for example, can last through time and remain numerically one and the same despite physical alteration over the years. If Hume is wrong in denying identity over time to physical particulars he might be every bit as wrong about identity over time for minds.

Fourthly, many would say that Hume's view that perceptions are ontologically distinct entities – that perceptions can exist independently of being perceived by any mind – is so counter-intuitive that it needs far more support than Hume gives it. Surely Berkeley is right that for psychological states their *esse is percipi*. Hume's physics of the mind, with its impressions and ideas as utterly distinct mental atoms (the only true substances), lacks the support for itself that might give it hope of supporting Hume's extreme doctrine that identity through change for any entity is a fiction.

And finally, it has to be asked how something consisting of nothing but a collection or bundle of perceptions could create new perceptions and remember old ones as Hume believes all human minds do. And how could a bundle of perceptions imagine persistence through change where according to Hume there is none? If the mind is just a bundle of perceptions then they just are the (overworked) imagination. But how could the imagination be misled, as Hume pictures it being: how could it be led from earlier to later perceptions and identify the later with the earlier if it did not itself persist from earlier to later? Does the mind not have to be outside the stream of perceptions and persisting parallel to it in order to observe repetitions and to create them as Hume says the memory does? Surely, in order to be duped into postulating a persistent self, the imagination must itself be a persistent thing.

CHAPTER 28

Hume's notion of consciousness

It must be confessed at the outset that Hume says very little about the nature of consciousness and subjectivity; or, rather, he equates consciousness now with thought in general, now with reflection, sometimes with experience. And he seems to have devoted little thought to differentiating among different sorts of conscious awareness: there are no explicit distinctions between the humblest sensation and the most sophisticated introspection; between peripheral awareness and concentrated attention; between mere animal wakefulness and deep philosophical reflection. In § "Conscious experience and introspection", below, I shall look at what little is to be found in the *Treatise* on phenomenal consciousness and say something further about introspection and the tensions in Hume's thinking that threaten his belief in the possibility of an objective science of the mind. Before that, the following two sections introduce Hume's theory of association of ideas and his views on what is distinctive (including versions of perceptual and access consciousness) of beings endowed with the capacity for thought.

The principles of association

Hume offers an original theory of the principles of association among ideas (T I.i.iv, 10–13). This theory is a source of considerable pride to Hume and has a legitimate claim to be regarded as pioneering work – however sketchy and preliminary – in modern psychological and phenomenological explanation of the workings of the conscious mind. Humean associationism was the natural precursor of, and possible formative influence on, William James's highly evocative and influential notion of "the stream of consciousness". Hume regards association of ideas, impressions, memories, imaginings and emotions in line with his principles of association as the only possible source of unity in the ever-renewing bundle of perceptions that he takes the human mind or self to be.

He begins his discussion "Of the connexion or association of ideas" by setting out the problem to which his account is the intended answer:

> As all simple ideas may be separated by the imagination, and may be united again in what form it pleases, nothing wou'd be more unaccountable than the operations of that faculty, were it not guided by some universal principles, which render it, in some measure, uniform with itself in all times and places.   (T I.i.iv, 10)

The (two-part) question is: what determines which of my present ideas are united or joined together into those complex ideas that I find myself currently having and, given that I am now entertaining whatever perceptions are currently before my mind, what determines what will come to mind next?

It is to the second part of this question that Hume directs his discussion. He begins by remarking that if ideas were "entirely loose and unconnected, chance alone wou'd join them" (*ibid.*). But fortunately this has not been left to chance. Our ideas are joined together by the "associating quality, by which one idea naturally introduces another" or, rather, by the three qualities of (a) resemblance, (b) contiguity or neighbourhood in time or place and (c) cause and effect. Recall that Hume aspires to be the Newton of the mind and Newton has the force of gravity as his bold new explanatory principle in physics. Hume offers his principle of association as *his* vital force or principle to explain conscious operations and the successive contents of mental histories. He says "these ... principles of union or cohesion among our simple ideas ... supply ... a kind of ATTRACTION ... in the mental world" (*ibid.*, 12).

But he is constrained from the outset by his conviction that there is no necessary connection between ideas, that nothing whatever connects ideas in such a way that they cannot be separated by the mind. So he must admit that there is a disanalogy between physics and psychology here: whereas no portion of matter is exempt from obedience to the stern law of gravity, association is only "a gentle force which commonly [but not invariably] prevails" (*ibid.*, 10). Shortly we shall see that this is an utterly crucial disanalogy.

It is worth asking what exactly Hume's three qualities qualify and what it is on which their influence is supposed to operate. In particular, does Hume think that it is ideas that have these qualities? Or are they properties of the objects the ideas are ideas *of*? And do these qualities operate on the mind (often called by Hume "the imagination") leading it from one idea to another? Or are they meant to operate on other ideas, one idea dragging another idea in its wake, so to speak? Awkwardly, Hume provides passages that support each rival answer to each question. It could be that Hume thinks ideas themselves produce their successors in our minds. But perhaps he thinks (or also thinks) that the imagination produces ideas that are associated in one of the three given ways with the ideas that precede them in a given subject's mind. The crucial difference, of course, lies in the presence or absence of an independent agent, distinct from the bundle of ideas.

How do the three different qualities accomplish their task? The following are invented examples designed to illustrate how Hume thinks the three associative qualities work.

- *Resemblance*: My idea of my friend may prompt (or prompt my imagination to think of) the idea of my friend's identical twin. This could be because the two ideas resemble each other, but that, in turn, is because the objects of the two ideas resemble each other.
- *Contiguity*: My idea of a particular student might bring to mind an idea of her roommate. This could be because the two ideas are "neighbours" in my mental storehouse, which would be, in turn, because the two roommates are often encountered together and are often in the same room at the same time.
- *Cause and effect*: My idea of a forest fire brings to mind the idea of a lightning storm. Perhaps two such ideas are related directly (as ideas) by cause and effect but perhaps again the ideas form a sequence because the objects they are ideas *of* have been experienced as cause and effect.

Plausible as some of this may sound there are numerous loose ends and difficulties in this picture of mental sequences. There are the difficulties that flow from Hume's equivocation as to the "target" of the power of association. Does it work on an agent (the mind or imagination) to influence its progress from idea to idea? Or does it work directly on and through ideas themselves? Only if Hume had an account of how the idea-bundle can have faculties and be itself a continuous mental agent would he be able to justify switching as he constantly does between talk of the imagination running easily along associative paths and talk of ideas themselves introducing and drawing associated ideas in their train.

Then there are all the difficulties connected with the notion that ideas might be kept in a mental storehouse or receptacle where some are close neighbours. Hume surprisingly indicates (very briefly [T I.ii.v, 60–61]) that he regards ideas and their deployment and retrieval as having a neurophysiological base. He describes the association, particularly between contiguous ideas, as being one that results from the fact that ideas that we think of as contiguous are stored in adjacent memory cells in the brain. But Hume is mistaken if he thinks this removes any of the mystery about how contiguity and resemblance are supposed to work to bring ideas "before the mind". Hume pictures animal spirits like library staff searching the stacks for a book for a reader, rummaging in brain cells for ideas the mind "desir'd … to survey". But there is nothing in Hume's story analogous to the catalogue the reader would have consulted to locate the book he wanted to see. Surely Hume is meant to be explaining how resemblance, contiguity and cause and effect suggest ideas to the mind, not how they turn out to be used for locating ideas the mind has already thought of in order to summon them. Indeed, if it has already thought of them no summoning is necessary.

All this might make us feel that the mechanical or physical model of mental history with which Hume is working is less than ideal. Worst of all is the failure of Hume's account of association to explain why it is sometimes resemblance, sometimes contiguity and sometimes a tie of cause and effect (and sometimes none of these) that operates to insert an idea into my mental history. It would seem natural to say that of course the "strongest" association wins out. But this answer is not available to Hume, whose "gentle force which commonly prevails" qualification amounts to conceding that association fails to work like gravitational force at exactly this point. There is no chance of weighing the forces of different associative qualities against each other literally and mechanically. Hume is all too aware that there is nothing in psychology corresponding to the way in which quantifiable physical forces such as gravity *necessitate* their effects unless outweighed by a measurably sufficiently strong countervailing force.

Hume does say that cause and effect is the most prevalent and efficacious of the three associative qualities and also the one most likely to bestow on an idea that extra vivacity that Hume thinks transmutes a merely entertained idea into a belief. Unfortunately, Hume is struggling to accommodate his view that thought is fundamentally free and autonomous within a scientific understanding whose guiding paradigm is one of governance by *inevitable* natural law. That fact, along with the fact that the raw materials he allows himself are so very few – just perceptions and the capacity to copy and repeat them to produce mental contents that differ in degrees of force and vivacity – make his science of the human mind, for all its originality and suggestiveness, ultimately equivocal and explanatorily unsatisfactory.

What distinguishes things with conscious minds from things lacking consciousness?

Except in the two paragraphs in the *Treatise* mentioned above (T I.ii.v), where Hume says ideas are stored in the brain to be retrieved for the mind by the animal spirits, Hume usually and repeatedly denies that he has anything to say about the causal basis or ultimate source of our perceptions (T I.iii.v, 84; see also, e.g. "unknown causes" [T I.i.ii, 7]). In his view we cannot know whether our mental states and capacities have a physical or some other cause. So we would not expect to find him venturing an answer to the question what in their physical properties accounts for the distinction between those physical things that are capable of having impressions and ideas and those things, such as rocks and writing desks, that have no such perceptions.

But some possible answers to this question are certainly ruled out by positions Hume adopts and defends. Consider Descartes's contention that human beings are conscious in a way that even very sophisticated animals – let alone rocks – are not and that this is because human beings alone among earthly creatures are endowed with a rational soul. Hume clearly rules out this way of accounting for the difference between conscious and non-conscious beings when he rejects the notion of substance, whether material or immaterial, as incoherent. For the same reason he would reject Leibniz's contention that non-human and human animals are the sorts of conscious creatures each is because they are endowed with appropriately sophisticated dominant monads (i.e. simple substances).

Hume does, however, agree with Leibniz that at least the higher non-human animals are conscious. Or, to speak more cautiously, he considers it "an evident truth" that "beasts are endowed with thought and reason as well as men" (T I.iii.xvi, 176). His evidence for the claim that the brutes have these mental capacities is primarily behavioural and his argument is an argument from analogy: we are conscious that *our* behaviour is deliberately and intentionally "guided by reason and design" when we act to achieve the ends of self-preservation, obtaining pleasure and avoiding pain: "When therefore we see other creatures, in millions of instances, perform like actions, and direct them to like ends, all our principles of reason and probability carry us with an invincible force to believe the existence of a like cause" (*ibid.*). We rightly judge, on Hume's view, that the "internal actions" (i.e. reason and design) of animals are as similar to ours as are the animal "external actions" or behaviour that we observe. Indeed, Hume is so convinced of our sharing vast amounts of our inner, mental life with non-human animals that he suggests that we can test any proposed theory of mind purporting to explain human minds by seeing if it can satisfactorily account for non-human animals' performance of any mental operation that is "common to men and beasts" (*ibid.*, 177). If it yields a satisfactory account of animal mentality then it should be trusted as an account of the minds of human beings as well.

Hume goes on to argue that non-human animals must possess what present-day writers might describe as "perceptual consciousness", or possibly a form of "access consciousness", since it is necessary "that there be some impression immediately present to their memory or senses, in order to be the foundation of their judgment" (*ibid.*, 177–8). He also credits animals with the capacity for inference "built on experience". Here, as in human beings, we can see "the influence of custom on the imagination". In Book II of the *Treatise* Hume tells us that custom or habit can build up the "relations of resemblance, contiguity and causation [to] operate in the same manner upon beasts as upon human creatures" (T II.i.xii, 327). He also credits at least "the nobler" beasts with passions and emotions similar in many respects to ours. Since there is never any suggestion in the *Treatise* that Hume recognizes the existence in the mental sphere of anything we would describe as "*unconscious* perception, thought or feeling" it seems fair to conclude that Hume thinks all these animal passions, emotions, reasonings and experiences are conscious.

Conscious experience and introspection

Phenomenal consciousness
Hume talks repeatedly of seeing colours (red, blue); hearing sounds (squeaky hinges, birdsong); feeling warmth and cold; tasting a variety of flavours and relishes and smelling fragrances. He is sure that we have a rich variety of impressions corresponding to each of the bodily senses and that each of these has its own distinct feeling, savour or qualitative character. It thus seems right to say that Hume credits human beings and non-human animals alike with what nowadays would be called "phenomenal consciousness".

Hume regards these tastes and colours (in modern terminology "raw feels" or "qualia") as examples of ideas restricted to those who have the requisite impressions. He maintains that where a subject lacks the relevant experience or an appropriate sense organ for having impressions of a certain sort (say impressions of colour or taste) there will be no impression and thus no idea of the corresponding quality. A congenitally blind person who has never seen red will lack any idea of red and we "cannot form to ourselves a just idea of the taste of a pine-apple, without having actually tasted it" (T I.i.i, 5). In this Hume is very much in line with those modern-day philosophers of mind and psychology who hold that direct acquaintance of one's own with phenomena such as tastes and colours is necessary before one can have knowledge of those things. We will never form "a just idea of the taste" of a pineapple unless we taste one. We will never know "what it is like" to see red unless we have that experience.

However, to the great surprise of his readers ever afterwards, Hume provides an excellent counter-example to this view in his thought experiment of the missing shade of blue. We are asked to imagine an adult well acquainted with colours of all kinds who has somehow never in his life encountered a particular shade of blue:

> Let all the different shades of that colour, except that single one, be plac'd before him, descending gradually from the deepest to the lightest; 'tis plain that he will perceive a blank, where that shade is wanting, and will be sensible, that there is a greater distance in that place betwixt the contiguous colours, than in any other.
>
> (T I.i.i, 6; and see EH I.ii.16, 20–21)

Hume's conclusion is that the man in the story would certainly be able "to supply this deficiency" and imagine the missing shade of blue despite the fact that he has never had the impression corresponding to this idea.

Numerous commentators have been outraged, not by the example, which is very neat and convincing, but by the fact that Hume immediately discounts it as "so singular that it is scarcely worth our observing". How can he fail to see that it is a perfect counter-example to his correspondence principle and as such wholly undermines the principle? How does he miss that this renders wholly doubtful his use of it to attack supposedly empty philosophical notions such as that of substance, necessary connection and identity over time?

More importantly for our present purposes, the case is not in fact at all singular: as one recent writer on consciousness points out "innumerable analogous examples can be generated across the sensory modalities".[1] And there exist in addition a number of different sorts of examples from the current literature on the epistemology of conscious experience designed to show that we *can* get a good grasp of the phenomenal feel of certain sorts of experience even where we have never had them ourselves. These examples include the way in which a composer or painter can "work in his or her head" and know how the planned music will sound, how the envisaged painting will look,

---

1. Owen Flanagan, *Consciousness Reconsidered* (Cambridge, MA: MIT Press, 1992), 88.

before a note is written or a brush applied to canvas. Again, there are the vast range of fictions – novels, plays, films – that somehow find a way of enabling us to imagine successfully what it is like to have a wide array of experiences and emotions that we have never experienced for ourselves.

Introspective consciousness
We saw above (Chapter 27, §§ "First-person authority" and "No unconscious perceptions") that Hume displays an uneasy mixture of beliefs about what introspection teaches. There is a clear tension between his oft-quoted pronouncement that "all actions and sensations of the mind ... must necessarily appear in every particular what they are, and be what they appear" and his suggestion that an opponent might need "serious and unprejudiced reflection" to gain particular self-knowledge of his own mental contents. The latter concessive (if ironic) suggestion challenges transparency, strong self-intimation and first-person authority: the mind can have secrets after all and it does not necessarily yield them up, at least to the casual inward glance. Introspection has mental appearances presented to it and appearances can deceive. The person introspecting must work hard to discern the mental reality behind any obstacles erected by prejudice. Introspective consciousness – although it is undoubtedly a rich source of information about our mind's workings and experiences – cannot be quite the infallible source of self-knowledge Hume had hoped.

And worse still we can now see that Hume is faced with another, closely related, tension, this time between the principle that "subjective experience of any phenomenon is necessary for genuine knowledge of that phenomenon" and his desire to produce a science of human mentality in general. For knowledge of the experiences and mental states of persons other than myself is, according to the principle just stated, something I could obtain only by having those experiences myself. But that is something no one can do. No one can literally have another's experiences or mental states for himself. Hume seems stuck: he cannot have knowledge of the subjective experiences or mental states of anyone other than himself and even the self-knowledge that he would like to say is infallibly provided by introspection cannot be guaranteed. So how is an objective scientific understanding of mind-in-general to be achieved?

There are two things Hume could say to this challenge. First he could say that just because a source of information proves fallible this does not mean that it cannot furnish knowledge under the right conditions. Provided that standards of accuracy and freedom from prejudice can be devised for introspection to measure itself against, it should be possible for the mental scientist to discover introspectively numerous features of his own mind that can plausibly be attributed to all human minds using an argument from analogy. Hume's frequent remarks about the importance of ever more accurate mental surveys and the superior probative value of multiple instances (e.g. T I.i.i, 2–3) show that he is amenable to the notion that introspection is a process that admits of different degrees of accuracy and success and could be required to be self-critical or self-correcting.

The second response Hume could make would be to recall his own "missing shade of blue" counter-example. But instead of dismissing it as too singular to matter he could accept that it *is* a counter-example and that it shows that we can in fact have knowledge of phenomena we have not experienced ourselves, including some that we could never experience. First-person impressions of others' minds and experiences are in principle unobtainable. But "missing shade of blue"-type examples (along with other examples such as those sketched in § "Phenomenal consciousness", above) can give us understanding of others' experiences and mental life sufficient to make an objective science of the mind a genuine possibility. This is especially true when such knowledge of others is integrated with the deliverances of hard-working self-critical introspection.

The trouble is that Hume, of course, cannot accept that his "missing shade of blue" reasoning disproves his correspondence principle. That principle is his main weapon against substance, necessary connections in nature, the persistent self and all the other traditional philosophical notions Hume regards as nonsense or, at best, unwarranted posits. Hume was proud enough of the reasoning in his story of the missing shade of blue to repeat it verbatim in the *Enquiry*. But he could not allow himself to see how radically his "missing shade of blue" disarmed his whole metaphysical position.

CHAPTER 29

Hume on mental causation

Does Hume believe that states of mind have causal efficacy? Can they either move the body or alter the mind of the person who has them? And supposing that the answer is yes, does Hume have any resources from which he could create a response to the modern-day causal exclusion argument against mental causation? In order to answer these questions we need to look first at Hume's account of the nature of causation as constant conjunction and his rejection of the notion of causal force or necessary connection. It will also be helpful to glance at his views on determinism, free will and miracles.

Causation not necessary connection

Contrary to persistent student myth, Hume does not deny that causation exists. Quite the contrary, Hume thinks that the relation of cause and effect is the most common relationship among things in the world and the foundation of "all reasonings concerning *matter of fact*" (T *Abstract*, 649). But what exactly can we observe in a simple example of cause and effect: say, a collision between a moving billiard ball and a stationary one? Strictly speaking we see only the first ball moving until it touches the second and then the second ball moving off. This "contiguity in time and place" and "priority of the cause to the effect" that we observe are two "requisite circumstances of causation". If we keep repeating the experiment with the same ball and then similar balls we will obtain similar results and eventually see that a third requisite circumstance of causation is "constant conjunction". In fact, the most important condition of causation, for Hume, is that "Every object like the cause, produces always some object like the effect" (*ibid.*).

But suppose that only a putative cause or effect is present and not its partner: I see only the first ball moving but look away before the collision. Or I arrive only in time to see the second ball cannoning across the table. In either of these cases I will need to make a causal inference. The newly created Adam seeing such an episode for the first time would not be able to predict the movement of the second ball from seeing just the movement of the first. What is needed is repetition: the multiplication of instances. Experience will teach Adam about the movement of colliding spheres and allow him to make inferences from cause to effect or from a perceived effect back to its cause. "All reasonings concerning cause and effect, are founded on experience, and … on the supposition, that the course of nature will continue uniformly the same" (*ibid.*, 651).

This last point means that such inferences or reasonings can never be demonstrations or deductions. Effects do not follow their causes by any kind of logical necessity since it is always conceivable that nature's course might alter. At this point Hume would like to say that this is all there is to cause and effect. In fact he often drops all reference to contiguity or priority; after all, there are plausible cases of action at a distance and of causes contemporary with (rather than prior to) their effects. Causation for Hume is essentially constant conjunction and nothing more. But he is aware that most philosophers would say that he has omitted something vital. Surely causes produce their effects by having a "power" or "force" or "productive quality".

Hume categorically denies that there is such a necessary connection between causes and effects (T I.iii.xiv, 157): there is no impression from which the idea of such necessary connection could be derived. In the billiard ball example there is nothing to be observed but regularity, contiguity and priority. We never see the first ball compelling the second to move. Experience of repeated examples gives only constant conjunction of the things dubbed "cause" and "effect". We never perceive any sort of necessary connection between the two or power in the first to produce the second. The only power or force in play is the force of habit or custom, which makes the observer expect the oft-repeated sequel.

The feeling of power?

In a passage added in the Appendix to the *Treatise* Hume considers the possible objection that we actually have direct experience of necessary connection in our own person; this happens on those constant daily occasions when "the motions of our body, and the thoughts and sentiments of our mind … obey the will" (T Appendix, 632). Having thus acquired "a just notion of force or power" from exercising our own power to move our body or change our mind, we know what we mean when we say the first billiard ball has the power to move the second or that there is a necessary connection between the first ball's movement and that of the second.

Consideration of this possible riposte to his position is largely an afterthought in the *Treatise* but Hume considers it at serious length in the *Enquiry* (EH I.vii.i.51ff., 64ff.). He is, of course, not convinced: he gives three main reasons why he remains sure that even when reflective consciousness tells us that "the motion of our body follows upon the command of our will" we remain ignorant of the *means* by which the will manages to pull off this feat. Hume thinks we are unable to discover "by the most diligent enquiry" the supposed force or energy by which the will moves the body. He then gives versions of the same three reasons against the possibility that we get the impression of power or necessary connection from awareness of our capacity to "raise up" ideas in our minds.

First, it would be astonishing if we had direct experience of the means by which the will moves the body for this would mean that we knew the answer to the perennial mystery of the nature of the union between soul and body. And that would mean that we knew "the nature of both these substances", which, of course, Hume strenuously denies. Equally, it would be extraordinary if we had any idea how the soul or mind produces an idea: this is a "real creation" *ex nihilo*. We no more know how we do it than we know how God creates the world out of nothing.

Secondly, we can voluntarily move our tongue and fingers, not our heart or liver. But we do not learn this prior to experience. Again, we are not directly aware of the limitations on our capacity to "raise up an idea", but there certainly are such limitations, especially where our sentiments and passions are concerned. All this suggests that we do not really have such powers. Similarly, someone who has lost the use of a limb will think he can still move it at will until he tries. If we know the limitations on our capacity to move our bodies or change our minds only from *experience*, this tells us that we do not have a direct impression of any such power.

Thirdly, science teaches us that a chain of physical causes connects any act of will with the bodily movement willed. I have not the slightest idea what these numerous causes and effects constituting the chain are. I certainly do not make the unknown brain event that initiates the chain the object of my will or have any impression of willing *it* to happen. Likewise, it would seem that our mental "self-command" is different at different times and situations. Health, time of day and proximity to a meal all affect the degree to which we are "master of our thoughts". And these variations seem very likely to result from unknown physical factors making "the [supposed] power or energy of the will" equally unknown.

261

But having argued vigorously against the notion that I might get an impression of power from my own power to move my body or alter my mental history Hume then comes close to admitting the point after all; he says in a footnote that we are aware of sometimes making a strong endeavour to overcome resistance (say when lifting a heavy body) and that this "animal nisus [effort, striving, impulse] which we experience enters very much into that vulgar inaccurate idea which is formed of it" (EH I.vii.53, 67). So we *do* have an idea of force from our own experience, albeit only a popular and "inaccurate" one. But Hume will not call this feeling "the impression from which the idea of power or necessary connection is derived" because this feeling of effort never enables someone to deduce what the effect of the exertion will be. To be a genuine experience of power, Hume thinks, an experience would have to be an infallible predictor of that power's effects. And, of course, for Hume no experience of a cause allows the person who has it to deduce without qualification what effect will follow.

Mental causes: liberty, necessity and miracles

Having now learned the fundamentals of Hume's account of causation and his rejection of necessary connection we are ready to address the questions asked in the Introduction: does Hume think that states of mind have causal efficacy? What response could he give if confronted with the modern-day problem of mental causation? Well, we know that he holds that what makes any event, whether mental or physical, a cause is the experienced constant conjunction of such events with events such as the one we take to be its effect. I am aware that events of the type "my arm rising" follow regularly on events of the type "my willing that my arm rise" so I know that, for Hume, it is correct to say that my willing causes my arm to rise. This is all there is to the fact that such willings cause such arm-risings. Again, I know that this decision to cross the road is the cause of my subsequent crossing of the road because all previous such decisions have led to such crossings. All there is to causation is constant conjunction. Hume can say with Locke (in turn echoing Descartes) that "we find by Experience, that barely by willing it, barely by a thought of the Mind, we can move the parts of our Bodies, which were before at rest" (*Essay* II.xxi.4, 235).

For Hume, mental states, events and acts easily meet his requirements for being causes of physical movement. Admittedly, we do not know *how* these causes bring about their effects. But Hume would say we neither need nor can answer Princess Elisabeth's question how mind, without contacting or pushing body, can nonetheless move it (see Chapter 4). The point is completely general: no more do we know how physical causes produce physical effects or how mental causes produce mental effects. There is, for Hume, no special problem of mind–body interaction. Hume gives only the haziest impression of whether he thinks of physical causes and mental causes as deeply different in kind or not. We can be sure he is no substance dualist. He may think the properties of perceptions and of body are metaphysically different. He may think mental properties are a kind of physical properties. He just does not say. What is clear is that mental causes are on the same footing with physical causes as far as Hume is concerned: if there is constant conjunction (and priority and contiguity) there is causation. Experienced constant conjunction amounts to causation.

Physical exclusion

But what if we were to press the "physical exclusion argument" that the physical world is causally closed; that my arm-movement or road-crossing must and will each have a sufficient, exclusively physical cause independent of my willing and deciding; that no event can be given more than one causal explanation; that the mental is thus pre-empted from having any causal efficacy?

Perhaps the simplest response would be for Hume to say that we have the evidence of constant conjunction to *prove* that such mental events *are* causes of such physical events and thus that the conjecture of causal closure of the physical must be mistaken. He could deny that all human bodily movements have complete physical causes that guarantee their occurrence whether or not there is any possible candidate to be the mental cause of those movements. But would Hume have been likely to adopt such a response and could he do so consistently with his other views on causation, necessity, freedom of the will and natural law? Is such a response really an option for Hume? Does he ever come close to adopting such a position?

In Book II of the *Treatise* Hume gives a detailed defence of the view that mental causes (motives, volitions, character) determine the happening of physical effects (bodily movements) and that they do so with the same "necessity" – as he is there using this term – as do physical causes (T II.iii.i, 400ff.). He gives an example of a causal chain some of whose links are "actions of the mind" and some physical, "natural causes" and describes that causal chain as perfectly natural, anything but deviant (T II.iii.ii, 406).

Liberty and necessity

Why does Hume set about arguing that mental causes can and do cause bodily movements and thus human actions? Hume is, like Hobbes, a "compatibilist"

263

in ethics. That is to say, he is forthright in maintaining (a) determinism about human action, (b) the possibility of a kind of freedom and (c) the full compatibility of determinism with free will, provided that the appropriate concepts of both causal determinism and freedom are employed.

The freedom we (some of the time) have, he thinks, is the freedom from constraint: I am free if, having decided what I want to do and how I want to act, I am not prevented from carrying out my intended action. And this is very frequently the case. To take a trivial example, I go to the cafeteria and, without constraint, choose the "healthy option" for my lunch. No one compels me to select the salad and decline the chips. I am offered a choice and I exercise it unimpeded.

But just as Hume is certain that there are features of the imagination, reason and understanding that are shared universally by all human minds and which can be studied scientifically (as he attempts to do in Book I of the *Treatise*) so too he is sure that there are "necessary and uniform principles of human nature" (T II.iii.i, 402) that govern our private and public behaviour and social intercourse of all kinds. The circumstances of birth, education, claims of family, friendship, national loyalty, craft or profession, national characteristics, and so on, all have a known causal influence on the will and thus on behaviour. We all realize how the presence or occurrence of these influences has been conjoined regularly in the past with subsequent appropriate acts of will on our part. There is in human affairs what Hume refers to as a "necessity" from which "the actions of the will ... arise" (*ibid.*, 405), and which means that "actions have a constant union and connexion with the situation and temper of the agent" (*ibid.*, 403). This is Hume's determinism as it applies to human life and action.

We are well accustomed to this regularity in human character and action. Our social and business encounters all rely on our ability to anticipate the responses and actions of our fellows: something we do using our understanding of everyday human psychology. In building his case for belief in this uniformity of human nature and motivation Hume gives many examples that are very reminiscent of those used by modern-day writers such as Jerry Fodor in arguing for the truth of (and realism about) folk psychology. "Folk psychology" is the term for our ordinary everyday common-sense psychological understanding of our family, neighbours, workmates, tradesmen, clients, customers and so on: all the people we encounter as we go about the business of daily life.

How could we rationally reject the view that people's actions are informally predictable from, if not entailed by, their situation and character and their presumed or known beliefs and desires, wants and wishes? How could ordinary social interaction avoid descending into chaos if people did not initiate actions conforming to the dictates of their particular situations and circumstances, guided by their knowledge of the myriad social and linguistic conventions operative in their environment? We know that most of the time people will keep appointments they have made; employees will look out for their employer's interests; parents will do what they think best in caring for their children; guards will prevent a prisoner's escape; the pain of a burn will make a person pull back from the fire; and so forth. Behaviour of certain sorts follows feelings, thoughts, motives, volitions and principles of certain sorts. Human actions are caused – indeed Hume says "determined" – by mental causes.

Natural law

This necessity of mental causes leading to physical effects is "of the same nature, and deriv'd from the same principles" as the physical necessity that links exclusively physical events. So, although it is not possible to *demonstrate* or *deduce* that certain future effects will flow from either sort of cause, this in no way diminishes the truth that I will always act in conformity with all the many influences that operate on my mind in planning my actions. Hume takes the causal regularities – both mental and physical – that are constantly revealed by experience to form a system of natural law. Newtonian scientific understanding of the physical, Humean scientific understanding of the mind, are achieved when these natural laws are inductively discovered and codified. Should such a natural law be transgressed that would constitute a miracle (EH I.x.90, 114).

What about those actions that seem to fall outside the causal system: the doings that seem to be done by chance? Hume says that where we feel that we act without cause, "the chance or indifference lies only in our judgment on account of our imperfect knowledge, not in the things themselves, which are in every case equally necessary" (T II.iii.i, 404). There are no chance actions; my behaviour is always caused. This is bound to seem surprising coming from the philosopher notorious for arguing that the principle that everything has a cause could, for all we know, have exceptions. But Hume is not being inconsistent: he can regard natural law as in fact exceptionless without believing that the proposition "Every event has a cause" can be demonstrated. A causeless happening is conceivable. It is just that there will never be one.

So Hume denies that anything happens by chance, sees mind and matter alike as governed by natural law and regards causeless events as conceivable but maximally improbable. The only way in which one of my actions might fail to be caused by "the natural and inherent principles and passions of human nature" is if God – whose omnipotence makes him alone capable of doing so – should elect "to new-mould the human mind, and change its character" (T III.ii.v, 521). That is, it would require a divine recreation of human nature and natural law. And although Hume does not deny outright the possibility of miracles (violation of natural law as opposed to recreation of it) it is clear from the Tenth Enquiry that he thinks them exceedingly unlikely.

Where does this leave Hume on the question of the causal closure of the physical realm and thus on the challenge of the modern-day epiphenomenalist position on mental causation? Earlier I suggested that Hume could respond by denying that the physical realm is causally closed. It seems to me increasingly that this is the response he would have favoured had he been faced with this challenge. We have seen that Hume would certainly refuse to deny the capacity of mental states and properties to affect the material world; of minds to move their bodies. He recognizes spirits as genuine causes every bit as much as he recognizes bodies as causes. He also insists that there is no such thing as chance behaviour. He is wholly persuaded of the law-governed character, and hence amenability to scientific understanding, of minds and mental causes. He is sceptical of the existence of miracles. It seems that if Hume believes in the causal closure or completeness of anything it is the closure of created nature, including efficacious human minds.

Postscript
Recalling that Hume does at one point in the *Treatise* say that ideas are somehow stored in the brain, we might wonder whether Hume could conceivably have been won over to some sort of identity theory: whether he could have been persuaded that the mental causes whose existence he never doubts are most convincingly accounted for by seeing them as very special types of physical properties, states or events. Had he been willing to come this far it might perhaps have been open to him to accept the causal closure of the physical realm while still retaining the causal efficacy of the mental, since (created) mental subjects and states would, under this supposition, be regarded as both physical and mental items.[1] But this speculation goes so far beyond any textual basis that it seems an appropriate time to accept that, speculation can and should be taken no further.

---

1. For a detailed and fascinating defence of such a theory of mind see Papineau, *Thinking About Consciousness*.

CHAPTER 30

Hume on representation

Whatever their other differences, all the early modern philosophers dealt with so far are agreed that the "aboutness" or intentionality of our ideas is *derived* rather than *original* intentionality. By one route or another, they all reach the view that it is God who bestows aboutness or meaning on our mental states. Either God furnishes us directly with innate ideas that are already about their objects or he endows us with the physiological mechanisms for acquiring – and endows things with the powers to cause in us – just those ideas that are best fitted to represent what we naturally take them to be ideas of. Either way, our ideas ultimately owe their "aboutness" to God, who appoints them to represent what they come to stand for in our thinking.

Does Hume agree with our other philosophers on this subject? In what follows I look first at the question whether Hume thinks that ideas in our minds represent things in the world external to our minds. The second section discusses *how* he thinks it is that mental states come to represent whatever they are about and the third section is about the problem of representing what does not exist. The final section looks briefly at the question whether Hume would say that perceptions owe their intentionality ultimately to the will of God.

Representing the external world

Hume's readers have always disagreed about his self-declared scepticism. On the one hand it is clear that he is highly sceptical about very many philosophical topics. These include at least: the existence of the self; the nature and existence of the external world; induction; material and immaterial substances; necessary connections and causal powers in nature; empty space; time in which no changes occur; identity over time for any objects and especially for persons. But how sceptical is Hume and what sort of scepticism does he subscribe to? Does he hold, for example, that there is no external world such as we may think ourselves to be informed about by our bodily senses? Or does he simply believe that we can never be justified in claiming *knowledge* of its existence?

At numerous points in the *Treatise* Hume declares his conviction that we never perceive or "have before the mind" anything other than perceptions (e.g. T I.ii.vi, 66–7; T I.iv.ii, 197, 212; T II.ii.ii, 343; T III.i.i, 456). As we know, he recognizes only two sorts of mental entities or perceptions; namely, what he calls "impressions" and "ideas". Impressions, most commentators agree, are sensations, products of interior reflection or of the bodily senses. Ideas are copies that the mind (the imagination) makes of those impressions. Some readers have elaborated on Hume's two terms, interpreting impressions as "the given", "experiences of the objective" or even "the real" and ideas as "images", "the imaginary", "concepts" or "meanings".

The exact spin put on the two terms is not as important for our immediate purposes as Hume's conviction that our thought and experience never go beyond these two sorts of conscious perception. He says: "since nothing is ever present to the mind but perceptions … 'tis impossible for us so much as to conceive or form an idea of any thing specifically different [of a different species or metaphysical kind] from ideas and impressions" (T I.ii.vi, 67). Since "we never really advance a step beyond ourselves, nor can conceive any kind of existence, but those perceptions", we are just inferring and going beyond the evidence when we think of what appear to us to be external objects as "specifically different" from perceptions (*ibid.*, 67–8).

Is Hume saying that the only things that exist as far as he is concerned are ideas and impressions (and the minds in which they appear, which are after all just bundles of perceptions)? Or is he just saying that we cannot in his opinion conceive of any other sort of existent thing (although there may be such)? Certainly he makes clear that he believes we never have unmediated contact with whatever reality there is outside the mind and that we therefore have absolutely no knowledge of what, if anything, exists beyond ideas and the impressions from which those ideas are copied.

Hume seems to be here confessing that he would subscribe to a form of idealism, he would think reality consists entirely of perceptions, were it not that the world outside our minds' perceptions is in principle unknowable. Ideas are copies of – and therefore representations of – our impressions. But the source of our impressions is a mystery. Impressions arise "in the soul originally, from unknown causes" (T I.i.i, 7). Their ultimate cause is, in Hume's opinion "perfectly inexplicable by human reason" (T I.iii.v, 84). They afford us no information about a world outside the mind. So, if they are representations at all we have no idea what it is that they represent.

Or so all the passages examined so far imply. They strongly suggest that Hume is an idealist in all but name. And yet the *Treatise* is also chock-full of references to material objects (including human bodies), which Hume speaks of as if they are, not Berkeleian collections of mental particulars, but public, space-taking, solid, movable, albeit in Hume's view not lasting, nonetheless mind-independent things. And, moreover, these pens, papers, desks, chairs, oceans, ferries, fires, stairs, doors, servants, letters, pictures and silver stand-ishes are represented by ideas – both simple and complex – in my mind.

In the *Abstract* Hume defines "impression" and "idea" as follows: "When we feel a passion or emotion of any kind, or have the images of external objects conveyed by our senses; the perception of the mind is ... an *impression* ... When we reflect on a passion or an object which is not present, this perception is an *idea*" (T *Abstract*, 647). This says that impressions, *inter alia*, are sensory *images of external objects*. It also says that ideas represent (thus enabling us to think about) absent *objects*.

One final quotation should confirm that Hume's scepticism on this subject is not (or not unequivocally) of the sort that declares the non-existence of what cannot be known to exist. Rather, it is a scepticism that denies our enti-tlement to claim knowledge of (the existence of) anything other than the contents of our minds:

> [A]s no beings are ever present to the mind but perceptions; it follows that we ... can never observe [a conjunction] between perceptions and objects. 'Tis impossible, therefore, that from the existence or any of the qualities of the former, we can ever form any conclusion concerning the existence of the latter, or ever satisfy our reason in this particular. (T I.iv.ii, 212)

There is no way in which we could experience both our impressions and their causes to see what those causes are, to see whether the impressions are reli-able guides to the nature of those causes, or even to discover whether some-thing "specifically different" from a perception exists. Any experience we might have of a supposed cause of our impressions would itself be an impres-sion, a perception, not something different in kind from a perception. As Hume says apropos Locke's representationalism, "our senses ... convey to us nothing but a single perception" and a "single perception can never produce the idea of a double existence" (*ibid.*, 189). That is, the impressions that enter our minds in sensation certainly exist but our sensations do not attest to the existence of a second, external thing causing each impression and which that impression resembles. Moreover, there is no justification for taking as true the inference we make from sense impression (considered as an effect) to independent external object (considered as the cause). Neither sensation nor inference can give us knowledge of the existence of anything beyond our perceptions, that is, outside our minds.

The upshot of all this for Hume's views on our mental representation of objects outside our minds is that he is prepared to say that our ideas represent the impressions that cause them. But for all we can know those impressions are all there is to the so-called external objects (pens, papers, desks, etc.) that we would list if making an inventory of the furniture of the world and which we ordinarily suppose to be of a different "species" or nature from that of perceptions. So he does not hold that impressions in turn represent external objects, although he sometimes talks as if he does; he is not prepared to venture an (official) opinion on what impressions represent, if anything. Ideas represent impressions and in so doing they somehow give us the wherewithal to think about the objects that furnish the world we experience.

Images and resemblance

If ideas represent impressions, what sort of representation is it and how is this representing accomplished? Recent writers on intentionality often cite Hume as a classic exponent of the view that one thing represents or is about something else when the first resembles the second.[1] And Hume certainly says some things that suggest that he thinks resemblance between ideas and the impressions they copy is the source of the intentionality of those ideas. He defines ideas as "faint *images*" of impressions (T I.i.i, 2) and says that "*all our ideas and impressions are resembling*" (*ibid.*, 3). He also says, when arguing that we have no idea of the substance of our minds, that there could be no idea of mental substance because there could be no impression of such a thing. "How can an impression represent a substance", Hume asks "otherwise than by resembling it?" Of course he proceeds to say that an impression cannot resemble a substance since it has none of the qualities or characteristics a substance is supposed to have (T I.iv.v, 232–3). The important point here is that Hume seems to be saying in the course of this reasoning that resemblance alone can make one thing represent another.

We have seen repeatedly in earlier chapters how difficult it would be to defend the view that representation depends entirely on resemblance. It

---

1. For example, see George Graham, *Philosophy of Mind: An Introduction*, 2nd edn (Oxford: Blackwell, 1998), 155.

is easy to think of things that represent or are about other things without bearing any resemblance to what they represent. To take just one obvious example, words represent or are about the things they are used to refer to but it is very difficult to produce a word that bears any resemblance of any kind to the thing it signifies. The words "magenta" and "mastodon" bear no resemblance to that colour or that prehistoric creature. Onomatopoeia (the formation of words that sound like the thing the word means) provides some words (for example "buzz", "dingdong", "whir") that have an auditory resemblance to the sound they are used to talk about. But such onomatopoeic words are surely very much the exception. Neither words nor ideas need to be like what they represent. In general we can say that resemblance is not necessary for representation.

Nor is resemblance sufficient. Identical twins, no matter how strongly they resemble each other, do not represent each other. And a house may resemble its blueprint in innumerable respects but that is not enough to make the house *represent* that blueprint; the house is not "about" its blueprint. This example is a reminder that resemblance differs from representation in being a symmetrical relationship. A symmetrical relationship works in both directions: if a portrait photograph resembles its subject then its subject resembles the portrait. Representation, on the other hand, is a one-way relationship: the portrait represents the person; the person is not about the portrait.

So if all there is to mental representation on Hume's view is resemblance, and in particular the resemblance of an image or picture to its subject, then this would seem to be something of a dead end. It is clear that Hume thinks ideas are the representatives in my mind of all the things in the world that I experience. But his account of how ideas manage to represent things is wholly inadequate to the task. Even strictly in its own terms it is confused and unpersuasive. There is the problem first off of how an idea (a wholly non-physical thing) could (pictorially) resemble or be the image of an impression (also a wholly non-physical thing). There is also the problem of how wholly non-physical ideas could resemble and thus represent physical things.

Then again there is the problem that, officially at least, impressions are not supposed to represent something beyond or external to the bundle of perceptions that constitute the mind, such as physical objects with sensible properties. In the special context just quoted, however, where Hume is arguing that there could not be an impression of mental substance, he says that this is because impressions share no features with substances and so an impression could not resemble a substance. This suggests that, at least in this context, Hume *does* think that impressions can and do represent objects beyond themselves and that this is by resemblance. The theory of mental

271

representation as founded on resemblance seems both fatally inadequate and self-contradictory.

However, it ought to be said in Hume's defence that he does not in fact rely solely on resemblance to underpin his view of how mental representation works. Recall that he defines ideas as copies that the mind makes of impressions. Whatever sort of copy and copying mechanism Hume has in mind it is clear that he believes there is a causal dependency of ideas on impressions. Lack of a particular sense organ (e.g. sight) robs the subject of the ideas in the production of which such sense impressions have a crucial causal role. Lack of a certain sort of experience or impression (e.g. the taste of pineapple) robs the subject of the corresponding idea. Hume repeatedly stresses the constant conjunction of simple ideas with precedent impressions, and constant conjunction as we know is the hallmark of causal relationship. Hume's ideas represent their causes. His theory of mental representation is at least as much a causal one as a resemblance one.

This does not mean, of course, that Hume's theory of mental representation is out of the woods. Crucially, Hume has no way of distinguishing those causes and causal factors – those items in the causal chain leading to an idea – that are relevant to that idea's intentionality and those that are not connected with its aboutness. Hume declines to engage in examination of our sensations, a study that he says belongs "more to anatomists and natural philosophers" than to himself in his present project (T I.i.ii, 8). But he makes the point in the *Enquiry*, when talking about the causal power of the will, that causal chains involving ideas often have a multitude of minute physical links of which the subject who senses, experiences, thinks, wills and acts remains wholly unaware. What then explains why some of the causes of any one of our ideas are connected with the aboutness of the idea caused while some are not? Not every cause results in its effect's being *about* that particular cause. So how does causality explain or account for intentionality? Hume has not told us.

Surprisingly, Hume has no theory of perception in the *Treatise*. One concomitant of this is that he has nothing to say about perceptual error. For all that we can find in the *Treatise*, Hume might believe that no one ever misidentifies anything and no idea ever comes into anyone's mind inappropriately in sensory experience. So he has no answer to either "the problem of misrepresentation" or "the disjunction problem", both of which have been discussed in earlier chapters as challenges to a causal theory of mental representation. He does think that resemblance between remembered and present sense experiences causes errors in reasoning: notably, it causes us to identify earlier objects with later ones and leads us into the mistake of thinking external objects preserve their identity as a single thing over time. But this is (for Hume) an error of logic rather than one that consists of misrepresenting one sort of thing as another.

Representing the non-existent

It is common ground among all writers on the subject that a central distinguishing feature of mental representation is that mental representations can be about the non-existent. I can have a thought that is about Pegasus, Mr Pickwick, Mrs Pickwick, round squares. I can also think about what no longer exists (Cicero, Great Aunt Vi) and what does not exist yet (an Aids vaccine, a longed-for but as yet unconceived baby). So any theory of mental representation worthy of attention must be able to accommodate thought about the non-existent. But it is difficult to see how Hume can meet this requirement.

To begin with, the conclusion of the previous section is that such explanation as Hume can give of how ideas represent things outside the mind makes causation (in conjunction with resemblance) the source of intentionality. An idea in the mind represents what it does because it is copied from (i.e. causally dependent on) an impression caused by that object. But what does not exist cannot cause anything. Try as I might I cannot get an impression of Cicero or Pegasus. So Hume would appear unable to account for my thoughts about historical figures or mythological beings.

Worse still, one of the leading precepts in Hume's theory of mind is the principle that every idea has a corresponding impression from which it is copied. We have seen him argue in the following way with respect to numerous philosophical notions as he does here about the idea of substance:

(i)   There is no impression of substance.
(ii) Thus there is no idea of substance.
(iii) Therefore, without an idea to act as its meaning, the term "substance" is literally meaningless or senseless.

Since a thing must exist to cause an impression and in turn an idea of itself in a perceiver, it would seem that Hume is committed to the view that we cannot think (or talk meaningfully) about something that does not exist.

There are a number of points that Hume would no doubt wish to make immediately in response to this very brief, broadbrush summary of his position. First of all, Hume could and should point out that the ideas of historical figures and situations that allow me to think about such things, although they have obviously not been copied from my own sensory

273

impressions, have been conveyed to me by histories and historical evidence. Plato and Cicero were accessible to their contemporaries, whose impressions of them provided those observers with corresponding ideas. An idea need have only a *possible* impression corresponding to it in order to be an idea in good standing. And it would seem that Hume thinks such genuine ideas can be conveyed in language from one mind to another.

Moreover, Hume would also doubtless point out that he specifically limits his correspondence principle to *simple* impressions and ideas (T I.i, 3). A complex idea such as the idea of the New Jerusalem is one that can be obtained by putting together simple ideas such as those of gold and of pavements, of walls and of rubies, all these simple ideas having been copied from impressions gained in experience. So imaginary and mythical things can be thought about because the simple ideas making up their complex ideas are readily obtainable. I can think of the New Jerusalem just as readily as I can think of Paris even though the first of these cities does not exist.

So Hume has an effective answer for the critic who accuses him of having a theory of thought and representation that does not allow thinkers to think about fictional or historical people and places. But the cost to Hume of using this answer could be more than he would be willing to pay. For if, in order to be genuine, an idea need only correspond to an in-principle-possible impression, not one I actually have, and if a complex idea can be made up of simple ideas drawn from all manner of experiences, it is difficult to see why I could not after all have an idea of causal power or empty space or of a persistent self. Of course admitting that such complex ideas are possible would not be equivalent to conceding that the things signified by those ideas exist. But it would completely undermine what Hume appears to regard as a powerful argument that they do not.

The ultimate source of intentionality?

Unlike his empiricist and rationalist predecessors, Hume does not say explicitly that the intentionality of perceptions derives ultimately from God's will. Nor does he deny that this is the case. He makes clear that he regards sense perception – particularly sight – as a natural mechanism whereby images are introduced to the mind via the impressions from which ideas are copied. And we have no reason to doubt that he took nature and the laws by which natural mechanisms operate to be God's creations.

Hume assumed that mental images just naturally represent what they resemble and that this requires no further explanation, any more than we need, or can, explain why the image in a mirror is the image of what is placed before the mirror rather than the image of anything else. Perhaps he should have seen that there is a profound problem here. But he did not. So it is at least fair to say that Hume is not guilty of explicitly consigning a problem he could not resolve scientifically to the incomprehensible will of God.

Conclusion

Personal identity

One topic that I have had to leave almost completely untouched in this book is the question what each of our philosophers would say accounts for personal identity or persistence of the self over time. Here is the briefest of catalogues of the answers I believe would be given. Criteria of personal identity are often said to fall into broadly two types: a criterion that stresses physical persistence of the body or one where psychological continuity is crucial. It could be said that each of our six thinkers (with the possible exception of Spinoza) adopts his own, highly distinctive *psychological* criterion.

Descartes

Descartes appears to have been very little interested in the subject of personal identity but if pressed to designate a principle of identity for the self he would say that personal survival for him is a matter of the persistence of the mind or rational soul. Since on Descartes's view the immaterial soul could exist even if there were no bodies of any kind, survival of human bodily death by the self is for him a genuine possibility. However, as far as I am aware he never says anything from which we could deduce whether or not he thinks it would be me surviving if at some future time my rational soul, although conscious, retained no memories or consciousness of any of my life or personal details. My guess would be that he would deny that this could occur, but that if *per impossibile* it did, the person would still be (a maximally amnesiac) me.

Spinoza

For Spinoza the self's survival during the life of the human being in question parallels the survival and stability of the complex bodily organism with its simpler organisms collaborating to make ever more complex higher-level organic systems. It is the ideas of these nested organic systems that go together to make the complex idea which is my mind or self. But he insists that mind and body do not interact in any way so we cannot read him as saying that the mind depends causally on the body for its survival. Although Spinoza thinks that, for those who attain what he calls "blessedness", a kind of immortality is possible, most readers find it very mysterious how this might happen. At any rate it appears that such immortality would not, for him, be survival of the individual mind and moral subject as such.

Leibniz

Leibniz equates the person with the dominant monad or soul, which governs the human body. Souls are created *ex nihilo* and are eternal even though, at the death of the body, they become dormant in a sort of utter waning of vitality and self-awareness that robs them of any presence detectable by themselves or others. However, this dormant state will not last forever, on Leibniz's view. For him the person is his or her whole "detail of changes" (collection of perceptions or mental contents) as specified by the pre-established harmony. The same person survives where there is the same detail of monadic changes or perceptions playing itself out, whatever different monads make up that person's body at any given period.

Locke

As we have seen, Locke equates personhood and personal identity with persisting individual consciousness rather than any substance either material or immaterial. He certainly leaves open the possibility of survival of bodily death: for any individual this would only require that some future person have exactly that consciousness and access to memories of his or her past self which that person now possesses.

Berkeley

Like Descartes, Berkeley would make personal identity depend on the survival of the mind, soul or spirit. Spirits alone, for Berkeley, are persistent substances as opposed to phenomenal things – such as stars, flowers, apples, trees in the quad and, of course, human bodies – which consist of ideas.

Hume

Finally, although Hume is famously sceptical about identity over time in general and the existence of a (lasting or even instantaneous) self in particular he never writes as if he, his readers and his philosophical opponents are anything other than lasting persons. And his notorious bundle-self notion gives him a Humean psychological criterion for personal identity: I survive from moment to moment throughout my history as the subject of experience and bundle of present perceptions, which inherits all my past self's impressions, ideas, memories and imaginings and imagines itself to be a lasting particular mind.

The evolution of a modern approach to mind?

A student might guess at the outset of a course on the early modern period that there is a progressive line of development – an evolution of thought as well as approach – from Descartes to Hume, with each successive later thinker responding to and building on his predecessor's ideas, until a Humean modern empiricism or even early positivism about the mind is achieved. What follows is a brief summary of the main answers given to the five questions posed to our six philosophers about their views on mind, which I have assembled in hopes of showing that such a "linear evolution of thought" picture is largely inaccurate. Far more helpful is the view that there is a highly reticulated complex of influences criss-crossing the period and providing a fertile ground in which both the Kantian idealism of the nineteenth century and the markedly different monistic materialism about the mind that has flourished in recent years are deeply rooted.

Is the mind a substance?
What can be learned about the development of views on the character of the human mind in the early modern period from the fact that only three philosophers of the six would affirm that the human mind is a substance? It is not as if (as might have been vaguely expected) it is the line dividing the earlier three (Descartes, Spinoza, Locke) from the later trio (Leibniz, Berkeley, Hume) that divides those who think the mind is a substance from those who do not. Nor is this a difference between those traditionally labelled rationalists and those labelled empiricists: of the rationalists, two regard the mind as an immaterial substance but one does not; of the empiricists, one denies that the human mind is a substance, one is agnostic and one does see the mind as a substance.

The last point might lend weight to the suggestion now supported by most commentators that the rationalist–empiricist dichotomy is not a hugely useful one.[1] To take just one illustration, it is certainly the case that Descartes is always

---

1. For a more detailed treatment of this issue see J. Cottingham, *The Rationalists* (Oxford: Oxford University Press, 1988), ch. 1.

eager to see how far unaided reason can take him in addressing any question (so far so rationalist). But equally certainly he labours to acquire knowledge about the scope and limits of the mind – in particular, the nature of sense perception and the springs of behaviour – from hands-on animal dissections and painstaking physiological research (in line with empiricist principles).

Of course Spinoza remains committed to a substance ontology so that for him the individual mind, while not a substance in itself, is nonetheless a part of the one divine substance. And Berkeley's empiricist label has often been questioned just because of his staunch defence of mind as a Cartesian imma-terial substance and his rejection of material substance. But even though Locke and Hume are both sceptical about the existence of substance and its role in individual human minds we cannot conclude that there is a simple trend here, let alone a pendulum swing, from an early unqualified (ration-alist) belief in the mind as immaterial substance to a later more enlightened (empiricist) outright rejection of such mind–matter dualism. Things are far more complicated than that.

What knowledge can we have of what goes on in our own minds?
We have seen that all six figures, in certain ways and in certain contexts, express allegiance to some sort of doctrine of mental transparency. Under the surface, however, there are pronounced differences between the views of the six on the question of self-knowledge. Descartes's position is far from the simple-minded and contradictory "Cartesian introspective model" often attributed to him: he makes clear that he thinks there are many ideas in the mind that lie ready to be discovered for the first time as well as memories that are out of sight until consciously adverted to. And it seems defensible to attribute to him the belief that a number of different types of advertence or consciousness characterize those various ideas or thoughts that he thinks appear ceaselessly before the mind.

For both Spinoza and Leibniz the mind of every individual holds ideas that can elude full consciousness for much or all of the subject's life. But, sad to say, Locke firmly rejects this revolutionary suggestion that there might be thoughts in my mind (for example, in dreamless sleep) of which I am unaware. Instead he declares that he can see no role that unconscious thought could occupy or mental work that such unconscious ideas could do. And although he certainly accepts that there are memories that remain in my mind without being conscious, his account of how these memories are retained and/or revived is so thin and sketchy that, to a modern eye, his unqualified allegiance to strong mental transparency seems highly retrograde: far less plausible and more naive than the earlier Cartesian view.

Berkeley believes that our ideas when made the focus of our discriminative attention are transparent to reflection but he also believes that ideas can lurk in the mind – in the shadows so to speak – awaiting that attention which will reveal their nature. Compared to Berkeley, Hume appears much less aware of the need for caution in declaring not only his immediate and privileged access to all his ideas, but his conviction that his ideas are all exactly as he takes them to be.

So, with the question of mental transparency, even more than with the question whether the mind is or is not a substance, there seems little trend or smooth line of development or refinement from Descartes's position to that adopted by Hume. If anything, Hume seems less aware than Descartes of the real possibility that a human mind might harbour thoughts and ideas that stubbornly resist awareness of them by their subject.

What account can be given of the nature of consciousness and subjectivity?
All six authors show a subtle understanding of numerous facets or aspects of conscious experience. Arguably, Descartes and Leibniz both recognize a number of different sorts of consciousness even if they do not explicitly distinguish them one from another. And they would agree that what are now called "access consciousness" and "perceptual consciousness" come to human beings as a result of their being animals.

There are also hints that Descartes, Berkeley and Hume would recognize phenomenal consciousness as a further distinct type of conscious experience (experienced by men and animals alike). Locke's subtle distinctions between different types and degrees of attention are also noteworthy, even though they do not in the end offer him a way of escaping the criticism that his all-or-nothing view of consciousness (an idea is either fully conscious or not there at all) contradicts everyone's everyday experience and indeed one strand in his own account of memory.

I have argued that Descartes and Leibniz have the beginnings of theories about consciousness that could stand as very early precursors of a higher-order-thought or "inner scanning" theory while Locke's and Berkeley's views do not admit of such a higher-order-thought reading.

Spinoza, disappointingly, says all too little about the source of consciousness beyond saying that each particular mind is part of the one great divine mind. We are left to wonder how he thinks individual subjectivity and consciousness are achieved, although he has a great deal to say about the nature of subjective experience itself that subtly enriches our understanding of that phenomenon.

And Hume, although he makes considerable use of introspection in his search for understanding of the mind never says anything to suggest he thinks that any sort of inner scanning explains the conscious character of his impressions or ideas. Like Locke he believes that consciousness, being in the mind and the having of ideas are all simply equivalent.

Have human mental states the power to initiate human movement?
All of our six figures but Spinoza credit human minds with the power to move their own bodies. Each has some response he can make to earlier and later problems of mental causation if only by attempting to shift the burden of proof to his opponent.

We have seen that Descartes thinks that a human mind can move its body by force of will, just as God – although wholly immaterial – moves matter by the power of his thought alone. Spinoza disagrees, denying the possibility of causal interaction between individual minds and their bodies and, in general, between the mental realm and the physical realm. Leibniz's complex position on mental causation is perhaps ultimately unsustainable: he wishes to agree with Descartes that human beings are free to choose and will, that their actions are guided by their thoughts and ideas, but it is difficult to see how he can square human freedom with his pre-established harmony.

Like Descartes, Locke believes that he has the evidence of everyday experience that mental states, in particular acts of will, cause our actions. But, as Spinoza observed, no matter how strongly I *feel* that I am making my body move by willing it to do so this is no proof that it is my will that does the moving. No matter how sure I am that what I do is caused by my mental states it is always possible that I am mistaken or under an illusion.

Berkeley has been accused of extinguishing all chance of mental causation for human beings by maintaining that all real ideas (such as the idea of any bodily movement), and thus all real movements, are caused not by their would-be human subjects, but by God. I have argued on the contrary that Berkeley believes God gives us (admittedly limited) powers to move ourselves, notwithstanding that God's unbroken will to sustain appearances as if there were an objective nature governed by natural law means that he is ultimately responsible for creating for every observer each appearance of every bodily change.

Hume believes firmly that human minds are efficacious. Granted, for him our choices, decisions and acts of will are governed by natural law, just as the motions of all bodies are governed. Human nature is a part of nature. However, he nonetheless holds that it is right to say that we are free and responsible with respect to those actions we perform when not constrained or coerced. Our mental states make a difference: they govern what we do when we are not compelled by conditions beyond our control.

281

How do our ideas represent what they are ideas of?
Whatever their other differences, all our thinkers up to Hume are agreed that
the "aboutness" or intentionality of our ideas is *derived* rather than *original*
intentionality. They are all persuaded that it is (either immediately or ultimately) God who bestows aboutness or meaning on our mental states. Either
they think we are furnished from birth with innate ideas that are already
about their objects (Descartes's innate ideas, Leibniz's monadic concepts
and Berkeley's divine archetypes), or we are endowed with the physiological
mechanisms for acquiring – and things are created with the powers to cause
in us – just those ideas that are best fitted to represent what we naturally take
them to be ideas of (Descartes's adventitious and invented ideas, Spinoza's
ideas of changes in his sense organs, Locke's ideas of sensation and reflection
and Berkeley's ideas copied from sensations). Either way, our ideas ultimately
owe their "aboutness" to God, who appoints them to represent what they
come to stand for in our thinking. In no case is it thought that ideas represent what they are ideas of simply as a result of their resembling those things
although there will of course be some sort of resemblance, in some respect or
other, between any idea and the thing it stands for.

Hume, however, says nothing that would indicate that he regards himself
as heir to this tradition. His view has much in common with Locke's and
Berkeley's view that ideas represent their experiential causes but he does not
mention God's role, if any. Our ideas for Hume represent and are copied from
our impressions. Their (original) intentionality is in large part a function of
their causal origin and to a lesser degree a result of such resemblance as exists
between idea and impression.

So, as far as theory of mind is concerned, there is certainly no smooth
line of development from Cartesian dualism to Humean rejection of all
substances, material or immaterial. It is true that each thinker after Descartes
is substantially influenced by him, some accepting and developing his ideas,
some rejecting one or another or all of them. But it is worth noticing that
there is here no battle between rationalists who refuse to leave their armchairs
and empiricists who reject any *a priori* propositions and restrict themselves
exclusively to arguing from the results of experiments.

And it would certainly be a travesty to picture each later philosopher as
devoting his career to taking his immediate predecessor's ideas and developing them before handing them on to the next generation. Each of these six
great philosophers responds to and is influenced by a personal selection of
past and contemporary thinkers while ignoring or even disparaging others.
Those philosophers who came after Spinoza were almost uniformly highly
censorious of him and found little if anything in his thought to respond (let

alone warm) to. And sometimes individuals failed to recognize any sort of kinship of outlook where later readers would detect it: Leibniz wrote, referring to his fellow idealist the young Berkeley, "the man in Ireland who impugns the reality of bodies seems neither to give adequate reasons nor to explain sufficiently". He then said that he suspected Berkeley of being "one of those people who seek to become famous by their paradoxes".[2]

Of course, it is true that Spinoza wrote a commentary on Descartes; that Leibniz wrote a commentary on Locke; that Leibniz and Berkeley evidently looked back to Descartes's view that the mind is the rational soul; and that Hume responded again and again to Locke, often disagreeing with him but sometimes echoing the *Essay* uncannily as he makes his own distinctive points in the *Treatise*.[3] To all this must be added the fact that each of the six is influenced to some extent by writers outside the circle, a list that includes Bacon, Arnauld, Mersenne, Hobbes, More, Malebranche, Boyle, Hutcheson and numerous others.

But if this book makes anything clear I hope it is that each of these six great philosophers is first and foremost an original thinker who merits our attention in his own right. Whether he is considering problems about the nature of knowledge or existence, substance or causation, God or the capacities and character of the human mind, each is a thinker whose unique views and voice it is worth making every effort to hear and to understand.

2. Letter to Des Bosses, 1715, cited in *Leibniz Selections*, Philip P. Weiner (ed. & trans.) (New York: Scribners, 1951), xli.
3. See, for example, the striking similarity between "All those sublime Thoughts, which towre above the Clouds … offered for its Contemplation" (*Essay* II.i.24, 118) and "Let us chace our imagination to the heavens … that narrow compass" (T I.ii.vi, 66–7).

Bibliography

Alanen, L. *Descartes's Concept of Mind* (Cambridge, MA: Harvard University Press, 2003).

Allison, H. E. *Benedict de Spinoza: An Introduction* (New Haven, CT: Yale University Press, 1987).

Almog, J. "Précis of What Am I?". *Philosophy and Phenomenological Research* **70**(3) (2005): 696–700.

Almog, J. *What Am I?* (Oxford: Oxford University Press, 2002).

Armstrong, D. M. "Introspection". In *Self-Knowledge*, Q. Cassam (ed.), 109–17 (Oxford: Oxford University Press, 1994).

Armstrong, D. M. *A Materialist Theory of the Mind* (London: Routledge & Kegan Paul, 1968).

Armstrong, D. M. "What *is* Consciousness?", in his *The Nature of Mind and Other Essays*, 55–67 (Ithaca, NY: Cornell University Press, 1981).

Ayers, M. "The Ideas of Power and Substance in Locke's Philosophy". In *Locke on Human Understanding*, I. C. Tipton (ed.), 77–104 (Oxford: Oxford University Press, 1977).

Ayers, M. "The Second Meditation and Objections to Cartesian Dualism". In *Early Modern Philosophy: Mind, Matter, and Metaphysics*, C. Mercer & E. O'Neill (eds), 24–45 (New York: Oxford University Press, 2005).

Ayers, M. *Locke: Epistemology and Ontology*, 2 vols (London: Routledge, 1991).

Baker, G. & K. Morris. *Descartes' Dualism* (London: Routledge, 1996).

Beardsley, W. H. "Berkeley on Spirit and its Unity". *History of Philosophy Quarterly* **18** (2001): 259–77.

Bennett, J. *A Study of Spinoza's Ethics* (Cambridge: Cambridge University Press, 1984).

Berkeley, G. *A Treatise Concerning the Principles of Human Knowledge*, J. Dancy (ed.) (Oxford: Oxford University Press, 1998).

Berkeley, G. *Philosophical Works including the Works on Vision*, M. Ayers (ed.) (London: Everyman, 1975).

Berkeley, G. *Three Dialogues between Hylas and Philonous*, J. Dancy (ed.) (Oxford: Oxford University Press, 1998).

Block, N. "Consciousness". In *A Companion to the Philosophy of Mind*, S. Guttenplan (ed.), 210–19 (Oxford: Blackwell, 1994).

Block, N. "On a Confusion about a Function of Consciousness". In *The Nature of Consciousness*, N. Block, O. Flanagan & G. Guzeldere (eds), 375–415 (Cambridge, MA: MIT Press, 1997).

Block, N., O. Flanagan & G. Guzeldere (eds). *The Nature of Consciousness* (Cambridge, MA: MIT Press, 1997).

Bogdan, R. (ed.). *Belief* (Oxford: Clarendon Press, 1986).

Brown, S. C. "Berkeley on the Unity of the Self". In *Reason and Reality*, Royal Institute of

Philosophy Lectures, Volume 5, 1970–71, G. N. A. Vesey (ed.), 64–87 (London: Macmillan, 1972).

Cassam, Q. (ed.). *Self-Knowledge* (Oxford: Oxford University Press, 1994).

Chalmers, D. *The Conscious Mind* (Oxford: Oxford University Press, 1996).

Clarke, D. M. *Descartes's Theory of Mind* (Oxford: Clarendon Press, 2003).

Cornman, J. W. "A Reconstruction of Berkeley: Minds and Physical Objects as Theoretical Entities". *Ratio* **13** (1971): 76–87.

Cottingham, J. (ed.). *Descartes* (Oxford: Oxford University Press, 1998).

Cottingham, J. *Descartes' Philosophy of Mind* (London: Phoenix, 1997).

Cottingham, J. *The Rationalists* (Oxford: Oxford University Press, 1988).

Crane, T. *The Mechanical Mind* (Harmondsworth: Penguin, 1995).

Crane, T. & S. Patterson (eds). *History of the Mind–Body Problem* (London: Routledge, 2000).

Cummins, R. *Meaning and Mental Representation* (Cambridge, MA: MIT Press, 1989).

Curley, E. *Behind the Geometrical Method* (Princeton, NJ: Princeton University Press, 1988).

Curley, E. *Spinoza's Metaphysics: An Essay in Interpretation* (Cambridge, MA: Harvard University Press, 1969).

Davidson, D. "Actions, Reasons and Causes". In his *Essays on Actions and Events*, 3–20 (Oxford: Clarendon Press, 1980).

Delahunty, R. J. *Spinoza* (London: Routledge & Kegan Paul, 1985).

Della Rocca, M. "Descartes–Inseparability–Almog". *Philosophy and Phenomenological Research* **70**(3) (2005): 701–8.

Della Rocca, M. *Representation and the Mind–Body Problem in Spinoza* (Oxford: Oxford University Press, 1996).

Descartes, R. *Meditations and Other Metaphysical Writings*, rev. edn, D. M. Clarke (ed. & trans.) (Harmondsworth: Penguin, 2001).

Descartes, R. *Oeuvres de Descartes*, 12 vols, rev. edn, C. Adam & P. Tannery (eds) (Paris: Vrin/CNRS, 1964–76).

Descartes, R. *The Philosophical Writings of Descartes, Vols I & II*, J. Cottingham, R. Stoothoff & D. Murdoch (eds & trans.) (Cambridge: Cambridge University Press, 1985).

Descartes, R. *The Philosophical Writings of Descartes, Vol. III*, J. Cottingham, R. Stoothoff, D. Murdoch & A. Kenny (eds & trans.) (Cambridge: Cambridge University Press, 1991).

Dicker, G. *Hume's Epistemology and Metaphysics: An Introduction* (London: Routledge 1998).

Donagan, A. "Spinoza's Dualism". In *The Philosophy of Baruch Spinoza*, R. Kennington (ed.), 89–102 (Washington, DC: Catholic University of America Press, 1980).

Dretske, F. "Misrepresentation". In *Belief*, R. Bogdan (ed.), 17–36 (Oxford: Clarendon Press, 1986).

Flanagan, O. *Consciousness Reconsidered* (Cambridge, MA: MIT Press, 1992).

Fogelin, R. J. *Berkeley and the Principles of Human Knowledge* (London: Routledge, 2001).

Foster, J. & H. Robinson (eds). *Essays on Berkeley: A Tercentennial Celebration* (Oxford: Clarendon Press, 1985).

Gallois, A. *The World Without, the Mind Within* (Cambridge: Cambridge University Press, 1996).

Gaukroger, S. *Descartes' System of Natural Philosophy* (Cambridge: Cambridge University Press, 2002).

Graham, G. *Philosophy of Mind: An Introduction*, 2nd edn (Oxford: Blackwell, 1998).

Grayling, A. C. *Berkeley: The Central Arguments* (London: Duckworth, 1986).

Guttenplan, S. (ed.). *A Companion to the Philosophy of Mind* (Oxford: Blackwell, 1994).

Hale, M. *The Primitive Origination of Mankind, Considered and Examined According to the Light of Nature* (London, 1677).

Hampshire, S. *Spinoza and Spinozism*, 2nd edn (Oxford: Clarendon Press, 2005).

Hatfield, G. *Descartes and the* Meditations (London: Routledge, 2003).

Hume, D. *Enquiries Concerning Human Understanding and Concerning the Principles of Morals*, L. A. Selby-Bigge (ed.), 3rd edn, P. H. Nidditch (ed.) (Oxford: Oxford University Press, 1975).

Hume, D. *A Treatise of Human Nature*, L. A. Selby-Bigge (ed.), 2nd edn, P. H. Nidditch (ed.) (Oxford: Oxford University Press, 1978).

Jolley, N. *Leibniz* (London: Routledge, 2005).

Jolley, N. *Locke: His Philosophical Thought* (Oxford: Oxford University Press, 1999).

Kenny, A. *Descartes: A Study of His Philosophy* (New York: Random House, 1968).

Kim, J. *Mind in a Physical World* (Cambridge, MA: MIT Press, 1998).

Kim, J. *Philosophy of Mind* (Boulder, CO: Westview, 1996).

Kirk, R. *Raw Feeling: A Philosophical Account of the Essence of Consciousness* (Oxford: Oxford University Press, 1994).

Kulstad, M. *Leibniz on Apperception, Consciousness and Reflection* (Munich: Philosophia, 1991).

Leibniz, G. W. *The Leibniz–Arnauld Correspondence*, H. T. Mason (ed. & trans.) (Manchester: Manchester University Press, 1967).

Leibniz, G. W. *Leibniz Selections*, P. P. Weiner (ed. & trans.) (New York: Scribners, 1951).

Leibniz, G. W. *New Essays on Human Understanding*, P. Remnant & J. Bennett (eds & trans.) (Cambridge: Cambridge University Press, 1997).

Leibniz, G. W. *Philosophical Essays*, R. Ariew & D. Garber (eds & trans.) (Indianapolis, IN: Hackett, 1989).

Leibniz, G. W. *Philosophical Papers and Letters*, L. E. Loemker (ed. & trans.) (Dordrecht: Reidel, 1969).

Leibniz, G. W. *Philosophical Texts*, R. S. Woolhouse & R. Francks (eds & trans.) (Oxford: Oxford University Press, 1998).

Leibniz, G. W. *Die philosophischen Schriften*, 7 vols, C. I. Gerhardt (ed.) (Hildesheim: Georg Olms, 1978).

Lennon, T. M. "Locke on Ideas and Representation". In *The Cambridge Companion to Locke's Essay Concerning Human Understanding*, L. Newman (ed.), 231–57 (Cambridge: Cambridge University Press, 2007).

Levine, J. "Materialism and Qualia: The Explanatory Gap". *Pacific Philosophical Quarterly* **64** (1983): 354–61.

Locke, J. *An Essay Concerning Human Understanding*, P. H. Nidditch (ed.) (Oxford: Oxford University Press, 1975).

Lowe, E. J. *Locke on Human Understanding* (London: Routledge, 1995).

Lyons, W. *The Disappearance of Introspection* (Cambridge, MA: MIT Press, 1986).

Martinich, A. P., F. Allhoff & A. J. Vaidya. *Early Modern Philosophy: Essential Readings with Commentary* (Oxford: Blackwell, 2007).

McRae, R. *Leibniz: Perception, Apperception, and Thought* (Toronto: University of Toronto Press, 1976).

Mercer, C. & E. O'Neill (eds). *Early Modern Philosophy: Mind, Matter, and Metaphysics* (New York: Oxford University Press, 2005).

Muehlmann, R. G. *Berkeley's Ontology* (Indianapolis, IN: Hackett, 1992).

Muehlmann, R. G. "The Substance of Berkeley's Philosophy". In his *Berkeley's Metaphysics: Structural, Interpretive, and Critical Essays*, 89–106 (University Park, PA: Penn State University Press, 1995).

Murray, J. A. H. (ed.). *A New English Dictionary on Historical Principles* (Oxford: Clarendon Press, 1888).

Nagel, T. "What Is It Like to Be a Bat?". Reprinted in his *Mortal Questions*, 165–80 (Cambridge: Cambridge University Press, 1979).

Newman, L. (ed.). *The Cambridge Companion to Locke's Essay Concerning Human Understanding* (Cambridge: Cambridge University Press, 2007).

Noonan, H. *Hume on Knowledge* (London: Routledge, 1999).

Papineau, D. *Thinking About Consciousness* (Oxford: Oxford University Press, 2002).

Patterson, S. "Epiphenomenalism and Occasionalism: Problems of Mental Causation, Old and New". *History of Philosophy Quarterly* 22 (2005): 239–57.

Pears, D. F. (ed.). *David Hume: A Symposium* (London: Macmillan, 1966).

Perkins, F. *Leibniz: A Guide for the Perplexed* (London: Continuum, 2007).

Pitcher, G. *Berkeley* (London: Routledge, 1977).

Rosenthal, D. "The Independence of Consciousness and Sensory Quality". *Philosophical Issues* 1 (1991): 15–36.

Ryle, G. *The Concept of Mind* (Harmondsworth: Penguin, 1963).

Savile, A. *Leibniz* (London: Routledge, 2000).

Scruton, R. *Spinoza* (Oxford: Oxford University Press, 1986).

Scruton, R. *Spinoza* (London: Phoenix Press, 1998).

Shoemaker, S. "Introspection and the Self". In *Self-Knowledge*, Q. Cassam (ed.), 118–39 (Oxford: Oxford University Press, 1994).

Spinoza, B. *Ethics*, E. Curley (ed. & trans.) (Harmondsworth: Penguin, 1996).

Stoneham, T. *Berkeley's World: An Examination of the Three Dialogues* (Oxford: Oxford University Press, 2002).

Strawson, P. F. "The First Person – and Others". In *Self-Knowledge*, Q. Cassam (ed.), 210–15 (Oxford: Oxford University Press, 1994).

Taylor, C. C. W. "Action and Inaction in Berkeley". In *Essays on Berkeley: A Tercentennial Celebration*, J. Foster & H. Robinson (eds), 211–25 (Oxford: Clarendon Press, 1985).

Thomas, J. "Does Descartes Deny Consciousness to Animals?". *Ratio* 19 (2006): 336–63.

Thomas, J. "The Solipsism Trap, the So-Called Master Argument, and the Pleasant Mistake". *History of Philosophy Quarterly* 23 (2006): 339–56.

Tipton, I. C. (ed.). *Locke on Human Understanding* (Oxford: Oxford University Press, 1977).

Warnock, G. J. "Hume on Causation". In *David Hume: A Symposium*, D. F. Pears (ed.), 55–66 (London: Macmillan, 1966).

Watson, R. *Representational Ideas from Plato to Patricia Churchland* (Dordrecht: Kluwer, 1995).

Williams, B. *Descartes: The Project of Pure Inquiry* (Harmondsworth: Pelican, 1978).

Wilson, C. *Descartes's* Meditations: *An Introduction* (Cambridge: Cambridge University Press, 2003).

Wilson, M. D. *Descartes* (London: Routledge & Kegan Paul, 1978).

Wilson, M. D. "Objects, Ideas, and 'Minds': Comments on Spinoza's Theory of Mind". In *The Philosophy of Baruch Spinoza*, R. Kennington (ed.), 103–20 (Washington, DC: Catholic University of America Press, 1980).

Woolhouse, R. S. *The Concept of Substance in Seventeenth Century Metaphysics* (London: Routledge, 1993).

Woolhouse, R. S. *The Empiricists* (Oxford: Oxford University Press, 1988).

Wright, C., B. C. Smith & C. Macdonald (eds). *Knowing Our Own Minds* (Oxford: Clarendon Press, 2006).

Yablo, S. "Almog on Descartes's Mind and Body". *Philosophy and Phenomenological Research* 70(3) (2005): 709–16.

Yolton, J. W. "Ideas and Knowledge in Seventeenth Century Philosophy". *Journal of the History of Philosophy* 13 (1975): 373–88.

Index

289

Noonan, H. 288

occasionalism 42*n*, 46*n*, 220, 288
occult qualities 140
Ockham's razor and Hume's hatchet
232–3
O'Neill, Eileen 23*n*, 285, 287
onomatopoeia 271
ontological primacy 2
organism consciousness 34, 35–7
original (intrinsic) intentionality *see*
intentionality (original or intrinsic)

panpsychism 85–7
panvitalism 85
Papineau, David 204*n*, 266*n*, 288
parallelism 69, 84–5, 95–6
particular self-knowledge 25, 74, 239–40,
257
Patterson, Sarah 42*n*, 46, 46*n*, 286, 288
Pears, D. F. 288
perception (bare) 115
Perkins, F. 288
perpetual thought 120, 148, 152–3, 155,
158, 161, 206, 209
personal identity 1, 7, 64, 66, 122, 140,
144, 162, 235–6, 276–7
petites perceptions (minute perceptions)
120, 124, 159
phenomena bene fundata (well-founded
phenomena) 105–6, 109
phenomenalism 109
physical exclusion problem, the 9, 42, 50,
166–7, 212, 213–14, 218–29, 263, 266
piece of wax 24
pineal gland 47, 77, 92, 128
Pitcher, George 191, 191*n*, 194*n*, 198–
200, 198*n*, 288
pre-established harmony 10, 105, 113,
125, 126, 128–31, 133, 277, 281
prime matter 3, 140
Princess Elisabeth of Bohemia 44–7, 50,
163–6, 213, 262
problem of universal divine mental
causation 219
prognostics 228
property dualism *see* dualism

qualia ("raw feels") 255

rationalism 1, 6, 141, 149, 170, 231–2, 246,
274, 278–9, 278*n*, 282
real distinction argument, the 14–17, 15*n*
reflection *see* apperception; reflex act
two senses of 116–17, 122–3, 194–6
reflex act 7, 194–7, 199–200, 202, 209
referential transparency 67
reliable indicators 55–7, 60, 177
Remnant, Peter ix, 118*n*, 287
representation (nature of) *see*
intentionality
Leibnizian "expression" 132, 135–6
stand-ins, surrogates 170–72
representational content 54
representativeness 10, 133
representative realism 169
res cogitans and *res extensa* 3
resemblance (as source of representation)
51–60, 134–5, 170–76, 270–73, 282
resignation (Spinoza) 76–7
Robinson, H. 216*n*, 286, 288
Rosenthal, David 124, 124*n*, 288
Ryle, Gilbert 12, 12*n*, 23, 288

salience 5, 121, 165
Savile, A. 288
scepticism 70, 128, 150, 166, 171, 196,
222–3, 226
Humean 235, 267, 269
Scrooge and Marley 177, 177*n*
Scruton, R. 288
secondary qualities, ideas of 57, 59, 125,
171, 174
Selby-Bigge, L. A. ix, 6*n*, 231*n*, 287
self-consciousness 7, 22, 108, 110, 116, 117,
122–3, 162, 202, 209
self-intimation 245
self-knowledge (two sorts) 4–5
Shoemaker, Sydney 235*n*, 288
sleepwalker 37
Smith, B. C. 26*n*, 288
something we know not what 139, 143,
184
Spinoza's three types of knowledge 71
Stoneham, Tom 182*n*, 216, 216*n*, 219*n*, 288
Stoothoff, R. ix, 12*n*, 286
Strawson, P. F. 288
stream of consciousness 250
subconscious 77; *see also* unconscious